MEL BAY'S COMPLETE BOOK OF GUITAR CHORDS, SCALES AND ARPEGGIOS

By William Bay

We believe this text to be the most complete and thorough book of its kind in print! The three sections (scales, chords, and arpeggios) contain a wealth of information useful to any guitarist, whether in daily practice or professional performance.

The **Scale Section** is a collection of helpful and frequently used guitar scales. Each major and minor scale is presented in numerous forms and positions on up the guitar fingerboard. Also, all scales are shown in diagram form, notation, and tablature. Finally, a special section on blues and rock scales is contained in the latter part of this section.

The **Arpeggio Section** contains a multi-octave presentation of each chord-related arpeggio. This means that the guitarist, by playing through each arpeggio, will continually move up the fingerboard from low positions to higher ones. This practice not only presents outstanding-sounding arpeggios but also serves as an invaluable daily practice routine. Indeed, practicing multi-position arpeggios like those presented here "makes the guitar fingerboard seem smaller and more manageable."

Finally, the **Chord Section** presents carefully voiced, powerful-sounding chords in each key. The chords are broken into "melody chord," "inside chord," "rhythm chord," and "bottom 4-string chord" classifications. These groupings serve as an aid to memorization and give an understanding in regard to possible uses of various forms. It is to be remembered, however, that the usage of each of these chord forms is interchangeable.

The guitar is an extraordinary instrument. No sooner does one complete a master course of study than he or she embarks on yet another. The possibilities on the guitar are endless! My hope is that this text will add something substantial to your knowledge of the guitar and will enhance your practical implementation of technical concepts.

William Bay

3 4 5 6 7 8 9 0

Scale Contents

Major Scales

C Scales 8
G Scales 10
D Scales 12
A Scales 14
E Scales 16
B Scales 18
G♭/F♯ Scales 20
D♭/C♯ Scales 22
A♭ Scales 24
E♭ Scales 26
B♭ Scales 28
F Scales 30

Minor Scales

A Minor Scales 34
E Minor Scales 36
B Minor Scales 38
F♯ Minor Scales 40
C♯ Minor Scales 42
G♯ Minor Scales 44
E♭ Minor Scales 46
B♭ Minor Scales 48
F Minor Scales 50
C Minor Scales 52
G Minor Scales 54
D Minor Scales 56

Rock Scales (Minor Pentatonic)

Key of C 60
Key of D 62
Key of G 64
Key of A 66
Key of E 68
Key of B 70
Key of G♭/F♯ 72
Key of D♭/C♯ 74
Key of A♭ 76
Key of E♭ 78
Key of B♭ 80
Key of F 82

#3 *Frets*

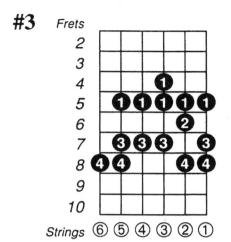

Strings ⑥ ⑤ ④ ③ ② ①

#4 *Frets*

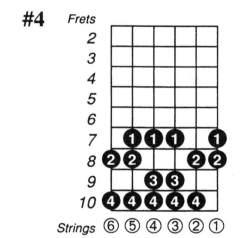

Strings ⑥ ⑤ ④ ③ ② ①

G Scales

#1 *Frets*

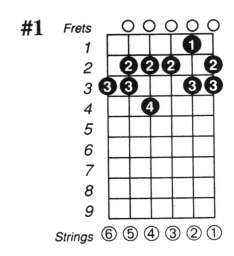

#2 *Frets*

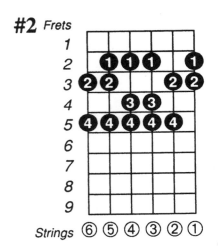

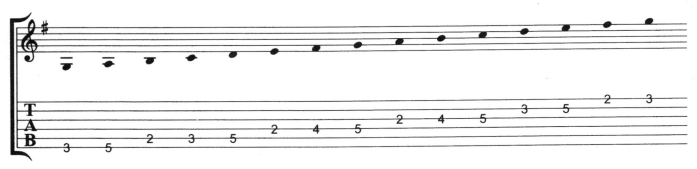

#3

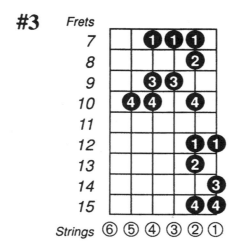

#4

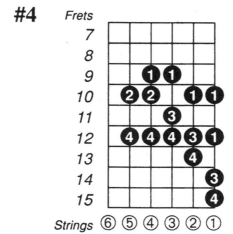

D Scales

#1

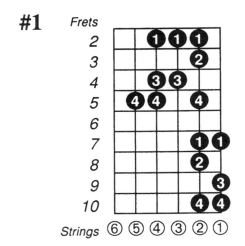

#2

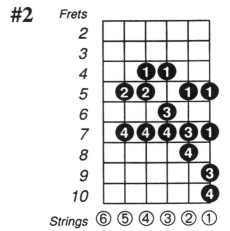

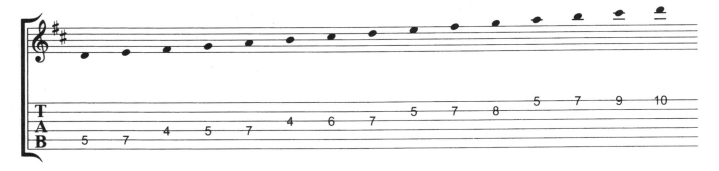

#3 *Frets*

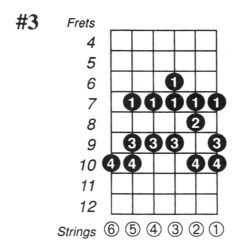

Strings ⑥⑤④③②①

#4 *Frets*

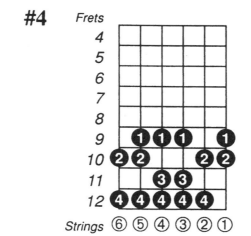

Strings ⑥⑤④③②①

A Scales

#1

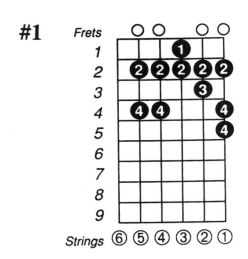

#2

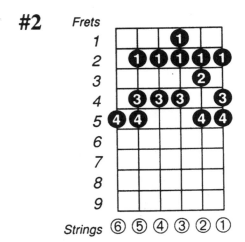

14

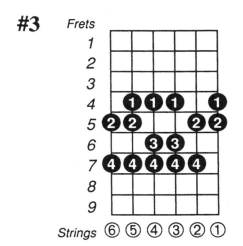

#3

#4

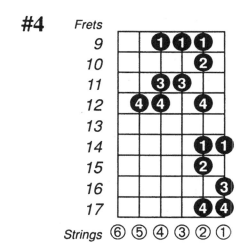

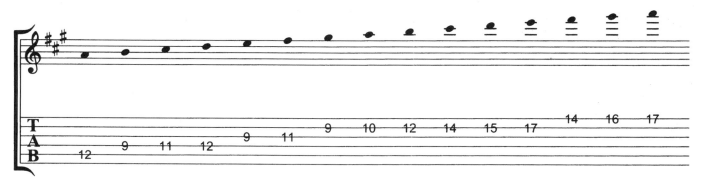

E Scales

#1

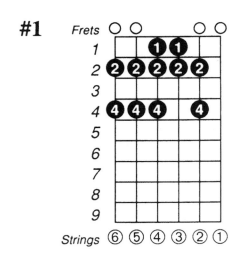

#2

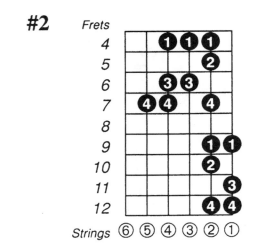

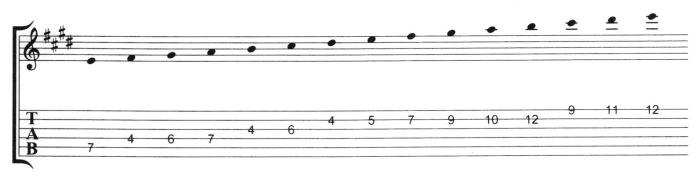

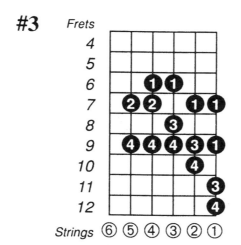

#3

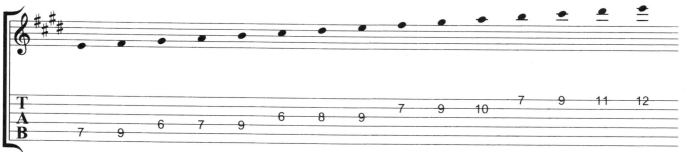

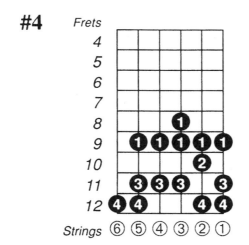

#4

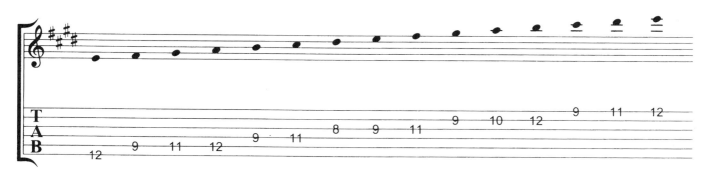

B Scales

#1 *Frets*

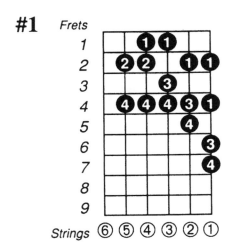

#2 *Frets*

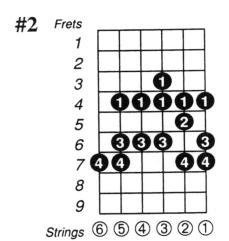

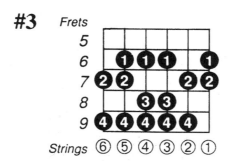

#3

G♭ / F♯ Scales

#1 *Frets*

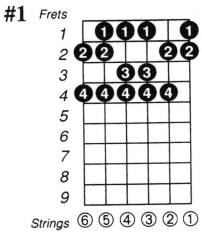

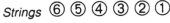

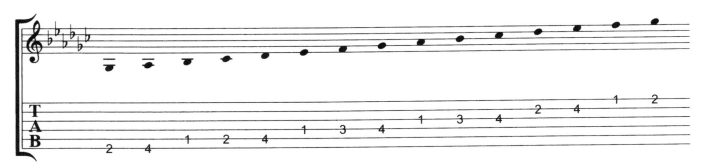

#2 *Frets*

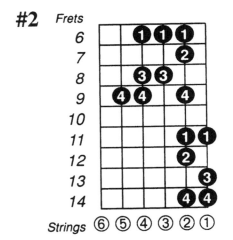

#3

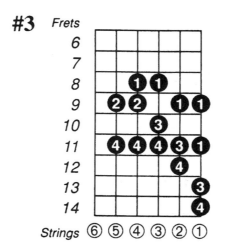

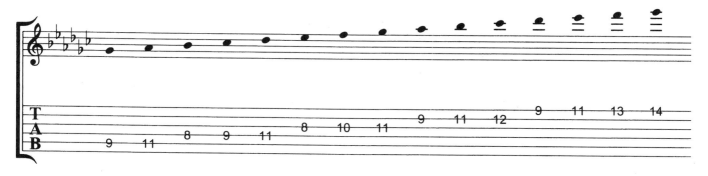

D♭ / C♯ Scales

#1

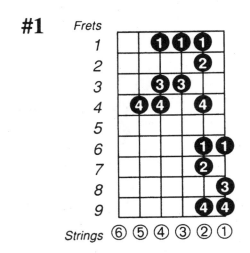

#2

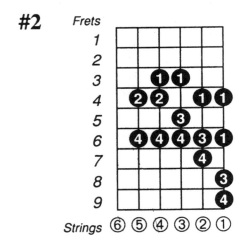

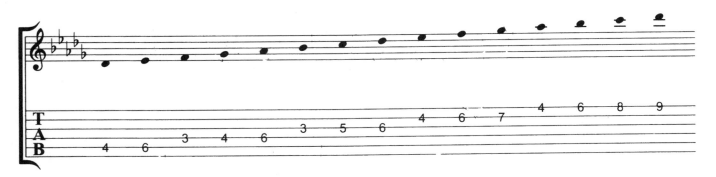

#3

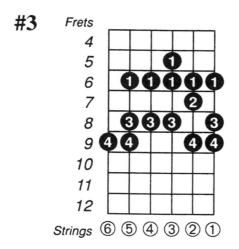

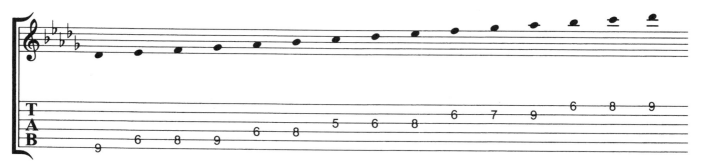

#4

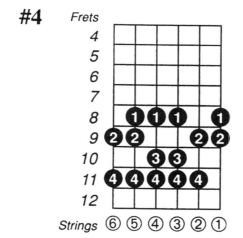

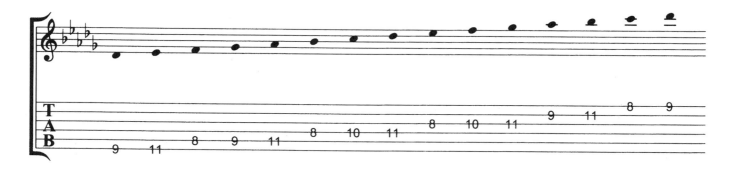

A♭ Scales

#1

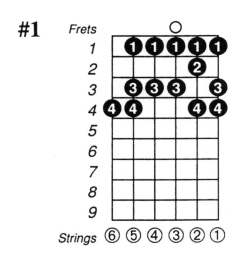

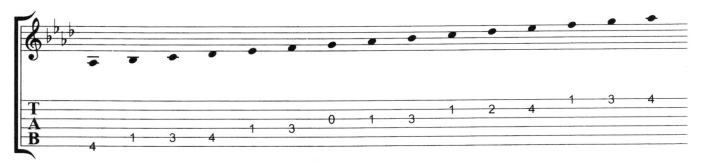

#2

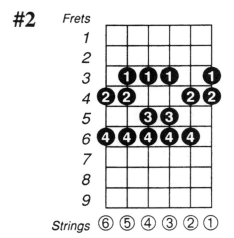

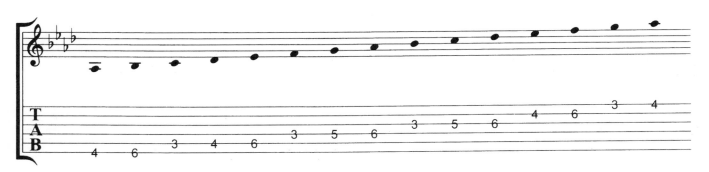

#3

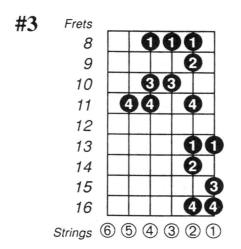

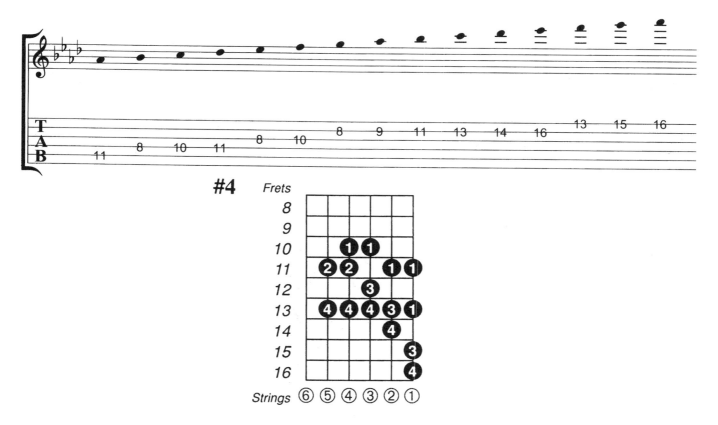

#4

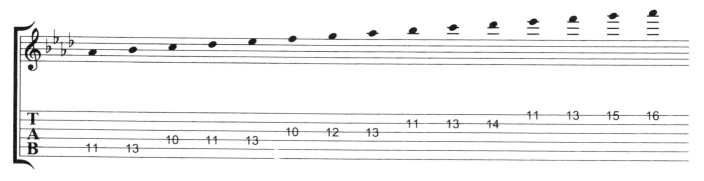

25

E♭ Scales

#1

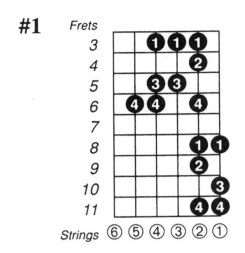

#2

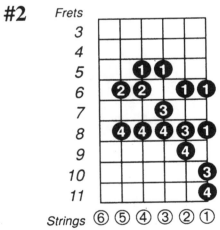

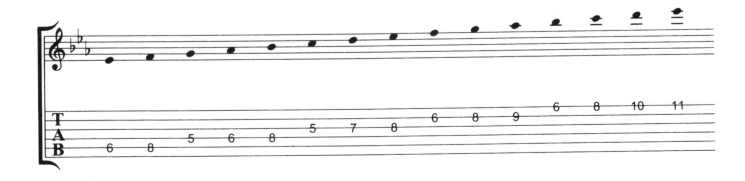

26

#3 *Frets*

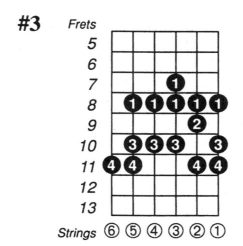

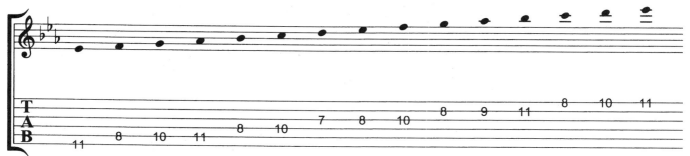

#4 *Frets*

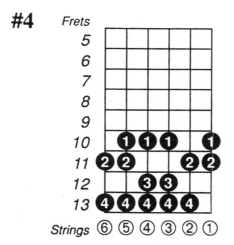

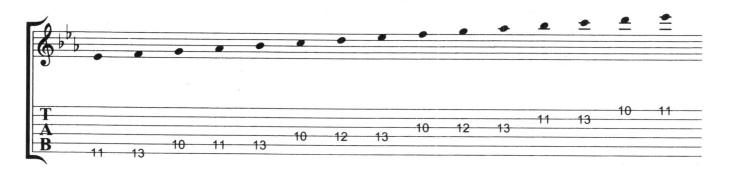

B♭ Scales

#1

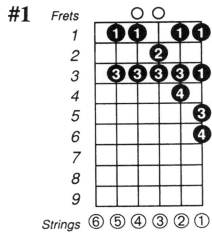

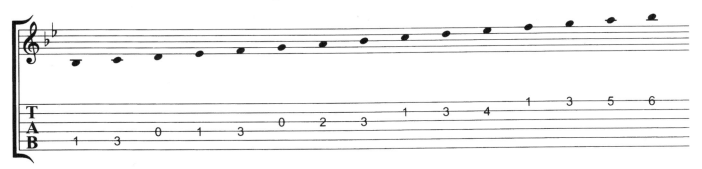

#2

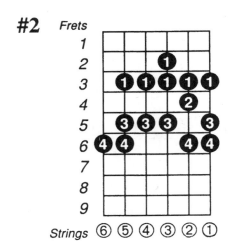

#3

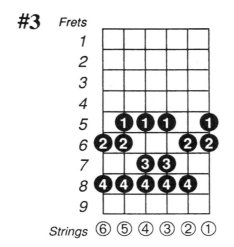

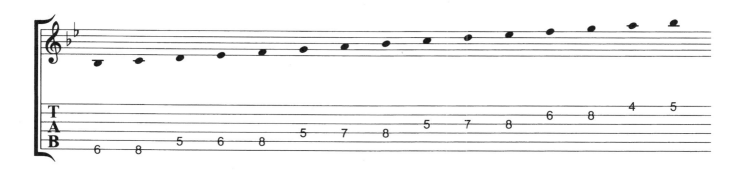

29

F Scales

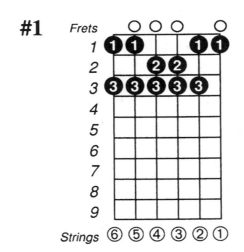

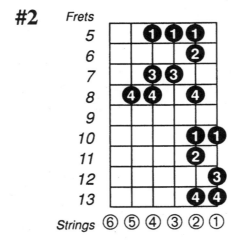

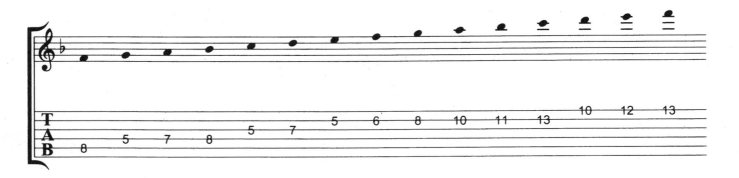

#3

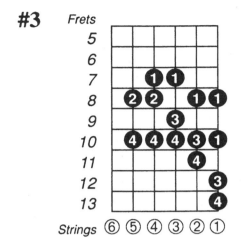

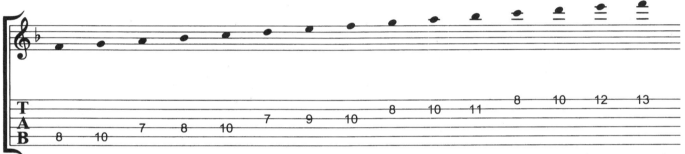

#4

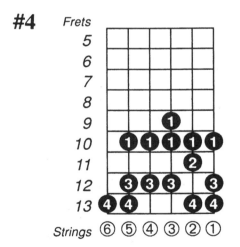

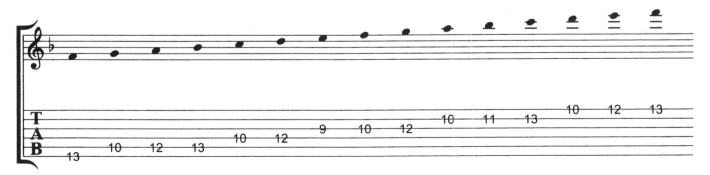

Minor Scales

A Minor Scales

#1

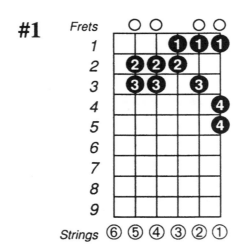

#2

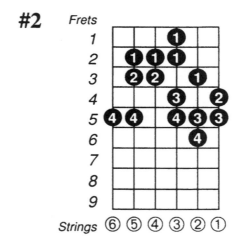

#3 *Frets*

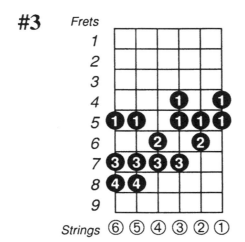

Strings ⑥ ⑤ ④ ③ ② ①

#4 *Frets*

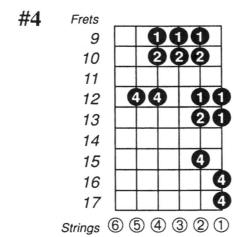

Strings ⑥ ⑤ ④ ③ ② ①

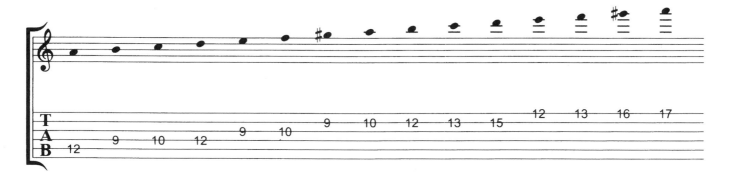

E minor Scales

#1

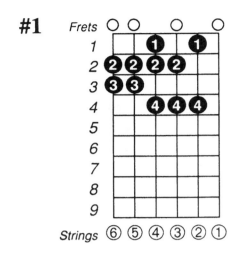

#2

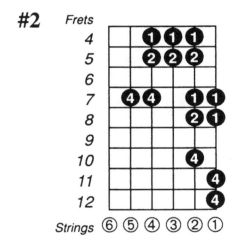

SCALES

36

#3   *Frets*

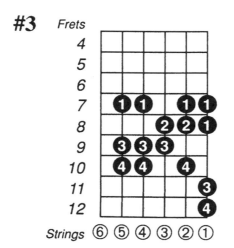

Strings ⑥ ⑤ ④ ③ ② ①

#4   *Frets*

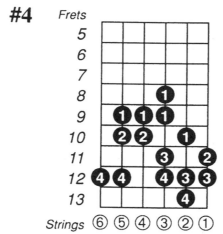

Strings ⑥ ⑤ ④ ③ ② ①

B minor Scales

#1

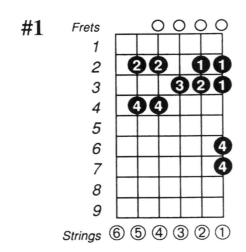

#2

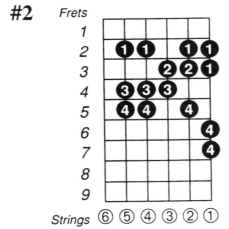

#3

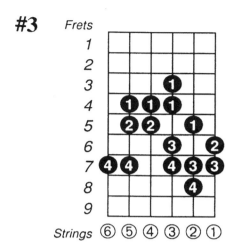

#4

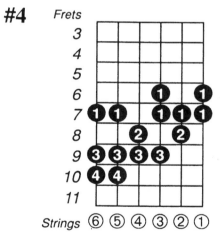

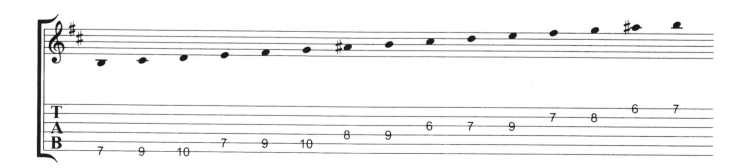

39

F♯ minor Scales

#1

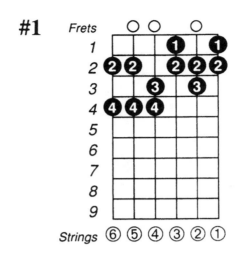

#2

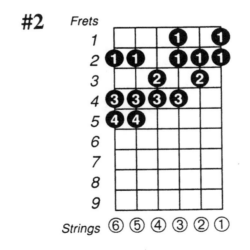

#3

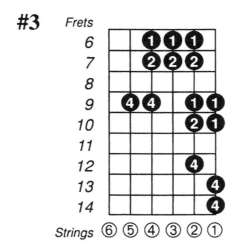

#4

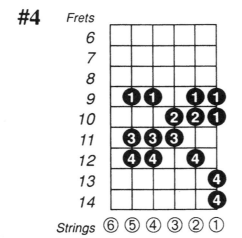

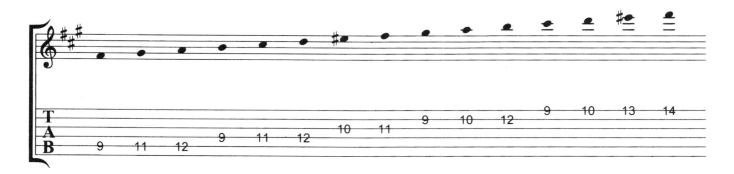

C♯ minor Scales

#1

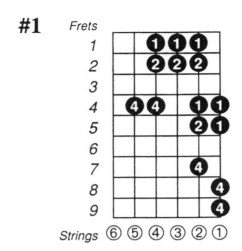

#2

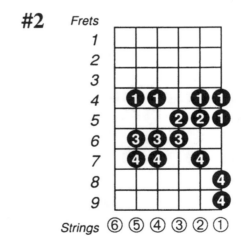

#3   *Frets*

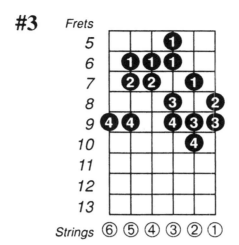

Strings ⑥ ⑤ ④ ③ ② ①

#4   *Frets*

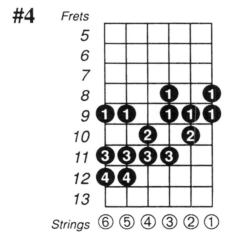

Strings ⑥ ⑤ ④ ③ ② ①

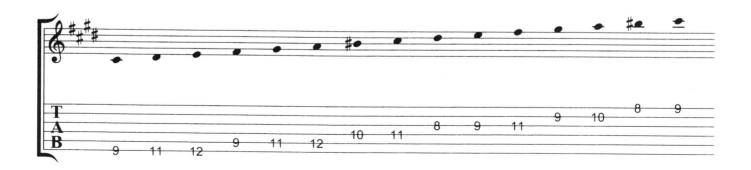

G♯ minor Scales

#1

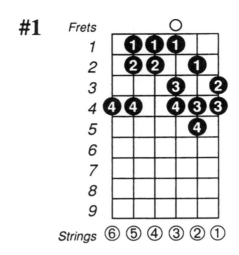

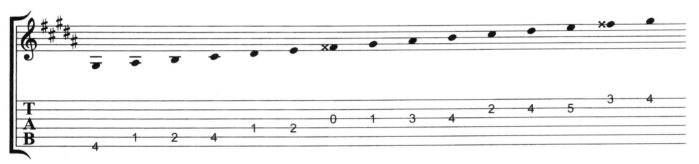

#2

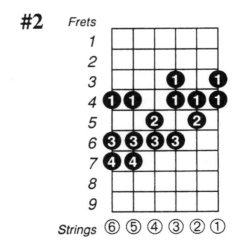

44

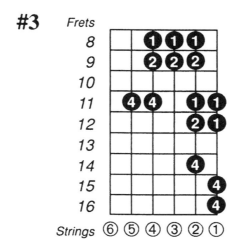

#3 Frets

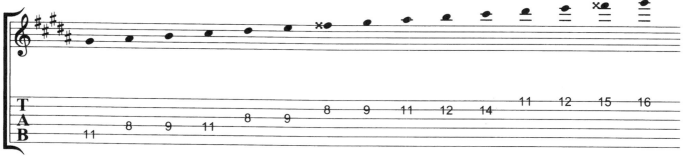

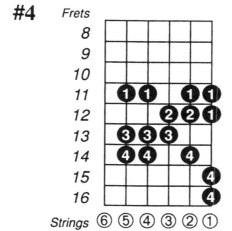

#4 Frets

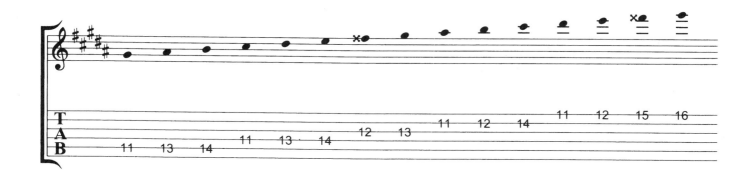

E♭ minor Scales

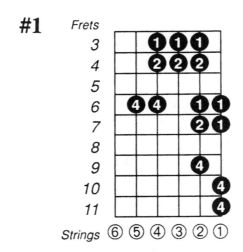

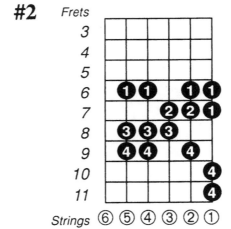

#3 *Frets*

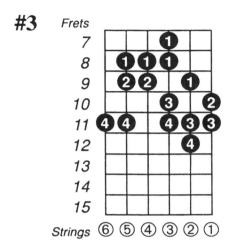

Strings ⑥ ⑤ ④ ③ ② ①

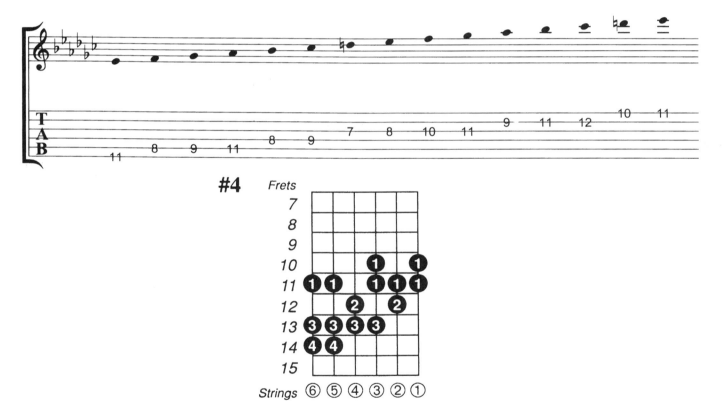

#4 *Frets*

Strings ⑥ ⑤ ④ ③ ② ①

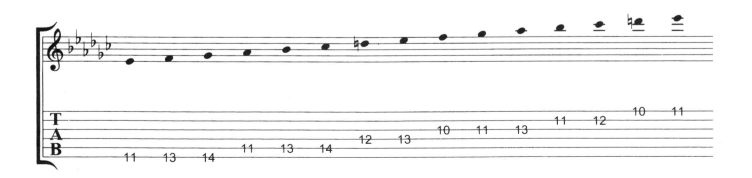

B♭ minor Scales

#1

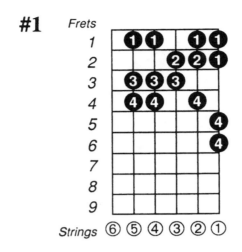

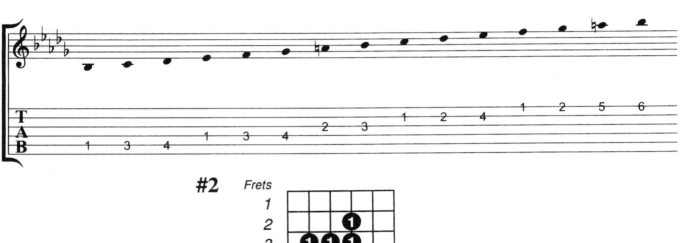

#2

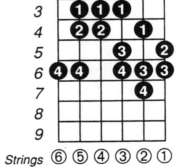

#3 *Frets*

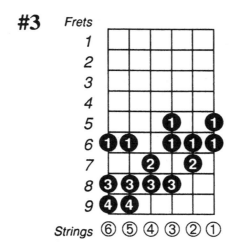

#4 *Frets*

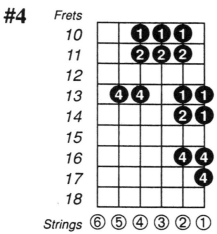

F minor Scales

#1

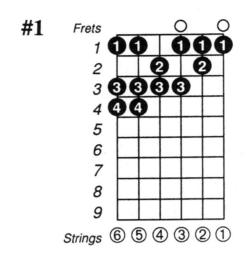

#2

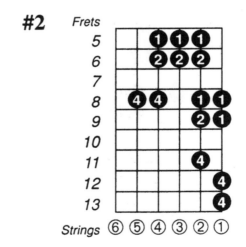

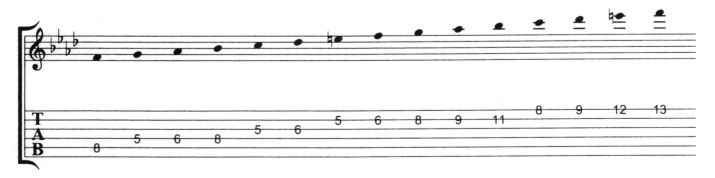

50

#3 *Frets*

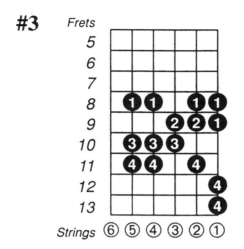

Strings ⑥ ⑤ ④ ③ ② ①

#4 *Frets*

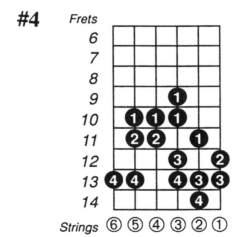

Strings ⑥ ⑤ ④ ③ ② ①

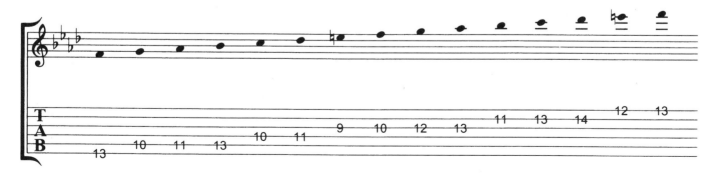

C minor Scales

#1

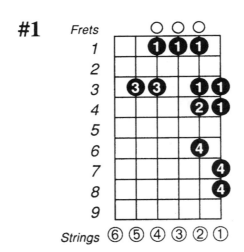

#2

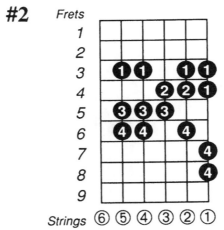

#3 *Frets*

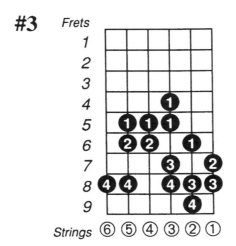

Strings ⑥ ⑤ ④ ③ ② ①

#4 *Frets*

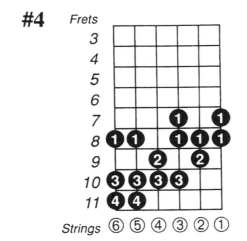

Strings ⑥ ⑤ ④ ③ ② ①

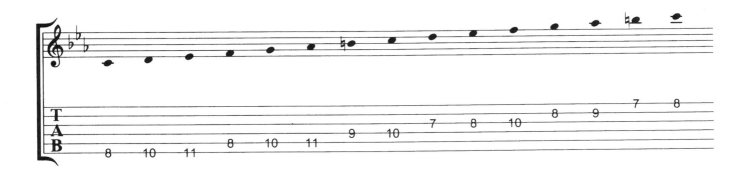

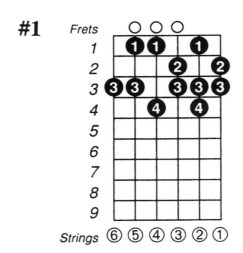

G minor Scales

#1

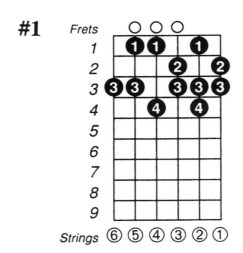

#2

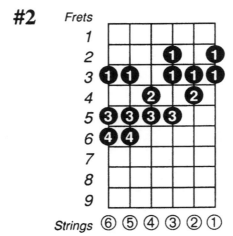

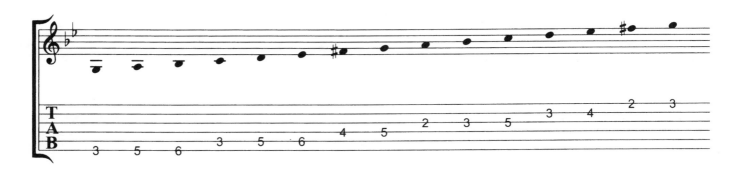

54

#3

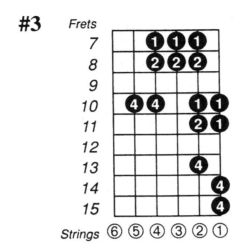

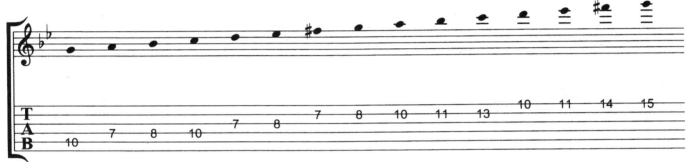

#4

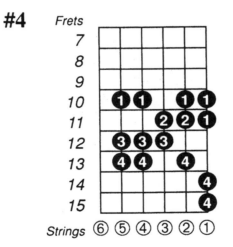

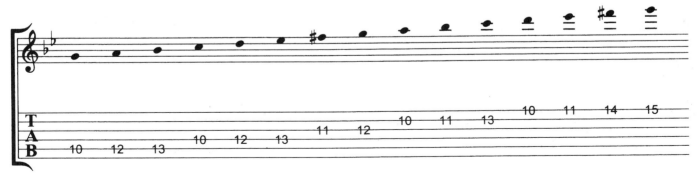

D minor Scales

#1

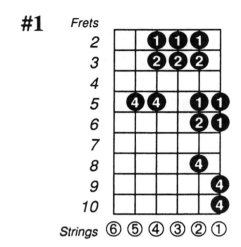

#2

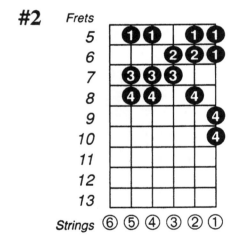

56

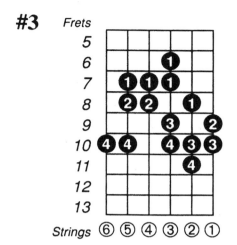

#3

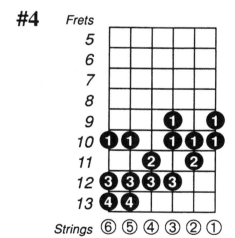

#4

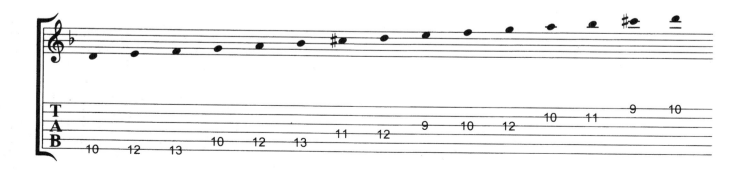

Rock Scales

(Minor Pentatonic)

Rock Scales
Key of C

#1

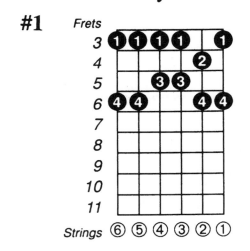

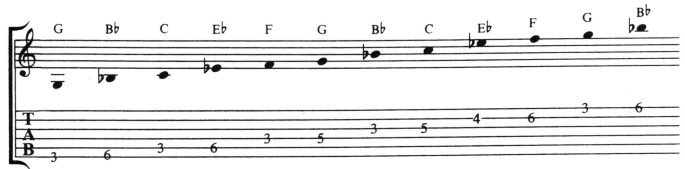

#2

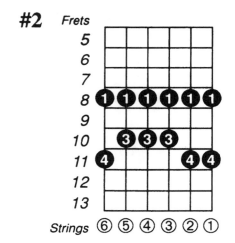

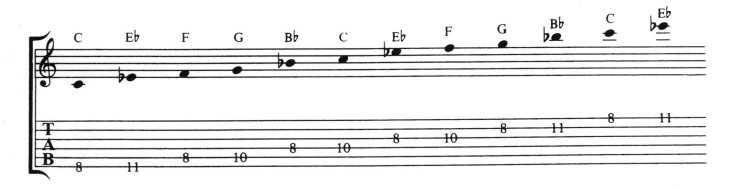

#3

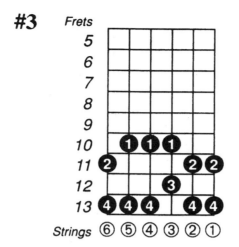

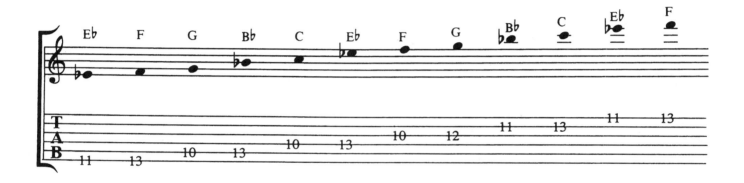

61

Rock Scales
Key of D

#1

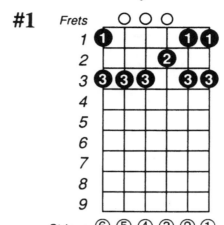

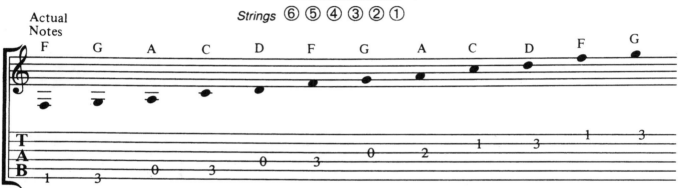

#2

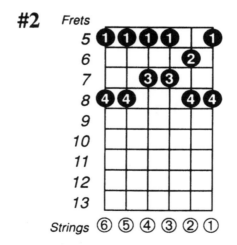

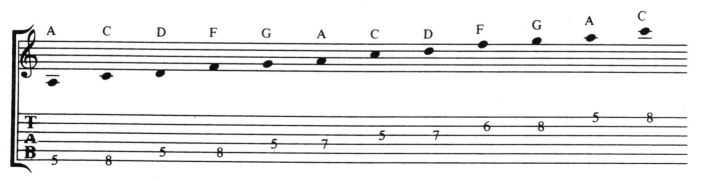

#3

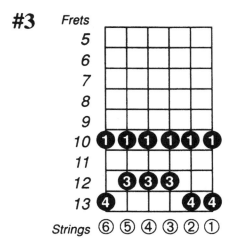

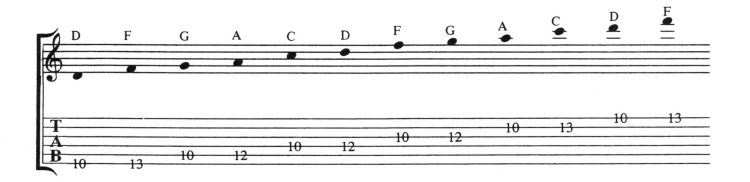

Rock Scales
Key of G

#1

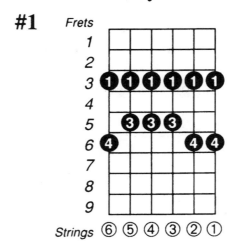

#2

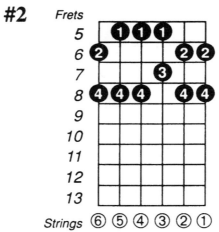

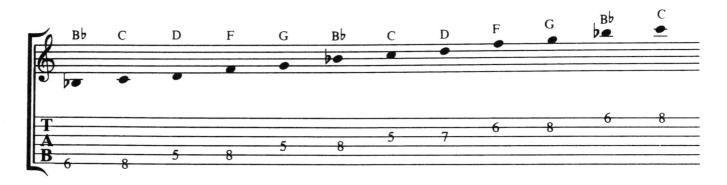

#3

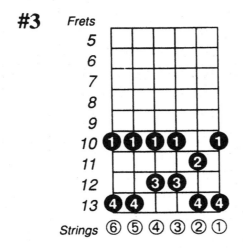

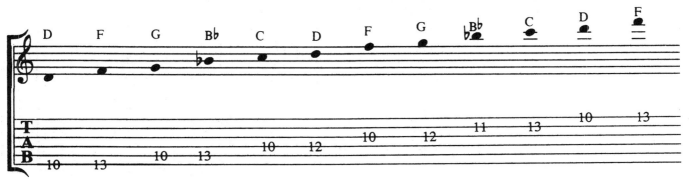

Rock Scales
Key of A

#1

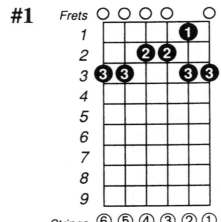

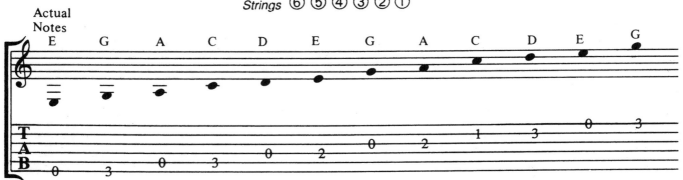

#2

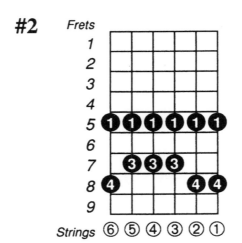

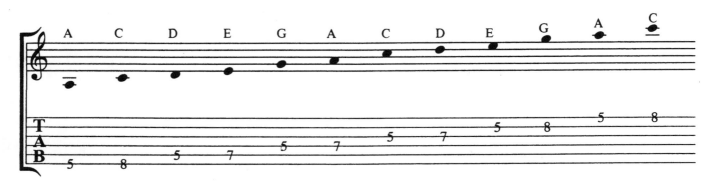

#3 Frets

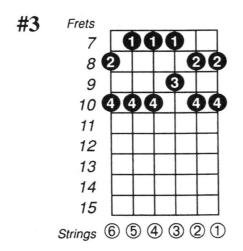

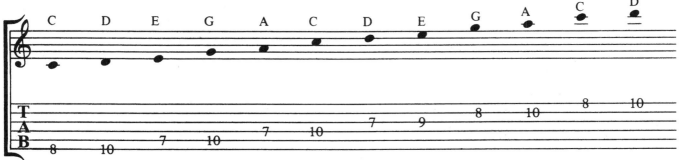

#4 Frets

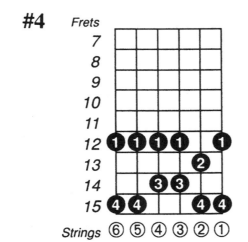

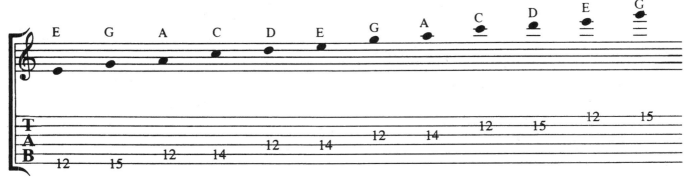

Rock Scales
Key of E

#1

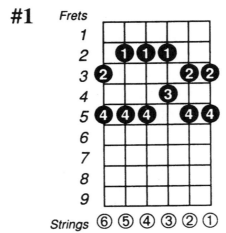

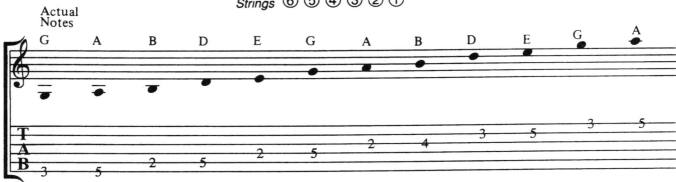

#2

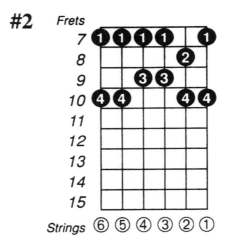

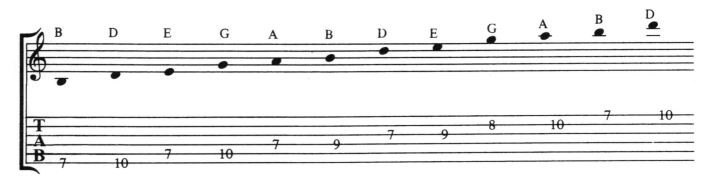

#3

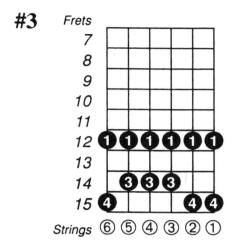

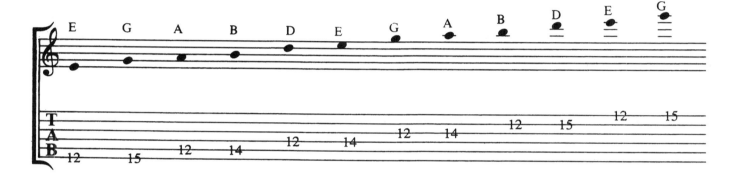

69

Rock Scales
Key of B

#1

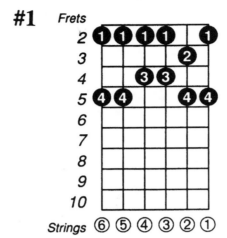

#2

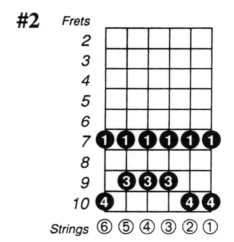

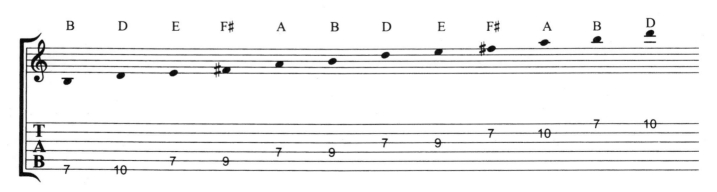

#3

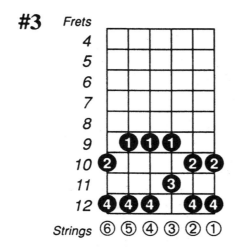

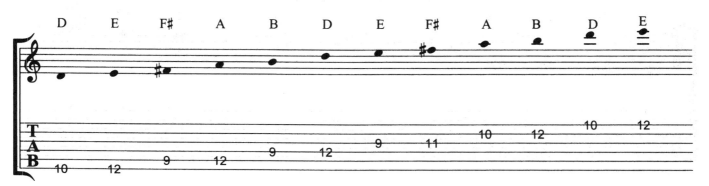

Rock Scales
Key of G♭ / F♯

#1

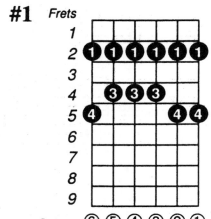

#2

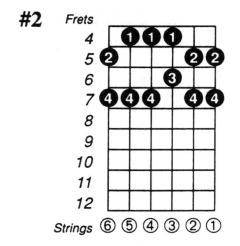

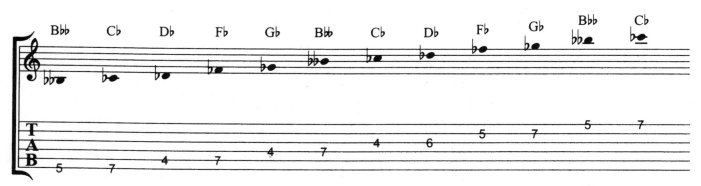

#3

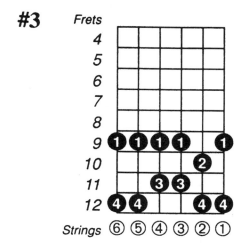

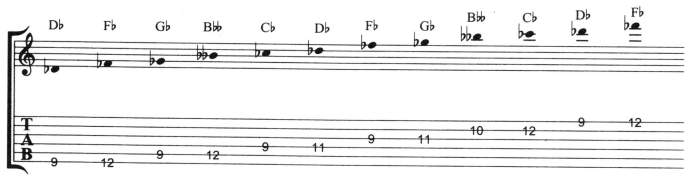

Rock Scales
Key of Db / C#

#1 *Frets*

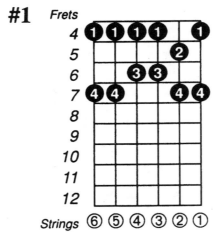

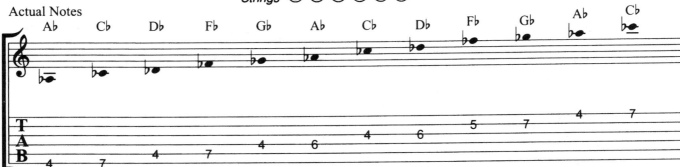

#2 *Frets*

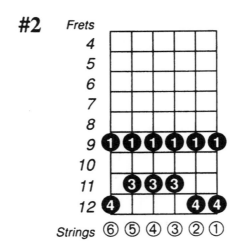

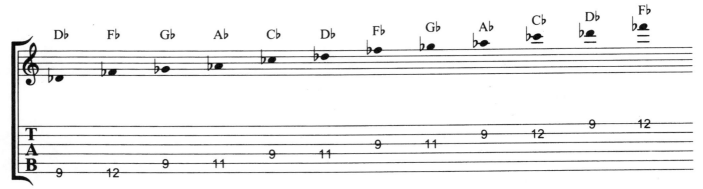

#3

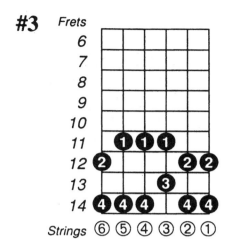

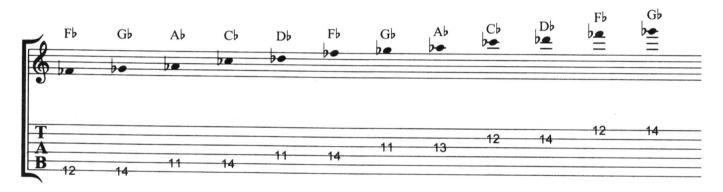

Rock Scales
Key of A♭

#1

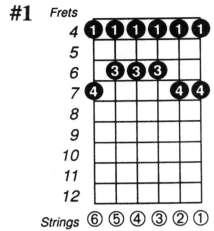

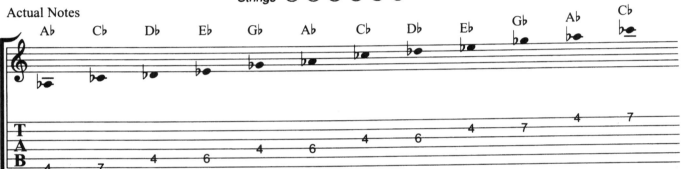

#2

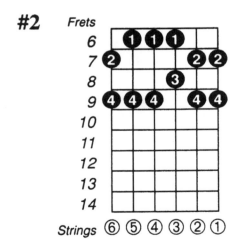

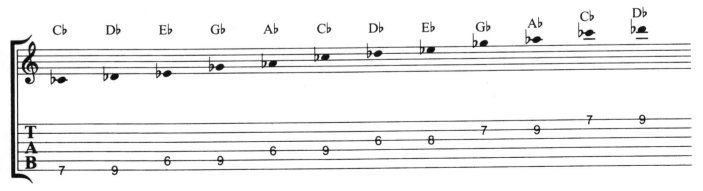

#3

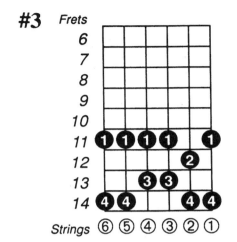

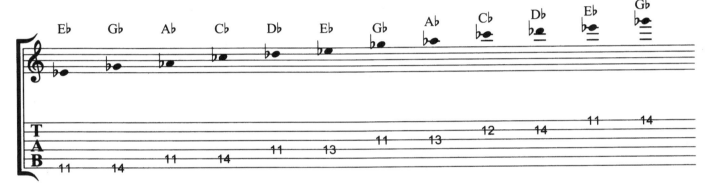

Rock Scales
Key of E♭

#1 *Frets*

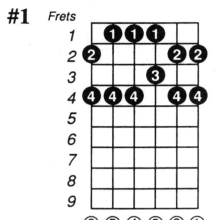

Strings ⑥ ⑤ ④ ③ ② ①

Actual Notes

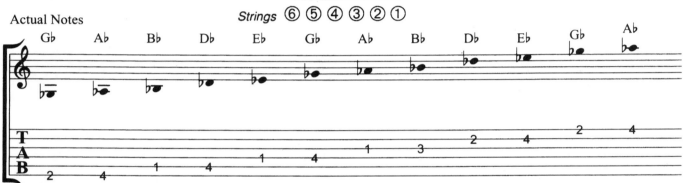

#2 *Frets*

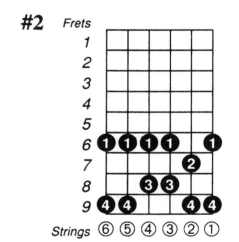

Strings ⑥ ⑤ ④ ③ ② ①

78

#3

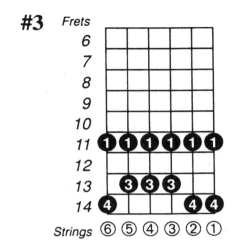

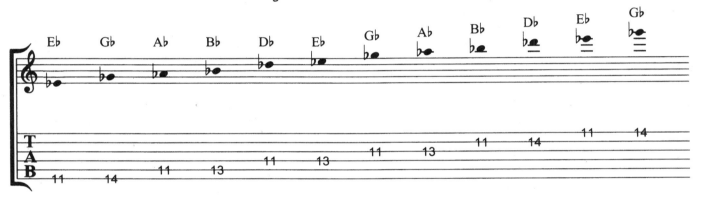

Rock Scales
Key of B♭

#1

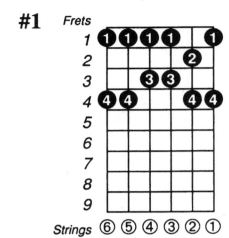

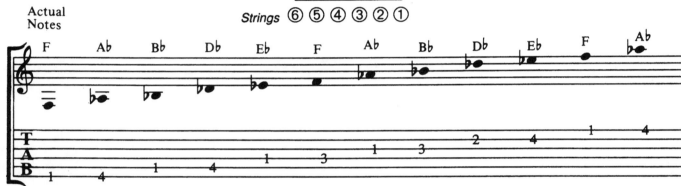

#2

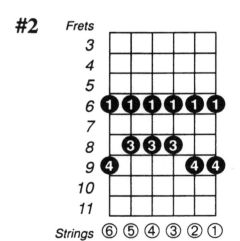

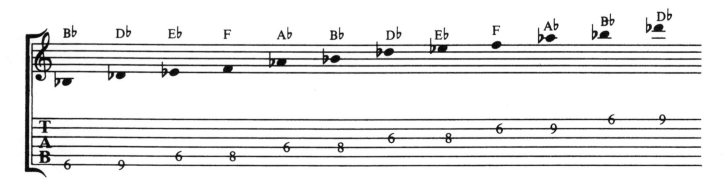

#3

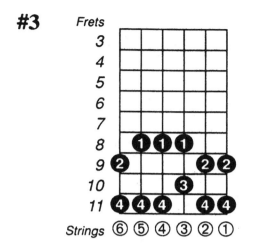

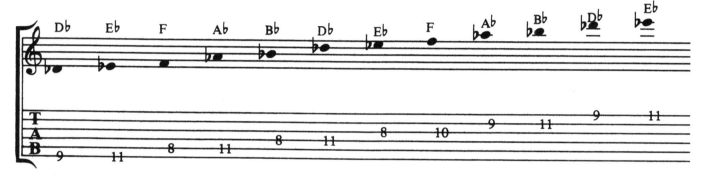

Rock Scales
Key of F

#1

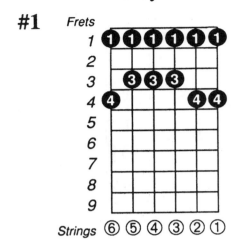

#2

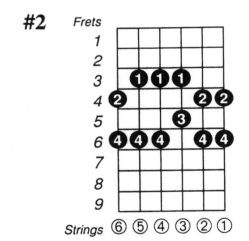

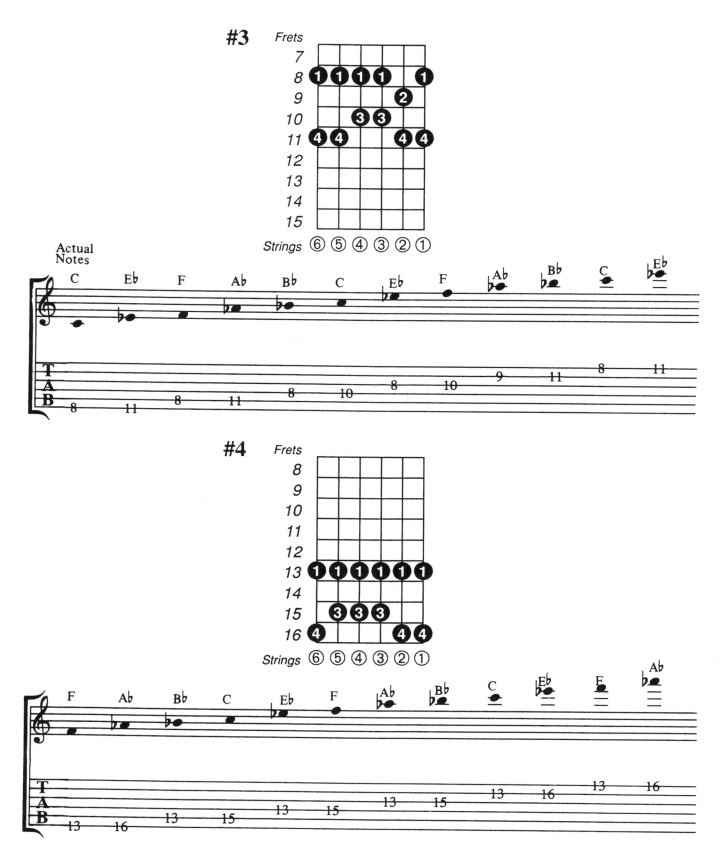

Arpeggio
Section

C Arpeggios

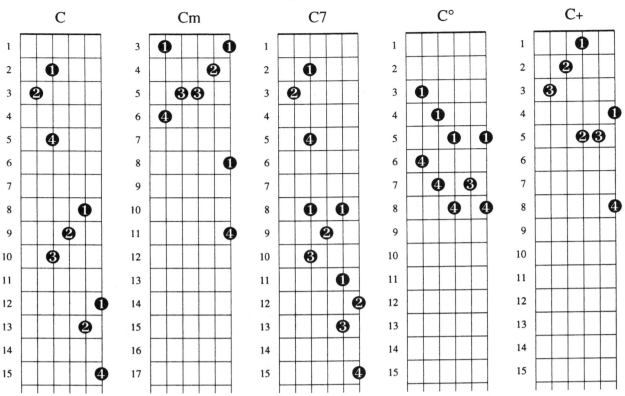

C   Cm   C7   C°   C+

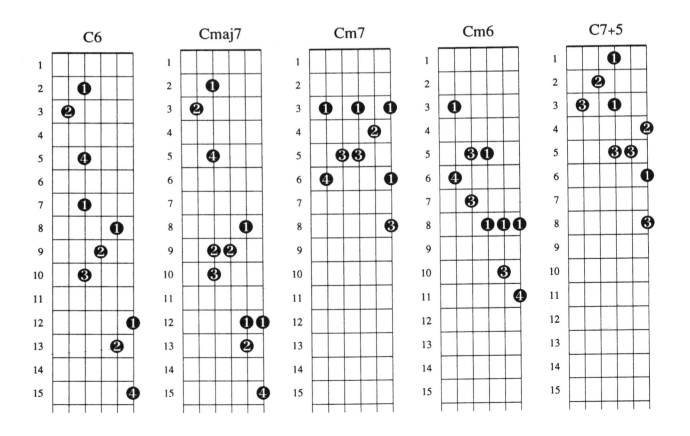

C6   Cmaj7   Cm7   Cm6   C7+5

86

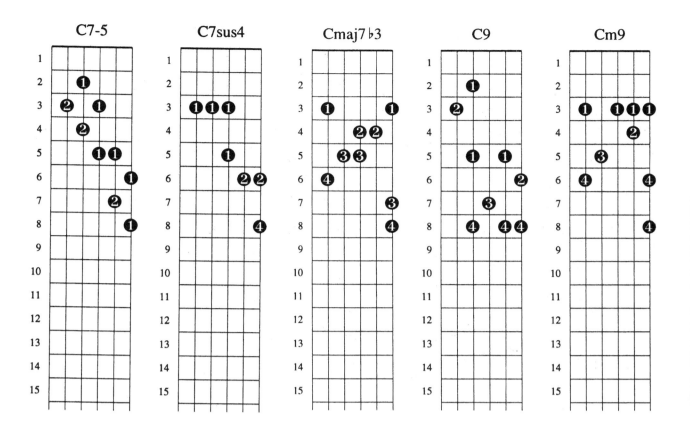

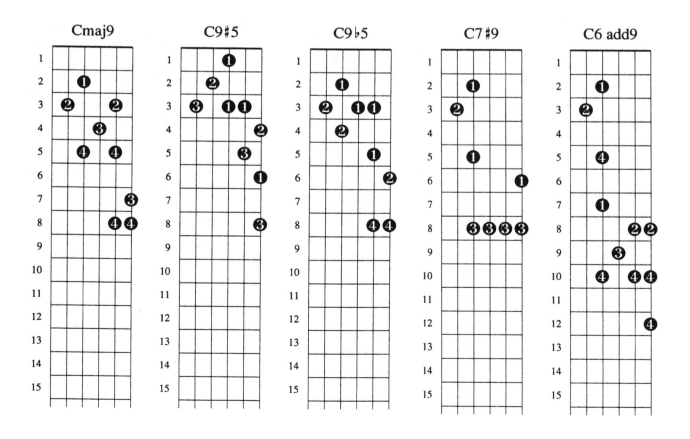

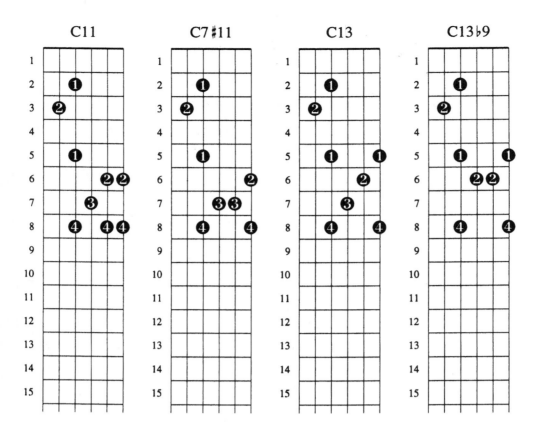

Db/C# Arpeggios

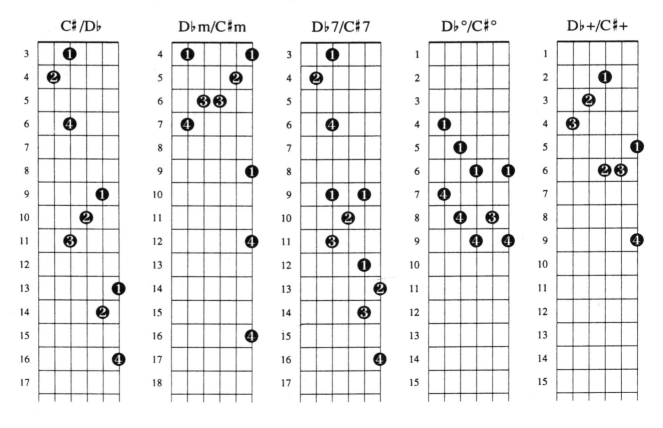

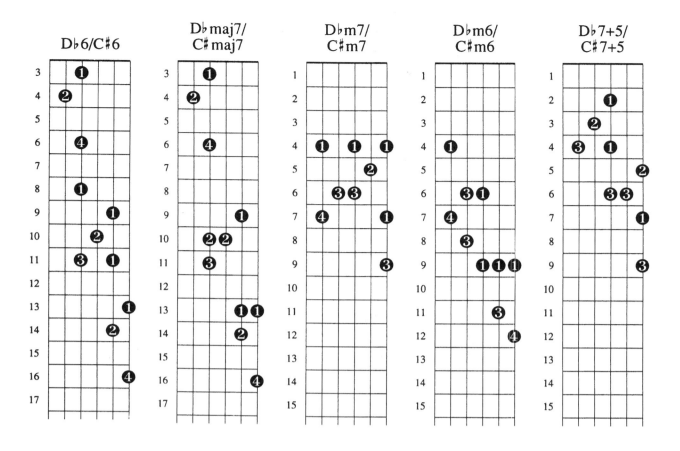

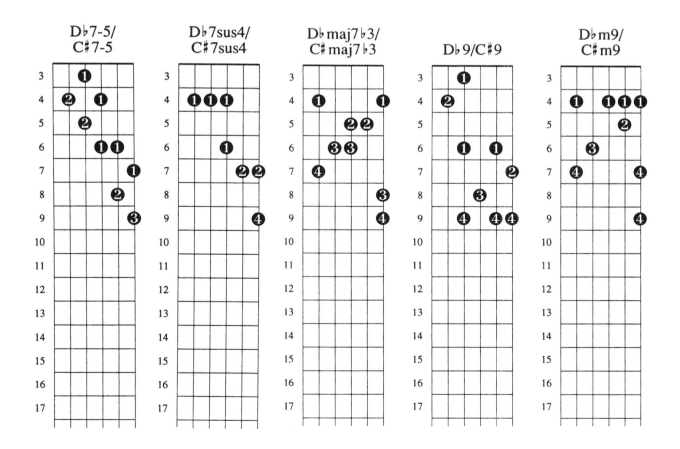

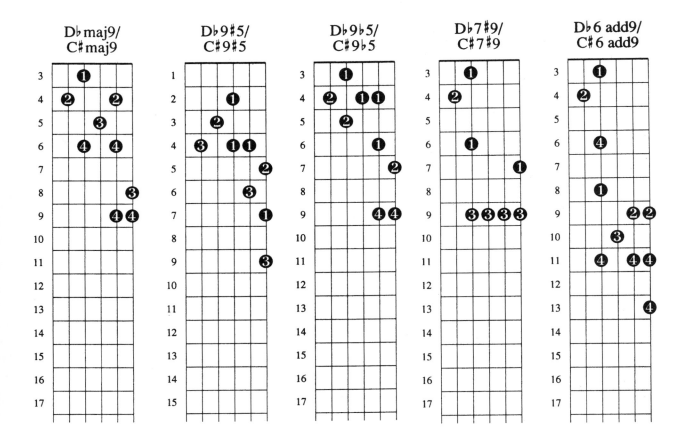

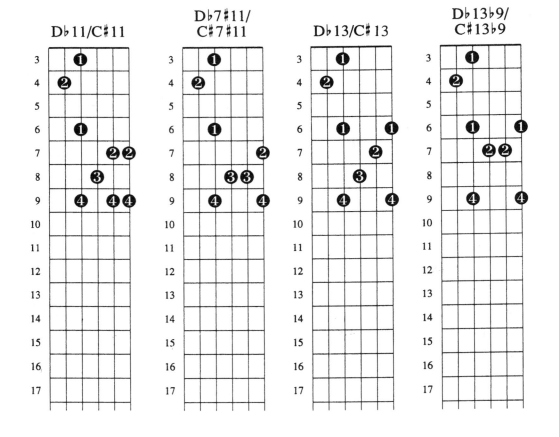

D Arpeggios

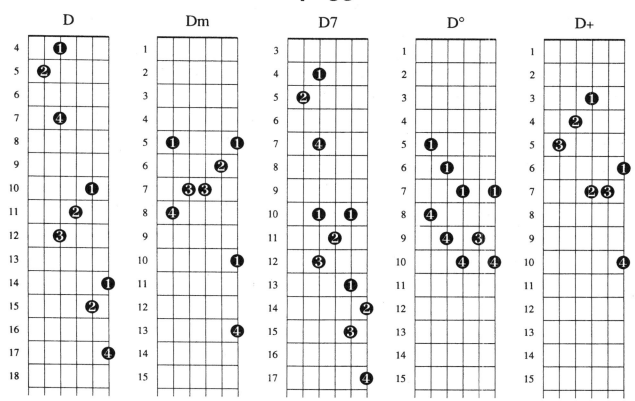

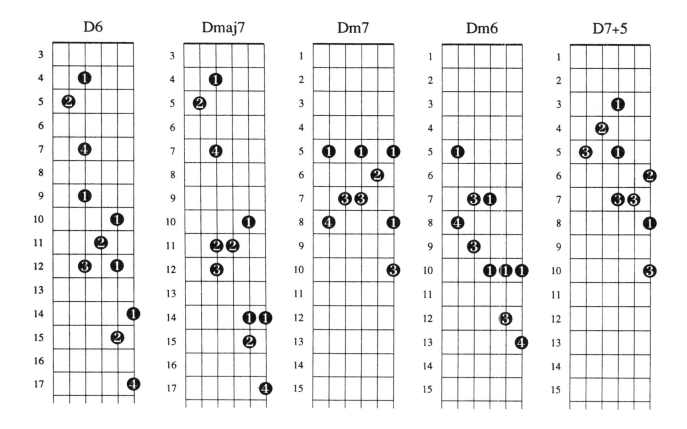

91

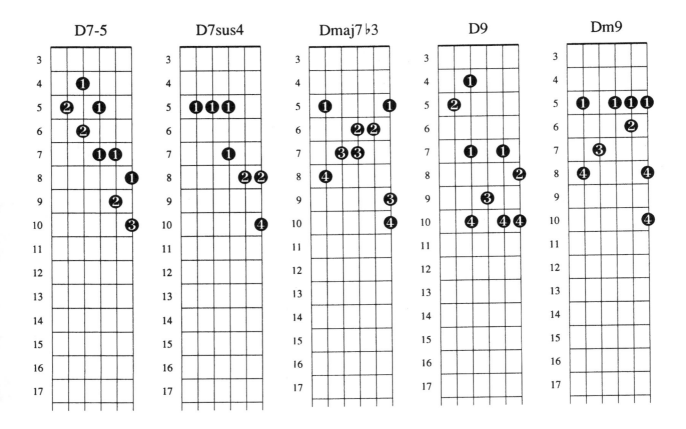

D7-5   D7sus4   Dmaj7♭3   D9   Dm9

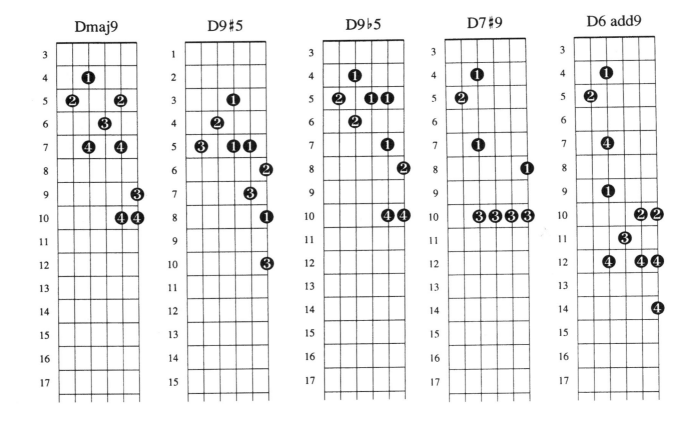

Dmaj9   D9♯5   D9♭5   D7♯9   D6 add9

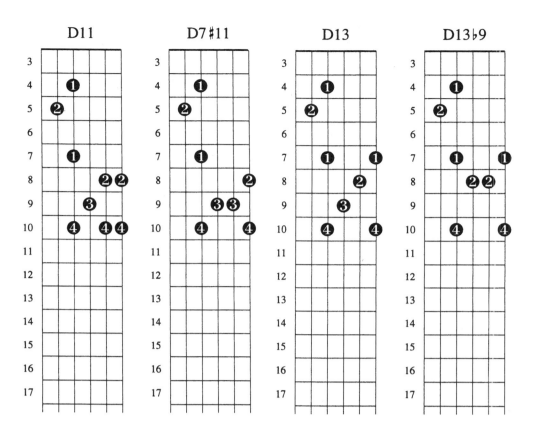

E♭ Arpeggios

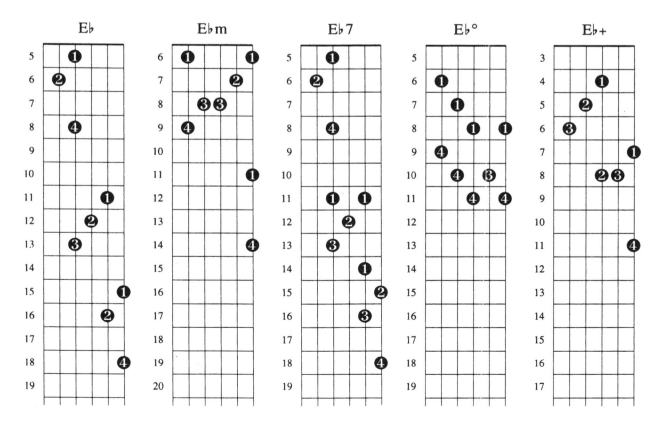

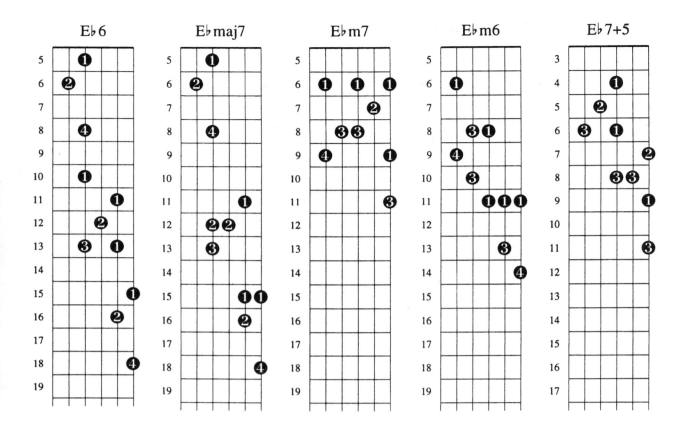

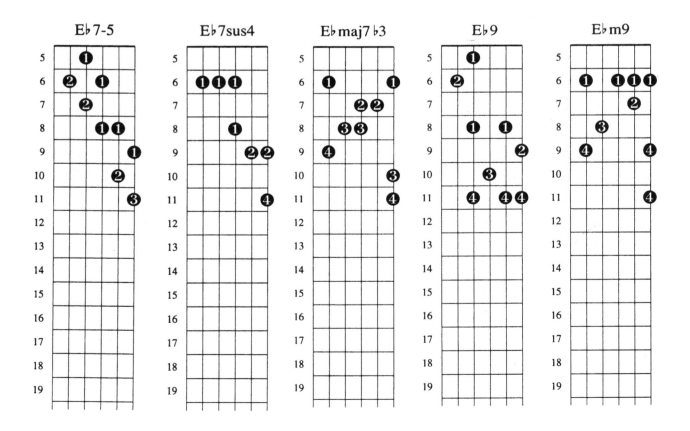

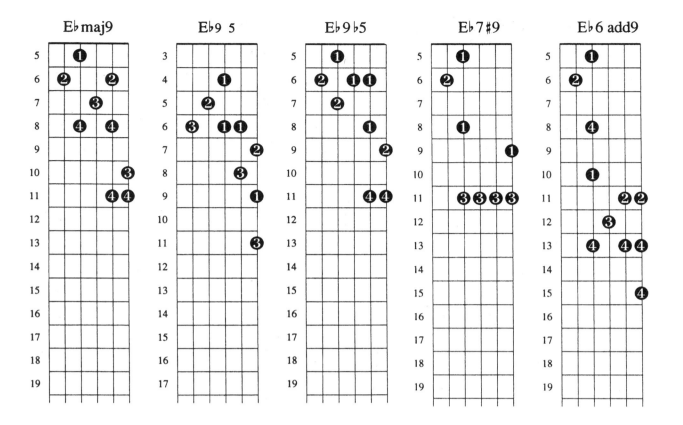

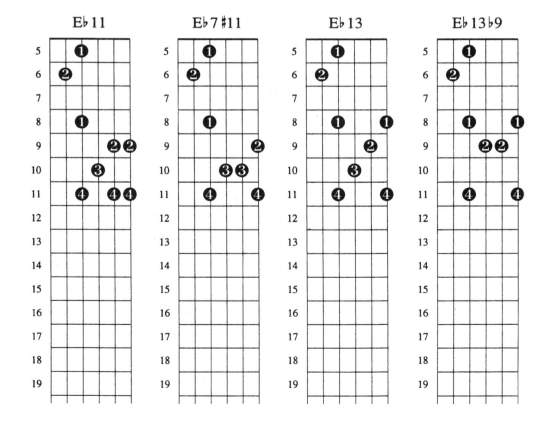

E Arpeggios

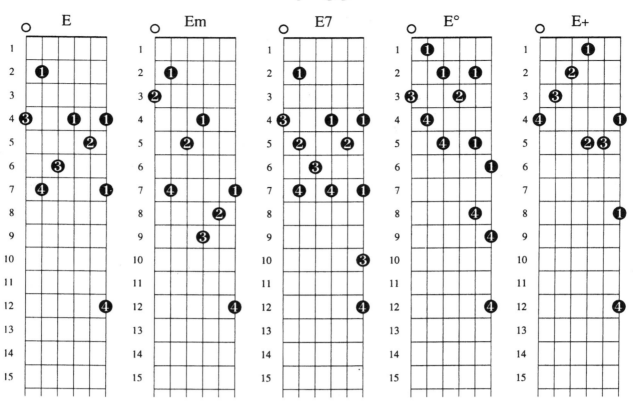

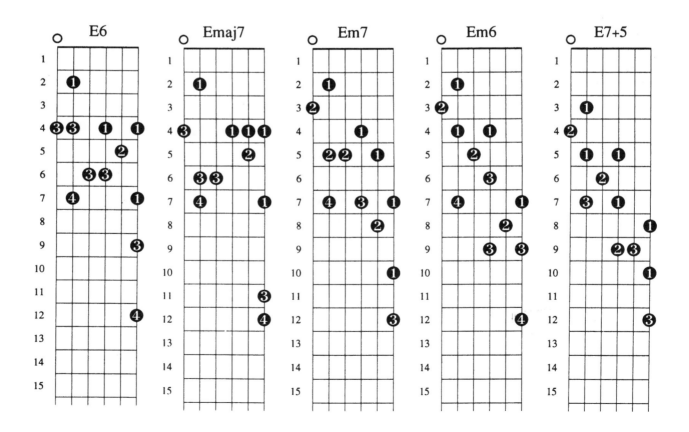

96

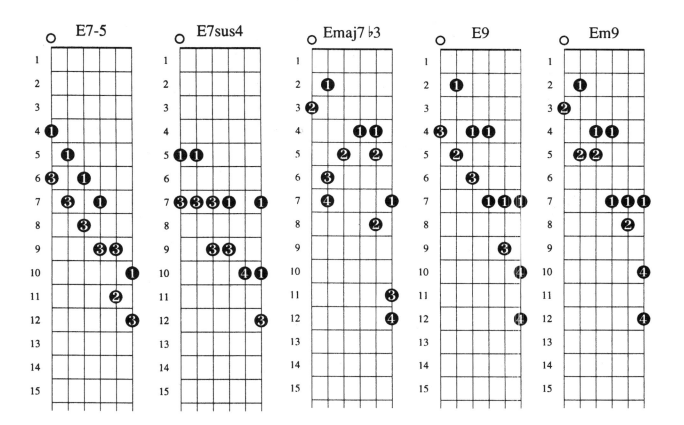

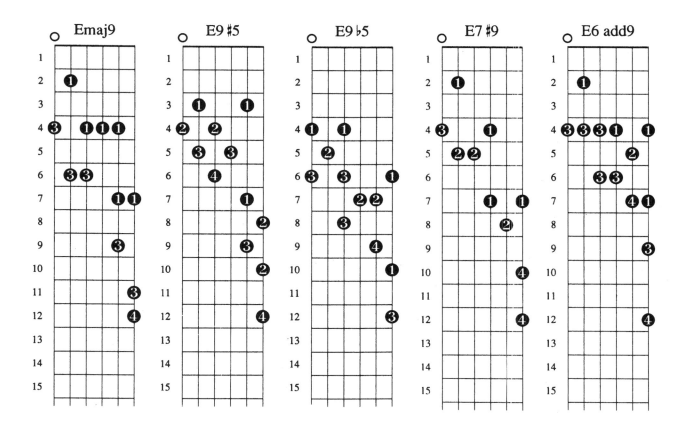

ARPEGGIOS

97

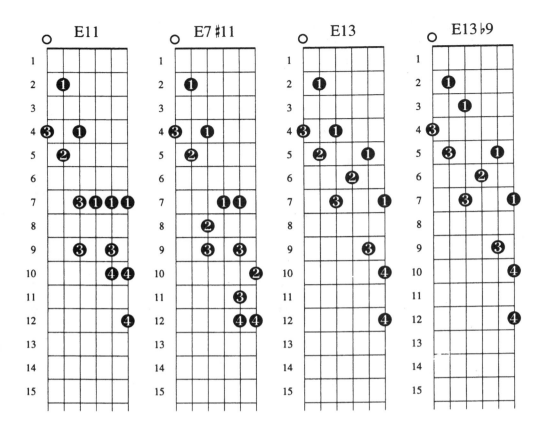

F Arpeggios

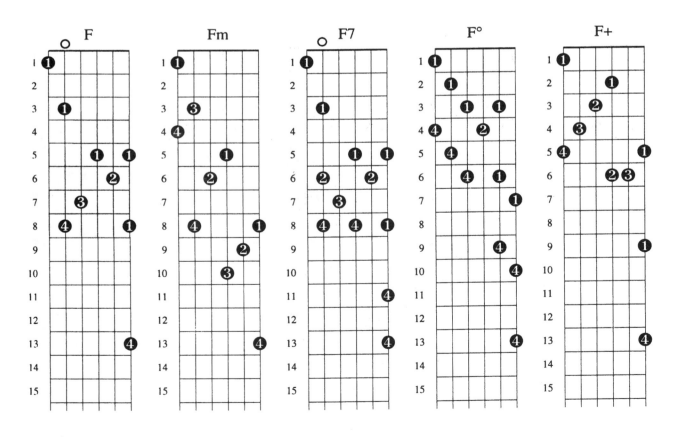

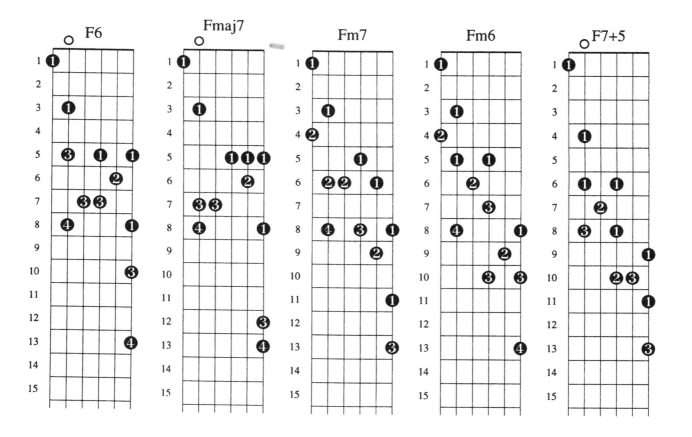

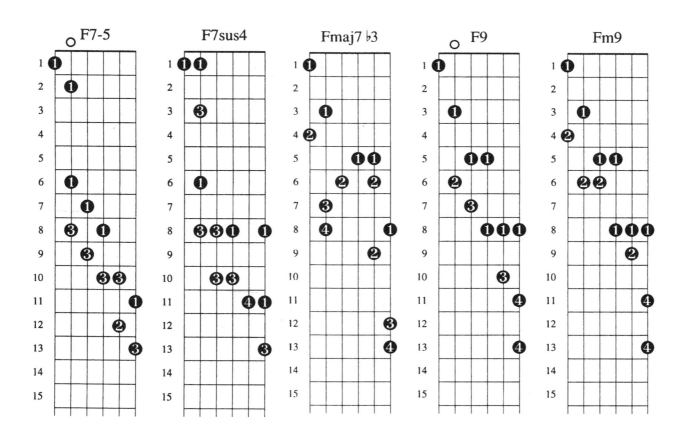

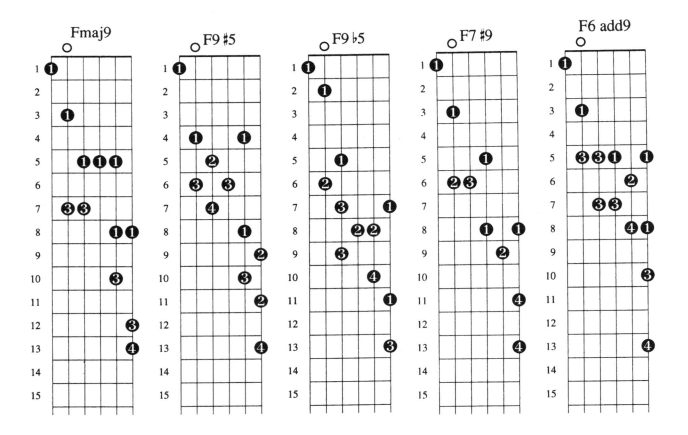

Fmaj9   F9 #5   F9 ♭5   F7 #9   F6 add9

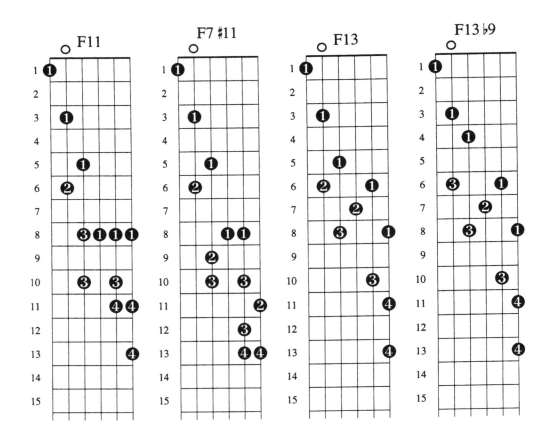

F11   F7 #11   F13   F13 ♭9

F#/Gb Arpeggios

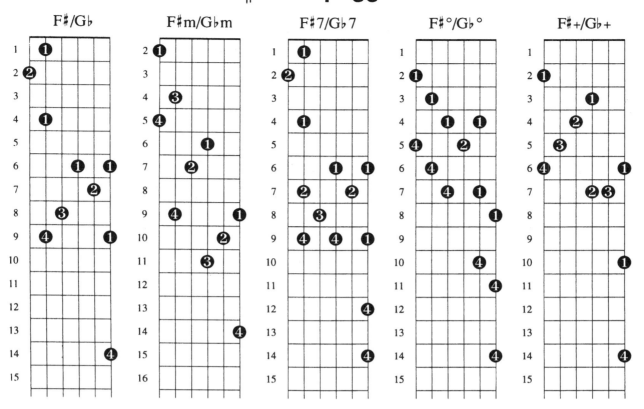

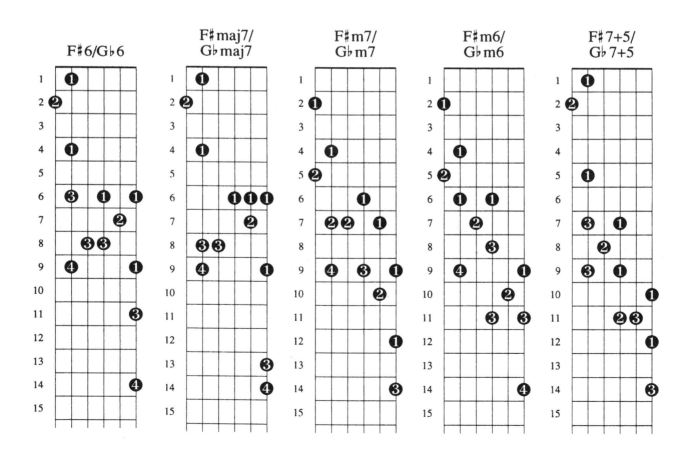

ARPEGGIOS

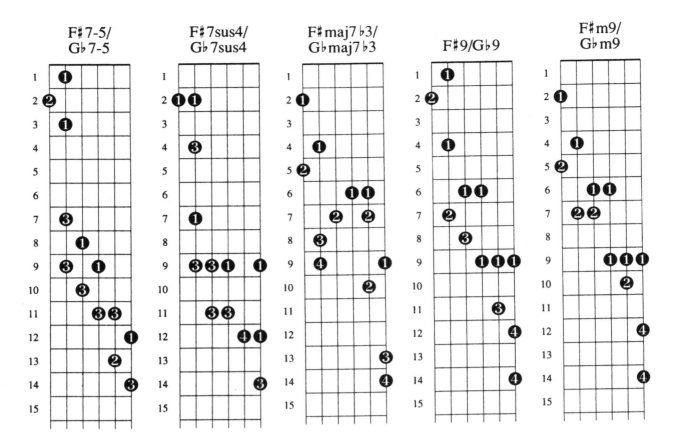

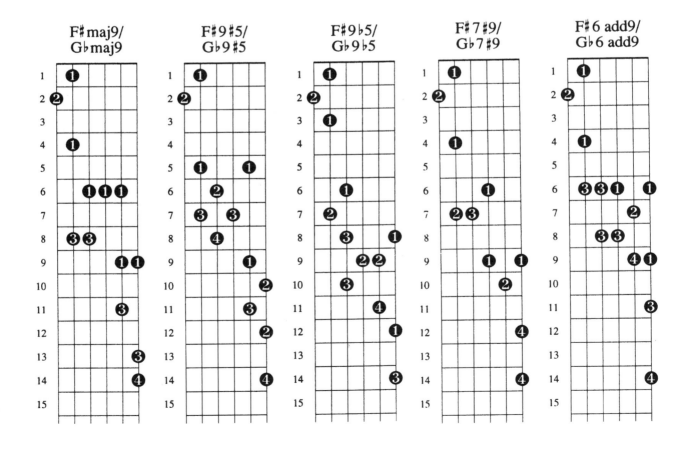

102

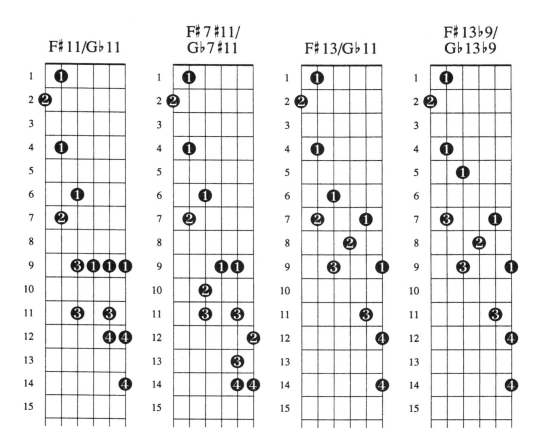

G Arpeggios

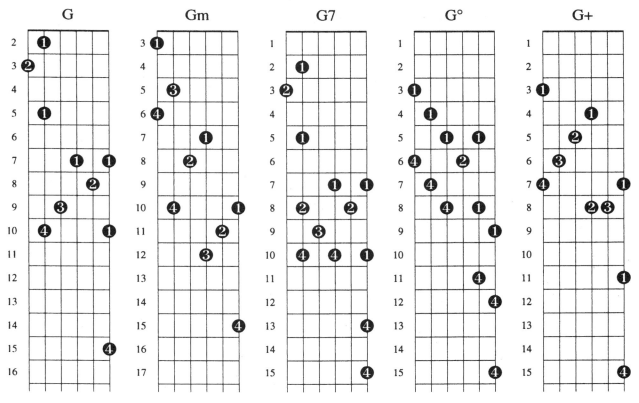

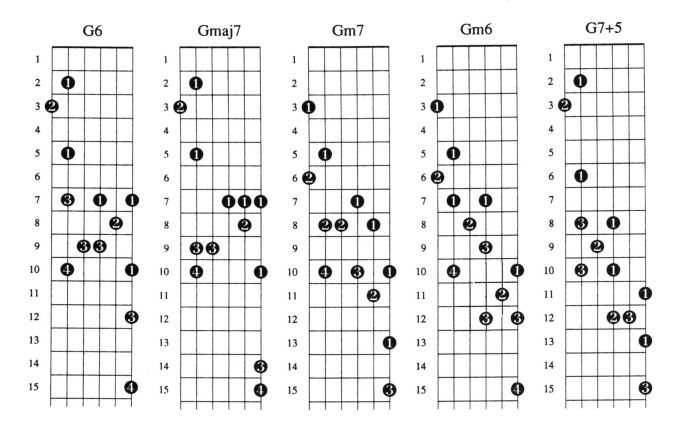

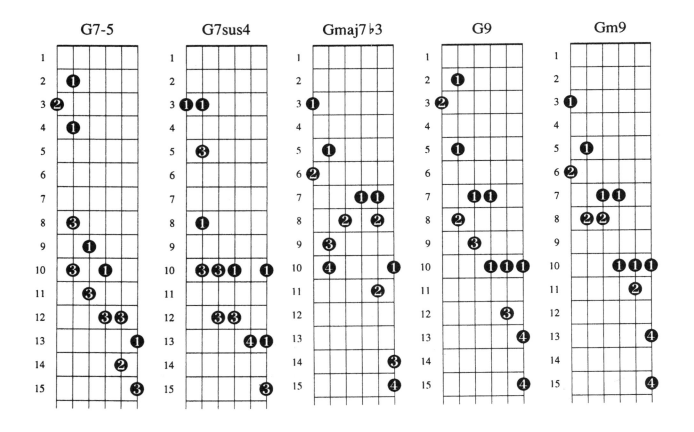

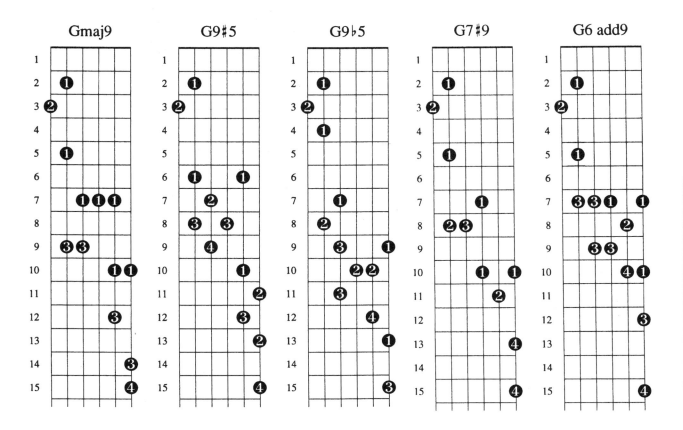

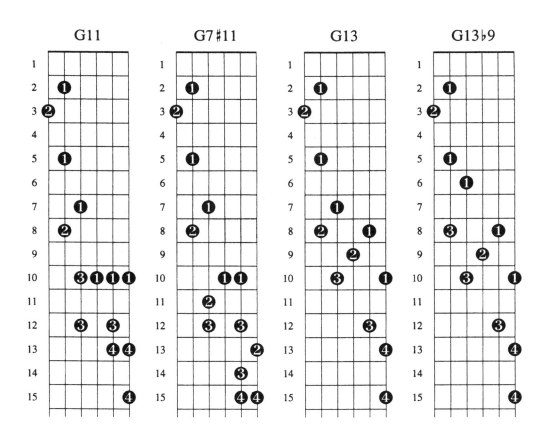

G♯/A♭ Arpeggios

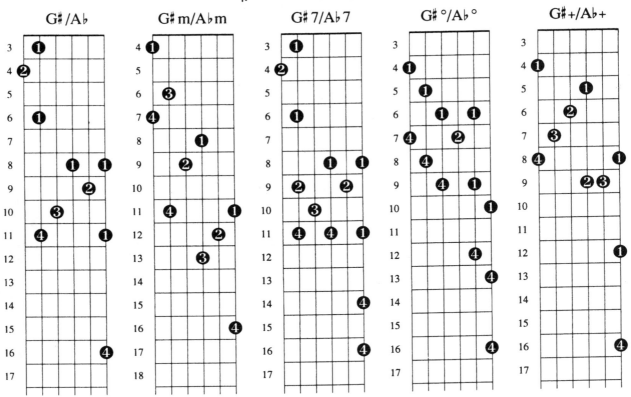

ARPEGGIOS

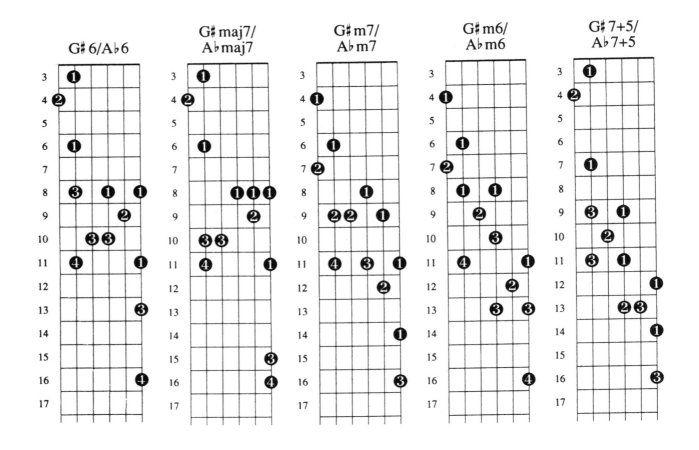

106

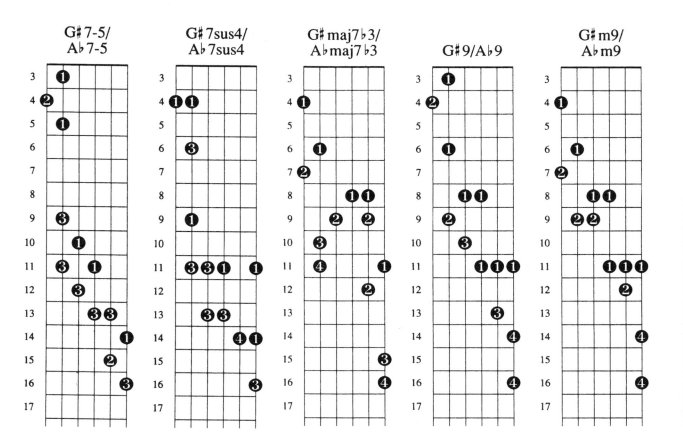

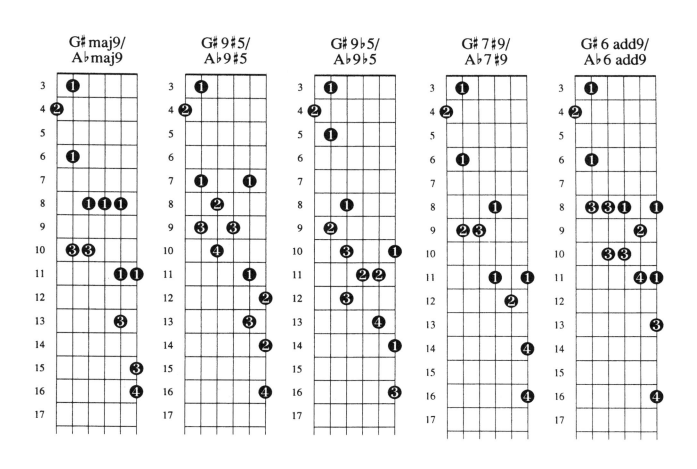

ARPEGGIOS

107

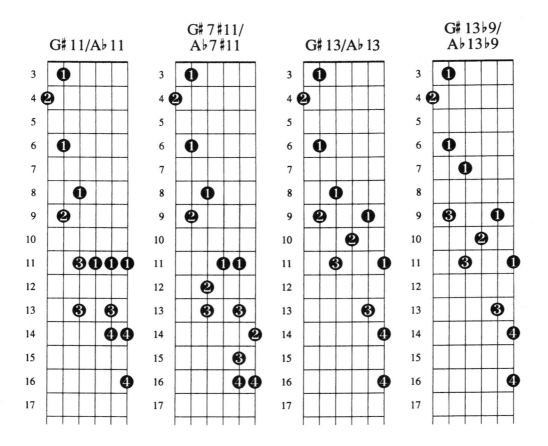

G# 11/Ab 11   G# 7#11/Ab7#11   G# 13/Ab 13   G# 13b9/Ab 13b9

A Arpeggios

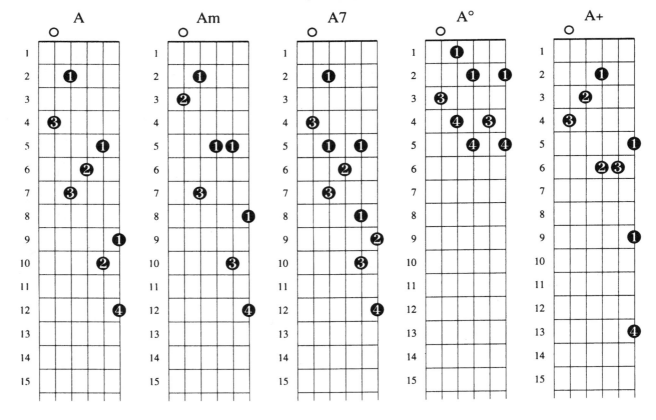

A   Am   A7   A°   A+

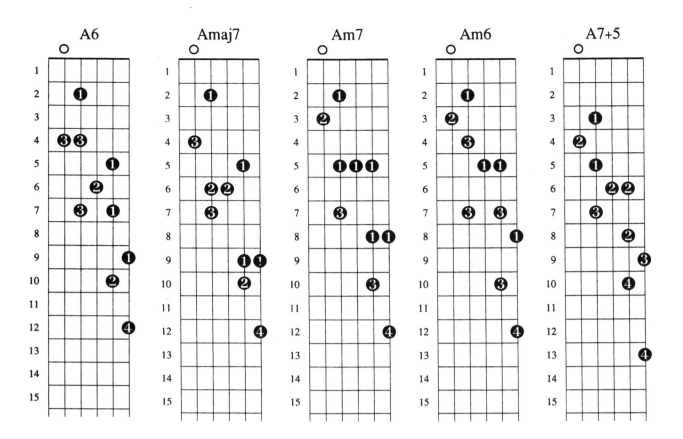

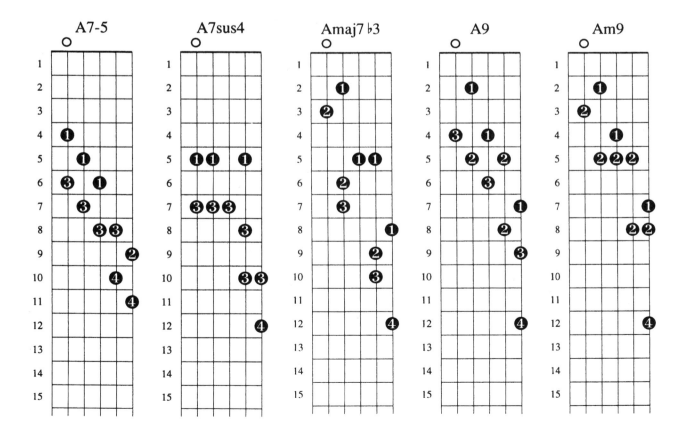

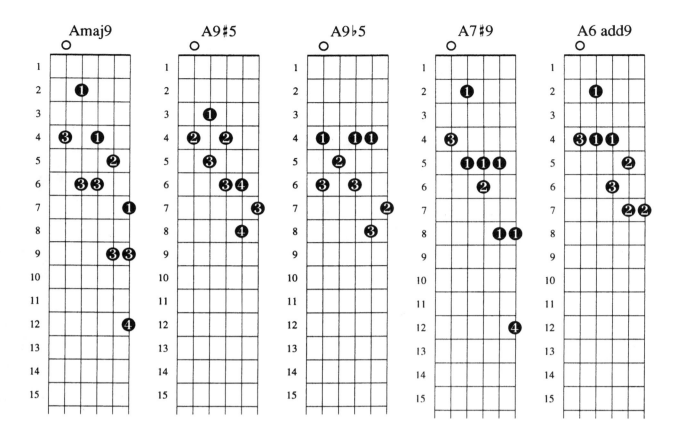

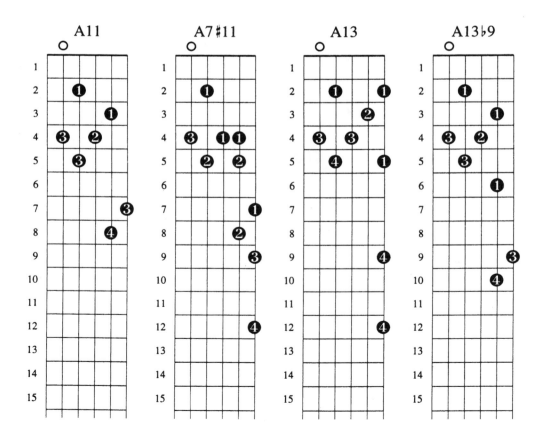

B♭ Arpeggios

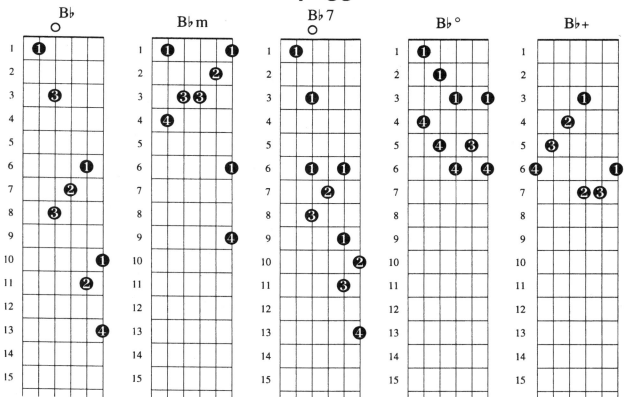

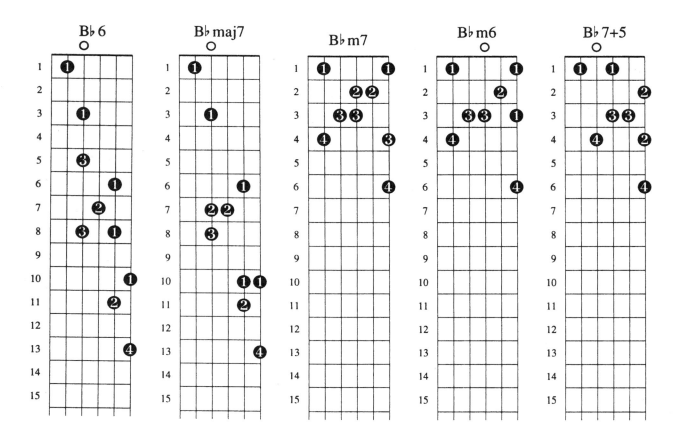

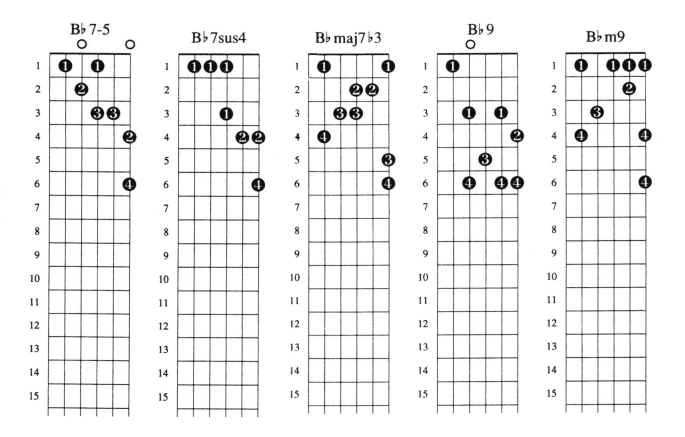

B♭7-5   B♭7sus4   B♭maj7♭3   B♭9   B♭m9

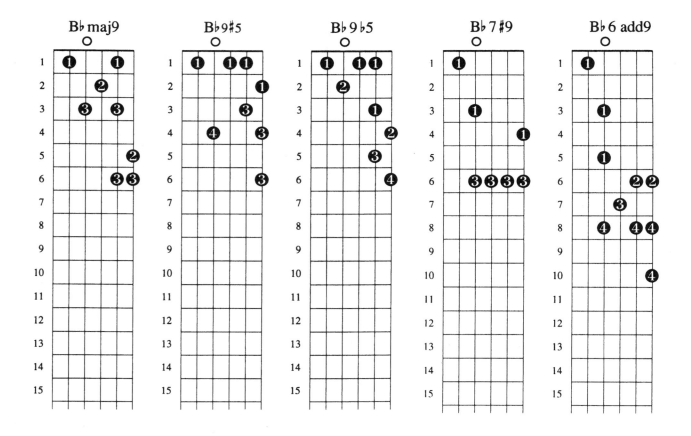

B♭maj9   B♭9#5   B♭9♭5   B♭7#9   B♭6 add9

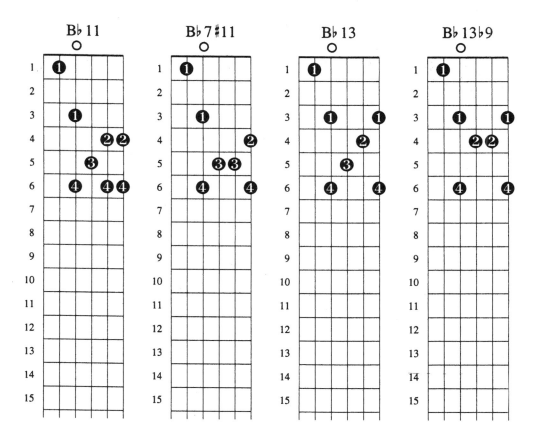

B Arpeggios

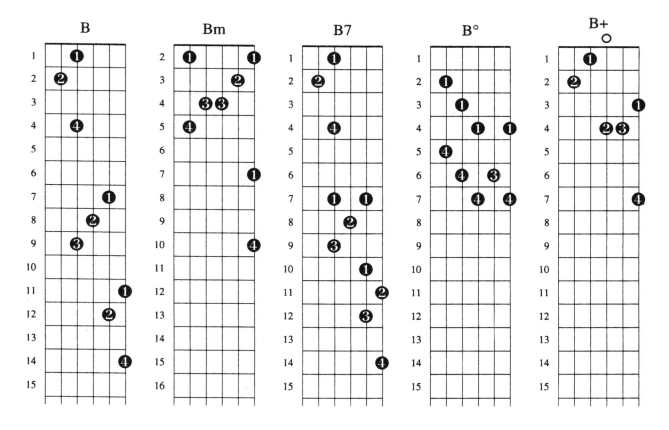

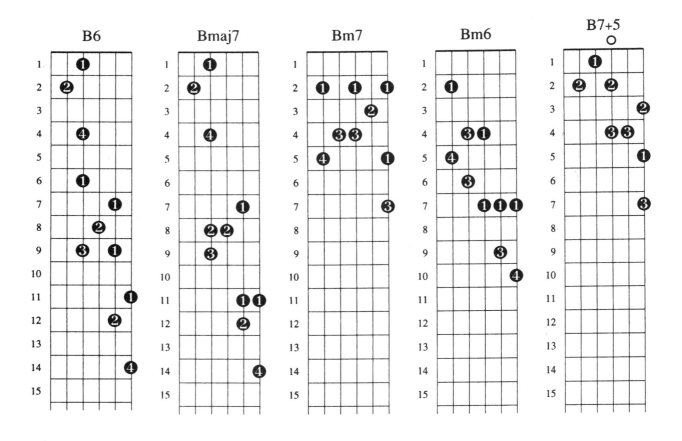

B6 Bmaj7 Bm7 Bm6 B7+5

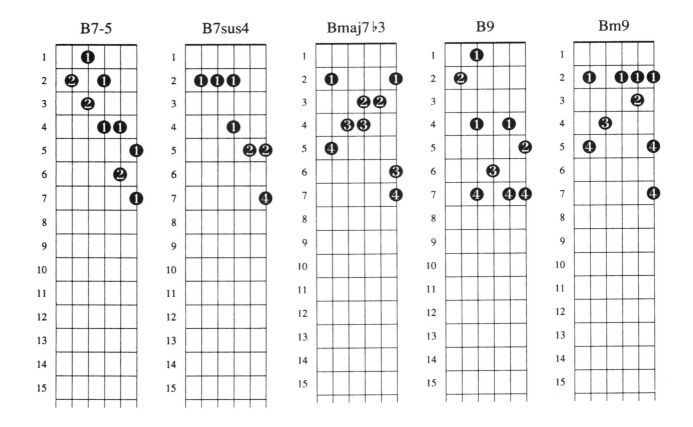

B7-5 B7sus4 Bmaj7♭3 B9 Bm9

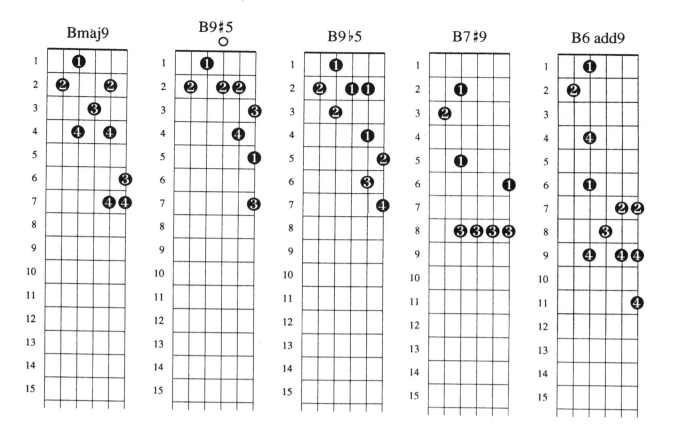

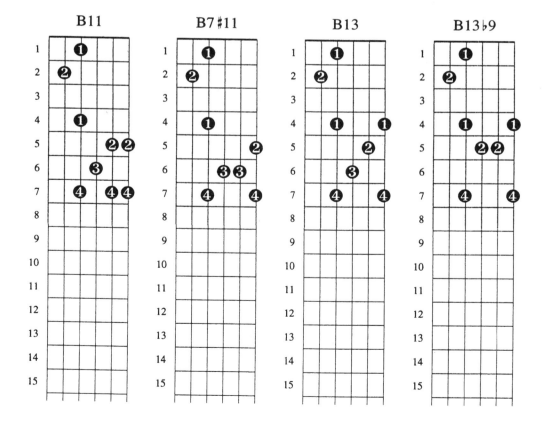

Chord
Section

C Major

Symbol (C)

G
E
C

5th
3rd
Root

Melody Chords

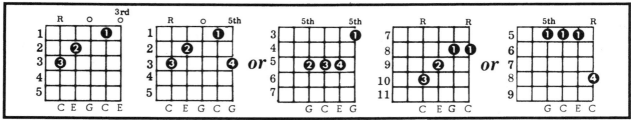

Inside Chords

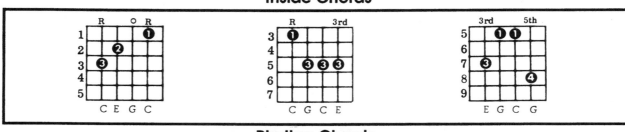

Rhythm Chords

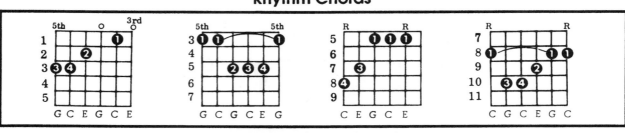

Bottom 4-String Chords

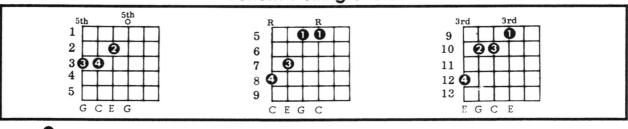

C Minor

Symbol (C m)

G
Eb
C

5th
b3rd
Root

Melody Chords

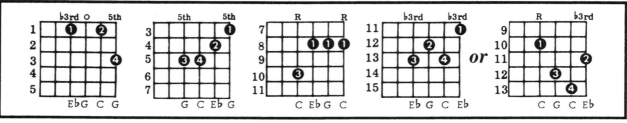

Inside Chords

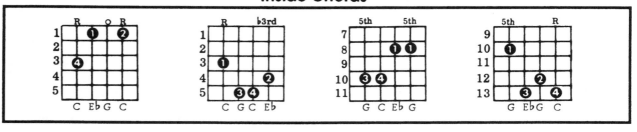

CHORDS

118

Rhythm Chords

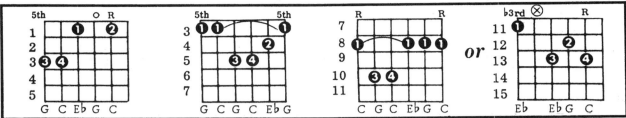

Bottom 4-String Chords

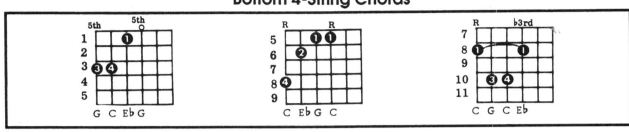

C Diminished

Symbols
(C-, C⁰, Cdim)

Melody Chords

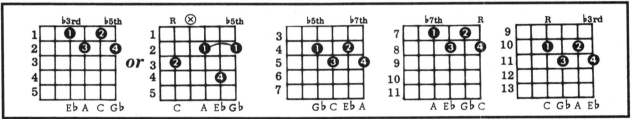

Inside Chords

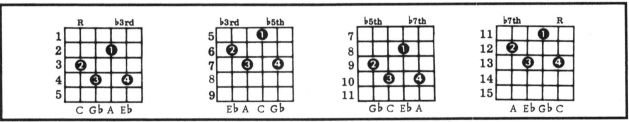

Rhythm Chords

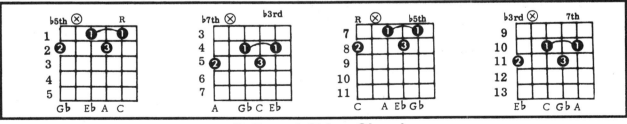

Bottom 4-String Chords

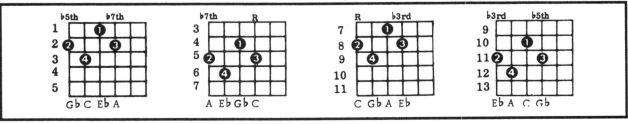

C Augmented

G# E C

Symbol (C +)

Melody Chords

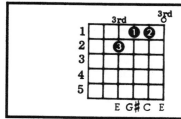 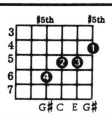 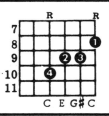

Inside & Rhythm Chords

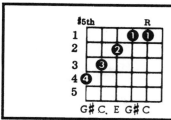 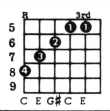 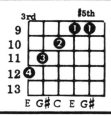

Bottom 4-String Chords

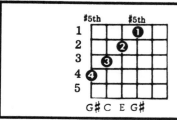 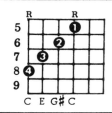 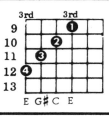

C 7th

Bb G E C

Symbol (C 7)

Melody Chords

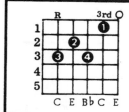 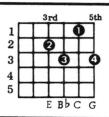 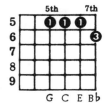 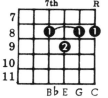 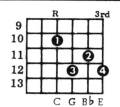

Inside Chords

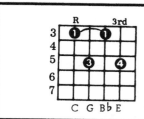 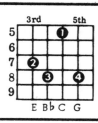 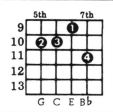 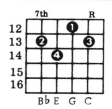

Rhythm Chords

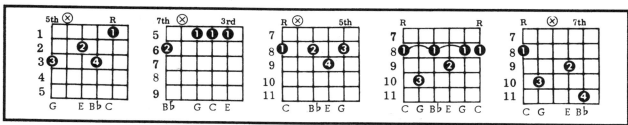

Bottom 4-String Chords

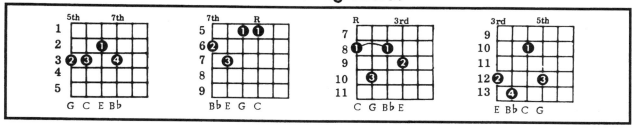

C Minor 7th

Bb 7th
G 5th
Eb b3rd
C Root

Symbol (C m7)

Melody Chords

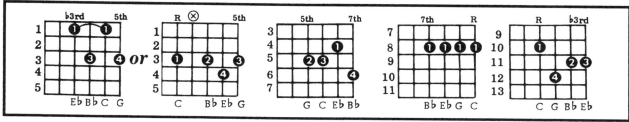

Inside Chords

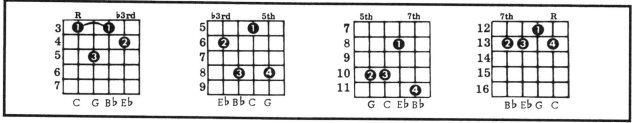

Rhythm Chords

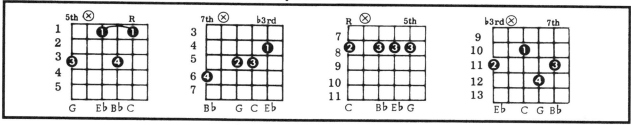

Bottom 4-String Chords

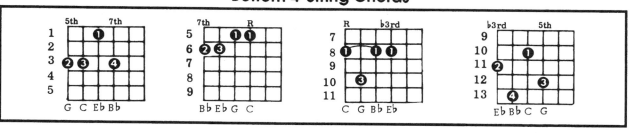

CHORDS

C 7th Aug. 5th

Symbols
(C 7 + 5, C 7 ♯ 5)

Melody Chords

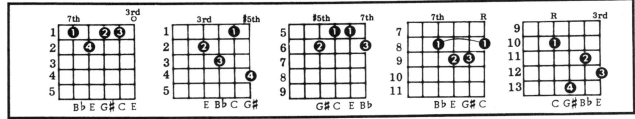

Inside Chords

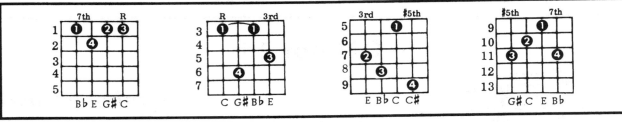

Rhythm Chords

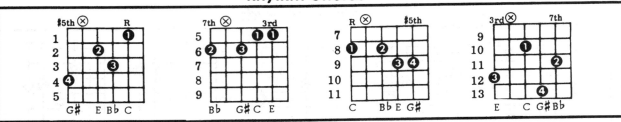

Bottom 4-String Chords

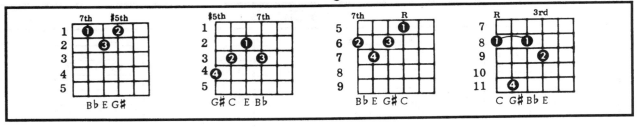

C 7th Flat 5th

Symbols
(C7-5, C7 ♭5)

Melody Chords

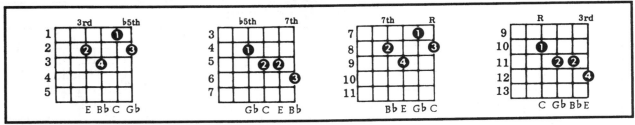

122

CHORDS

Inside Chords

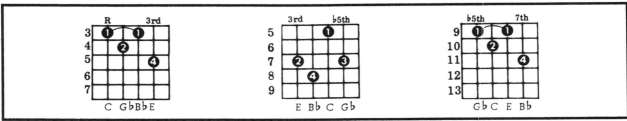

Rhythm Chords

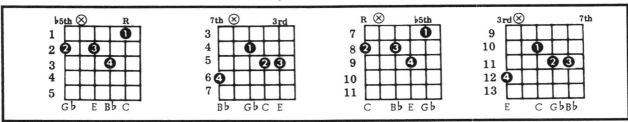

Bottom 4-String Chords

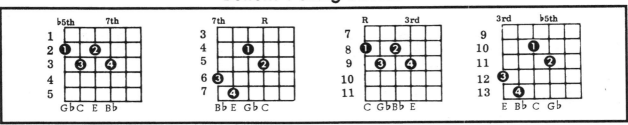

C Major 7th

Symbol (Cma7)

Melody Chords

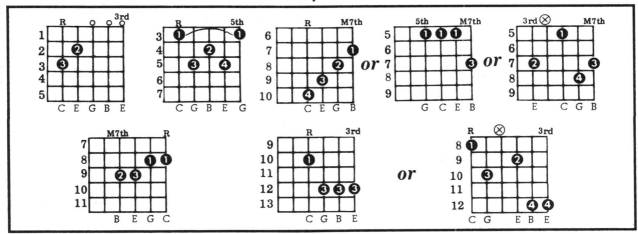

Inside & Rhythm Chords

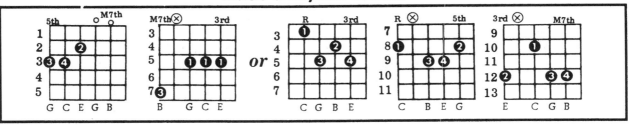

Bottom 4-String Chords

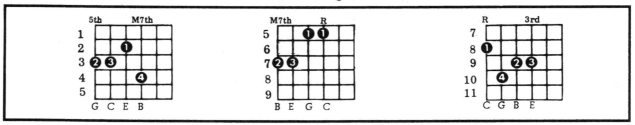

C Major 7th Flat 3rd

Symbols
(Cma7♭3, Cmin-maj7)

Melody Chords

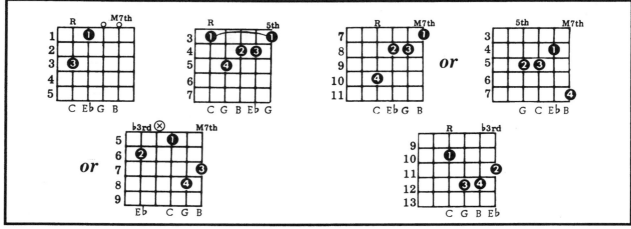

Inside & Rhythm Chords

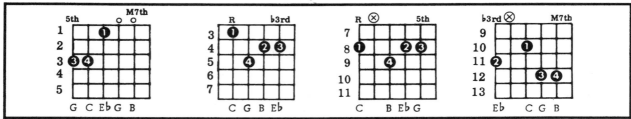

C Minor 7th Flat 5th

Symbol (Cm7♭5)

Melody Chords

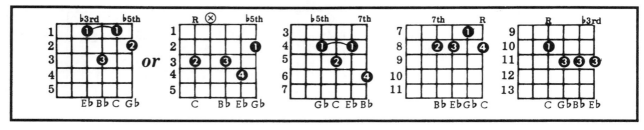

124

Inside Chords

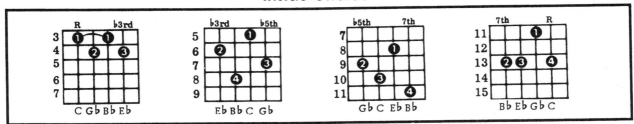

Rhythm Chords

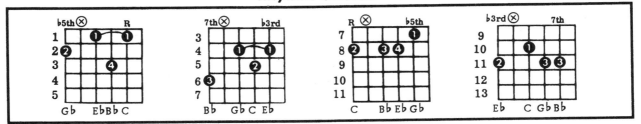

C7 Suspended 4th

Bb — 7th
G — 5th
F — 4th
C — Root

Symbol (C 7sus4)

Melody Chords

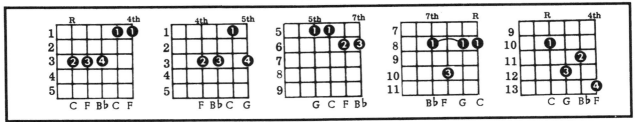

Inside Chords

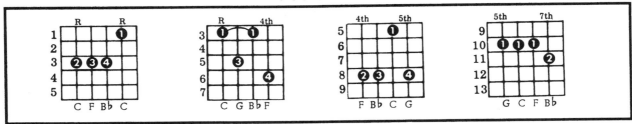

Rhythm Chords

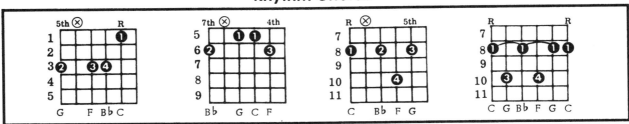

CHORDS

C 6th

A
G
E
C

6th
5th
3rd
Root

Symbol (C6)

Melody Chords

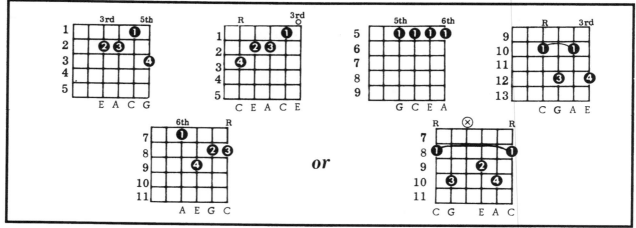

Inside Chords

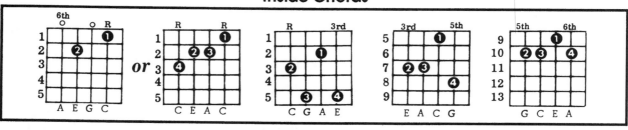

Rhythm Chords

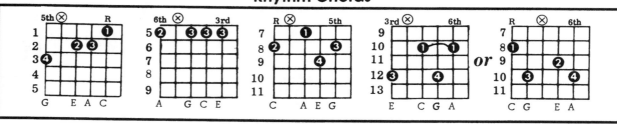

Bottom 4-String Chords

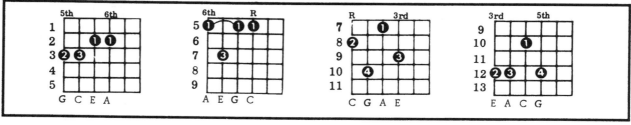

CHORDS

126

C Minor 6th

Symbol (Cm6)

Melody Chords

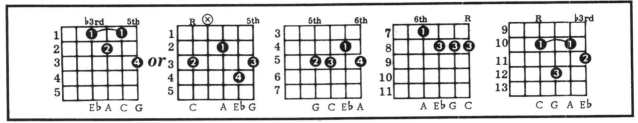

Inside Chords

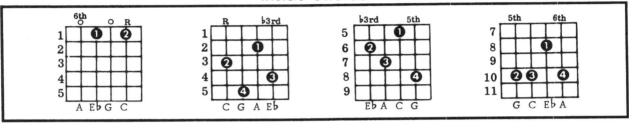

Rhythm Chords

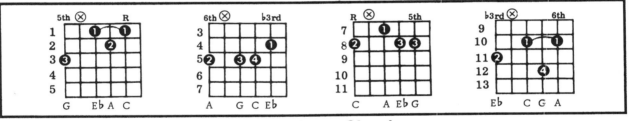

Bottom 4-String Chords

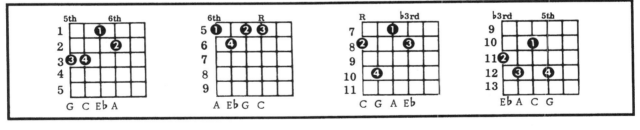

C 9th

Symbol (C9)

Melody Chords

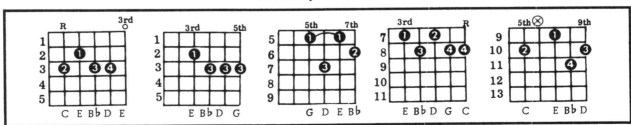

127

Inside & Rhythm Chords

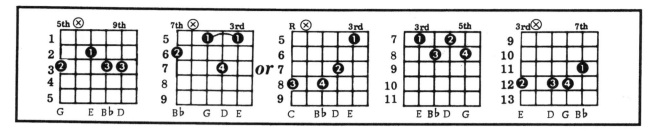

C Minor 9th

Symbol (C m9)

Melody Chords

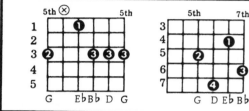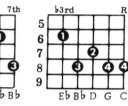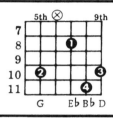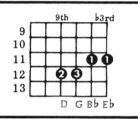

Inside & Rhythm Chords

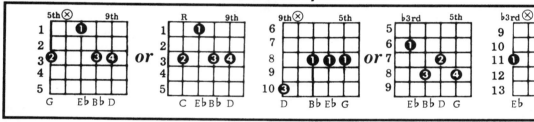

CHORDS

C Major 9th

Symbol (C ma 9)

Melody Chords

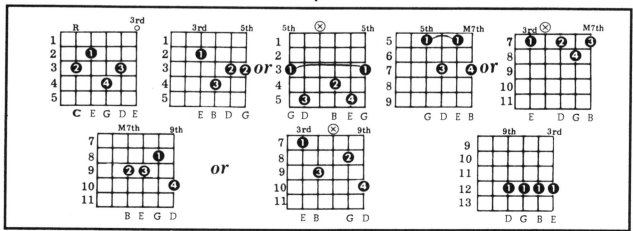

Inside Chords

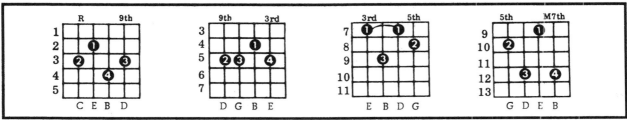

Rhythm Chords

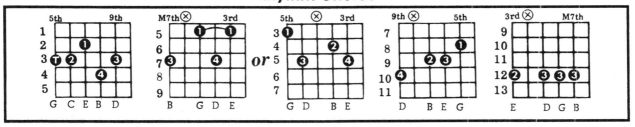

C9 Sharp 5th

Symbols
(C9 + 5, C9#5)

Melody Chords

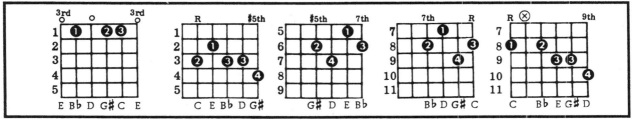

Inside & Rhythm Chords

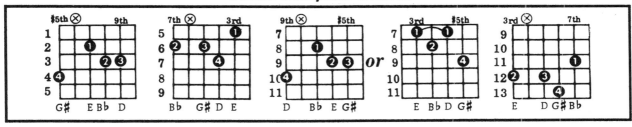

C9 Flat 5th

Symbols
(C9-5, C9♭5)

Melody Chords

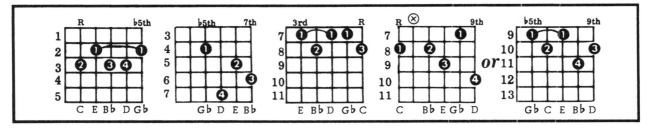

C9 Flat 5th cont.

Inside & Rhythm Chords

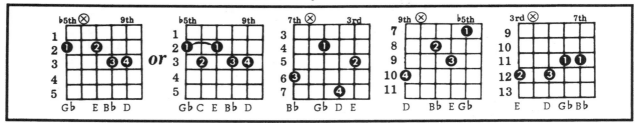

C7 Flat 9th

Symbol (C 7♭9)

Melody Chords

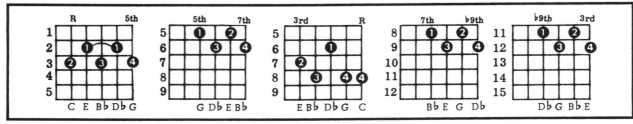

Inside & Rhythm Chords

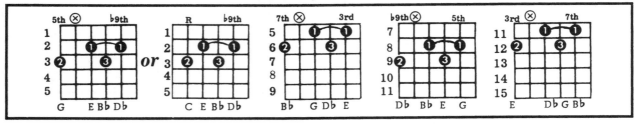

C7 Sharp 9th

*Symbols
(C 9+, C7#9)*

All Forms

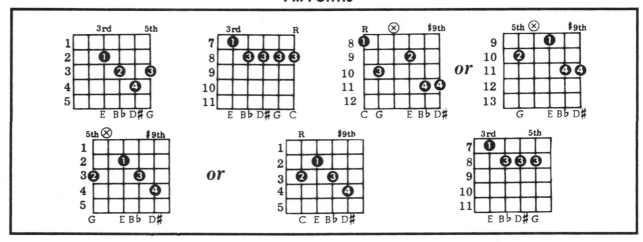

CHORDS

C6 Add 9th

Symbols
(C6 add 9, C⁹⁄₆)

All Forms

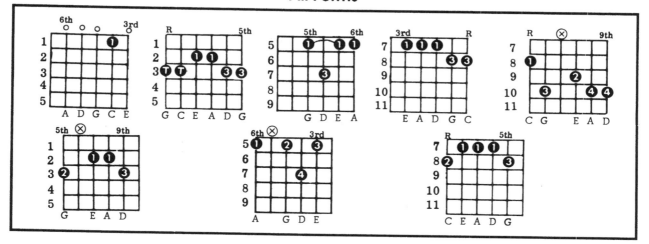

C 11th

Symbol (C 11)

Melody Chords

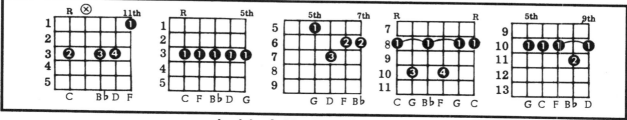

Inside & Rhythm Chords

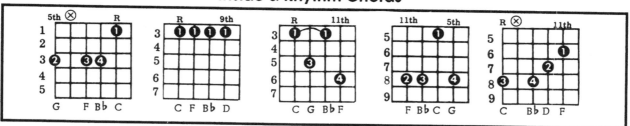

CHORDS

131

C Aug. 11th

Symbols
(C11+, C7#11)

All Forms

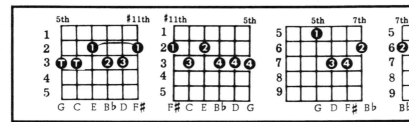

C 13th

Symbol (C 13)

All Forms

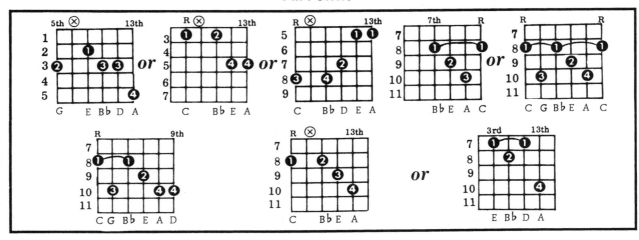

C 13-9

Symbol (C 13-9)

All Forms

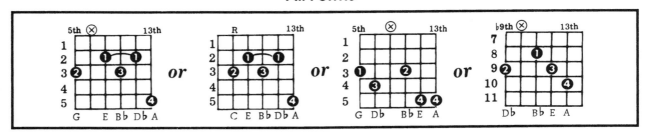

CHORDS

C 13-9-5

Symbol (C 13$^{-9}_{-5}$)

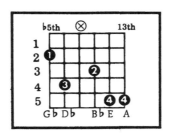

D♭ Major

Symbol (D♭)

Melody Chords

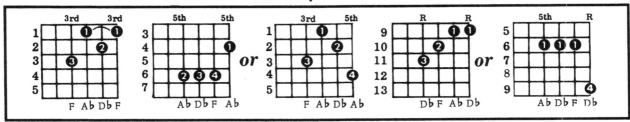

Inside Chords

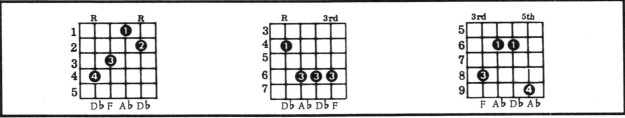

Rhythm Chords

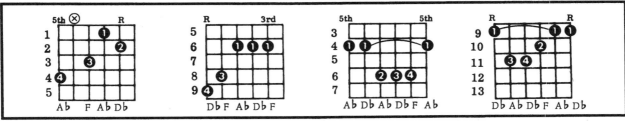

Bottom 4-String Chords

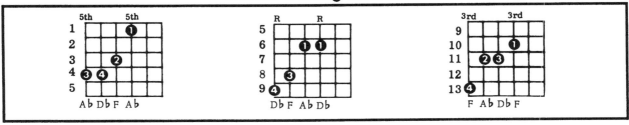

D♭ Minor

Symbol (D♭m)

Melody Chords

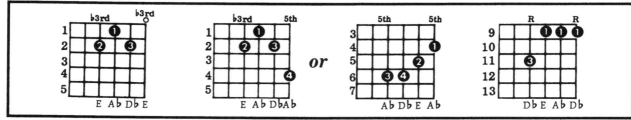

Inside Chords

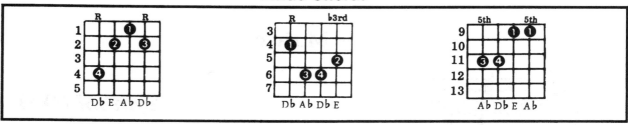

Rhythm Chords

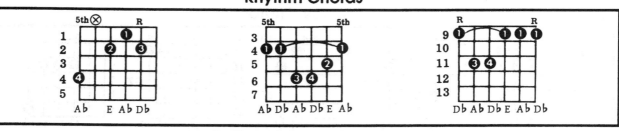

Bottom 4-String Chords

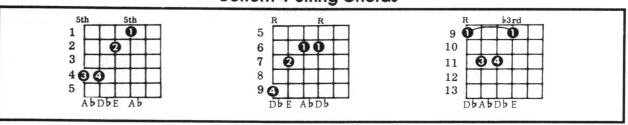

D♭ Diminished

Symbols (D♭-, D♭⁰, D♭dim)

Melody Chords

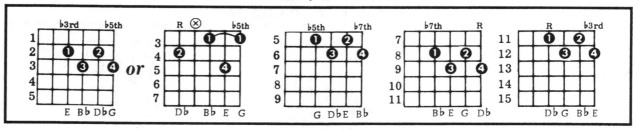

Inside Chords

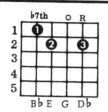

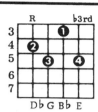

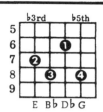

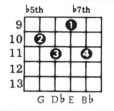

Rhythm Chords

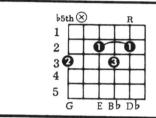

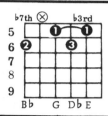

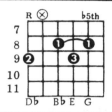

Bottom 4-String Chords

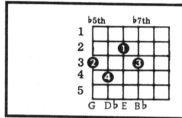

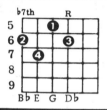

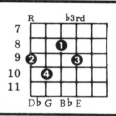

D♭ Augmented

Symbol (D♭+)

Melody Chords

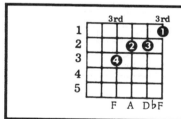

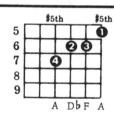

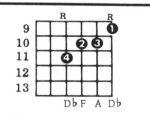

Inside & Rhythm Chords

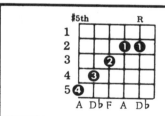

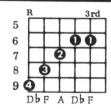

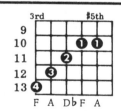

Bottom 4-String Chords

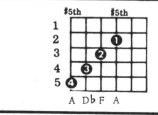

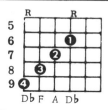

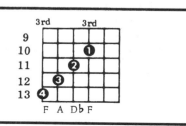

CHORDS

135

D♭ 7th

Symbol (D♭7)

Melody Chords

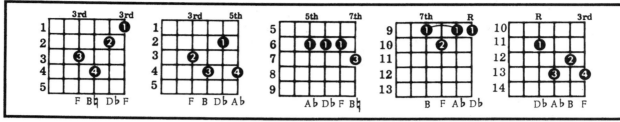

Inside Chords

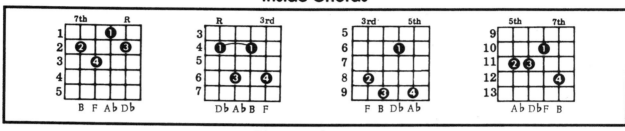

Rhythm Chords

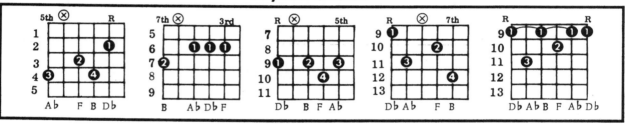

Bottom 4-String Chords

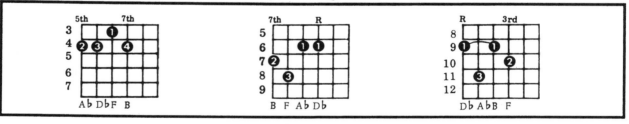

D♭ Minor 7th

Symbol (D♭m7)

Melody Chords

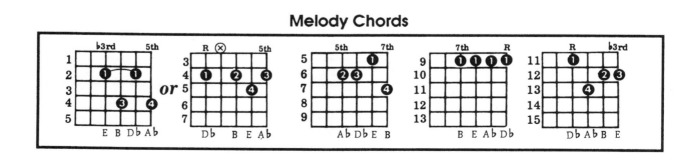

CHORDS

Inside Chords

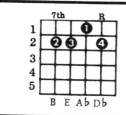 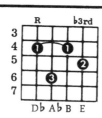 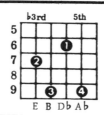 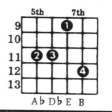

Rhythm Chords

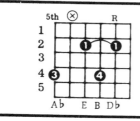 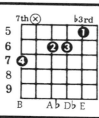 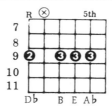 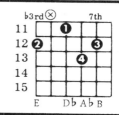

Bottom 4-String Chords

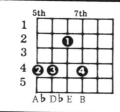 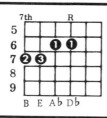 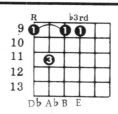

D♭ 7th Aug. 5th

Symbols
(D♭7+5, D♭7♯5)

Melody Chords

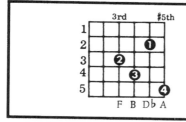 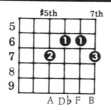 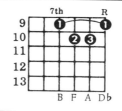

Inside Chords

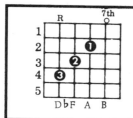 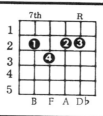 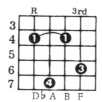 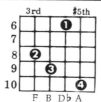 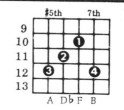

Rhythm Chords

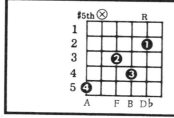 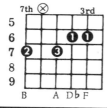 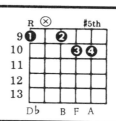

137

Bottom 4-String Chords

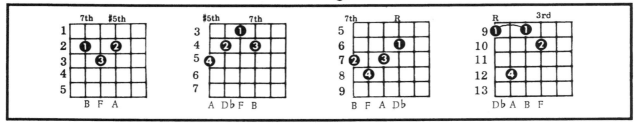

Db 7th Flat 5th

Symbols
(Db 7-5, Db 7b5)

Melody Chords

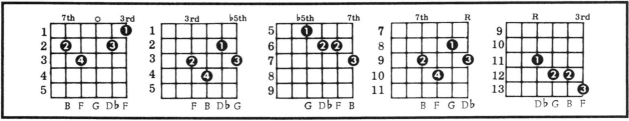

Inside Chords

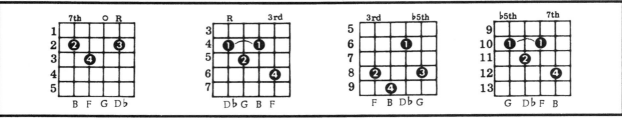

Rhythm Chords

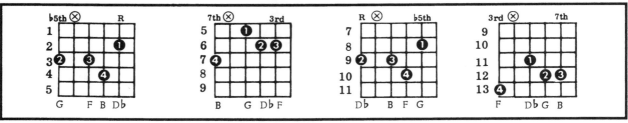

Bottom 4-String Chords

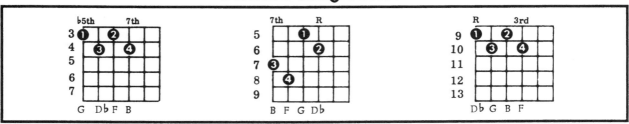

CHORDS

D♭ Major 7th

Symbol (D♭ma7)

Melody Chords

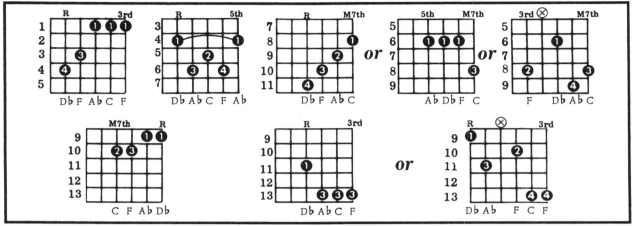

Inside & Rhythm Chords

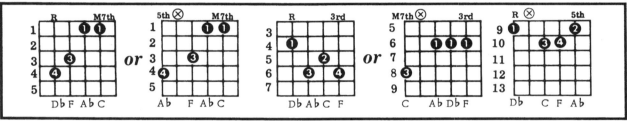

Bottom 4-String Chords

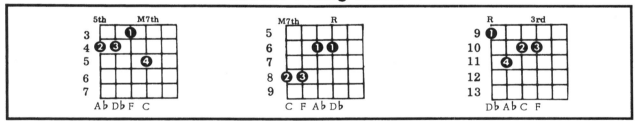

D♭ Major 7th Flat 3rd

*Symbols (D♭ ma7♭3,
D♭ min-maj7)*

Melody Chords

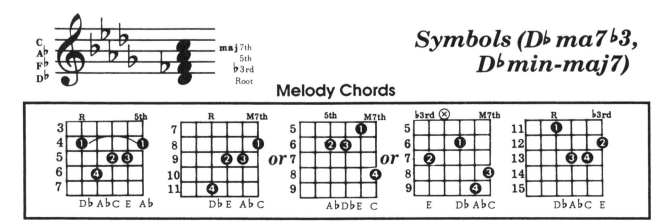

Inside & Rhythm Chords

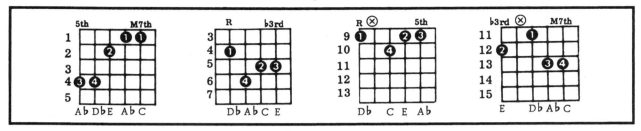

D♭ Minor 7th Flat 5th

Symbol (D♭m7♭5)

Melody Chords

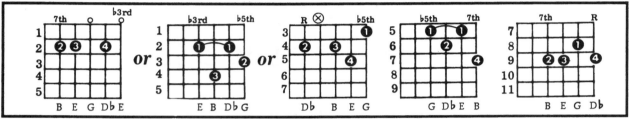

Inside & Rhythm Chords

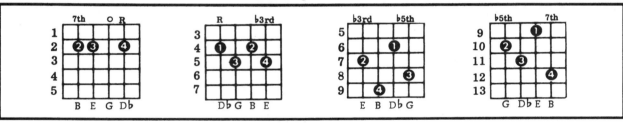

Bottom 4-String Chords

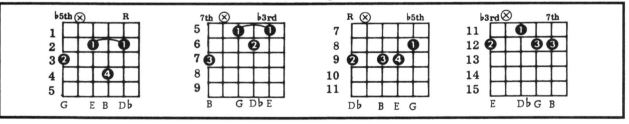

D♭7 Suspended 4th

Symbol (D♭7sus4)

Melody Chords

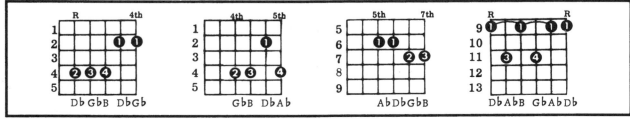

140

Inside Chords

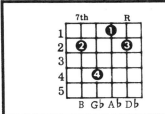 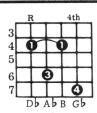 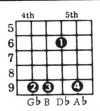 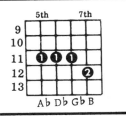

Rhythm Chords

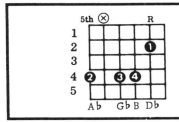 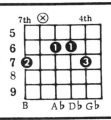 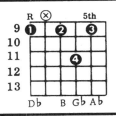

D♭ 6th

Bb
Ab   6th
F   5th
Db   3rd
            Root

Symbol (D♭6)

Melody Chords

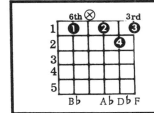 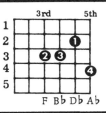 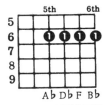 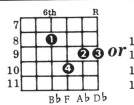 *or*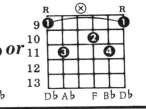

Inside Chords

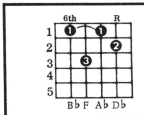 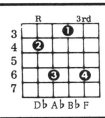 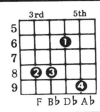 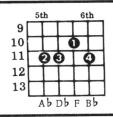

Rhythm Chords

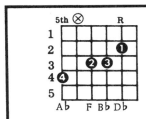 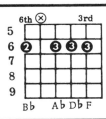 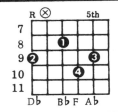 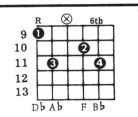

Bottom 4-String Chords

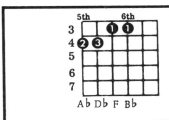 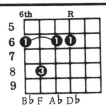 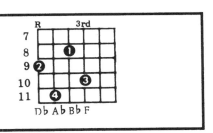

CHORDS

141

D♭ Minor 6th

Symbol (D♭m6)

Melody Chords

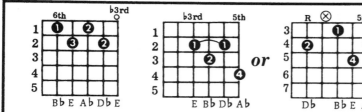

or

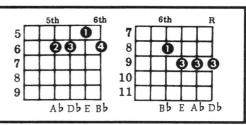

Inside Chords

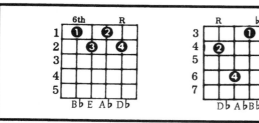

Rhythm Chords

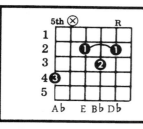 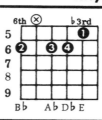 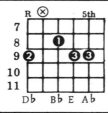 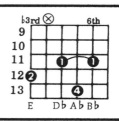

Bottom 4-String Chords

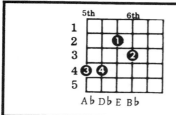 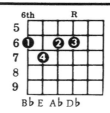 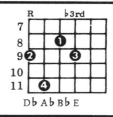

D♭ 9th

Symbol (D♭9)

Melody Chords

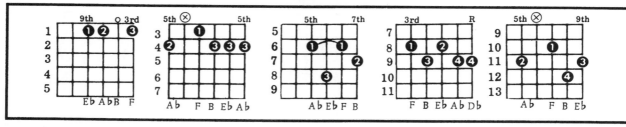

CHORDS

Inside & Rhythm Chords

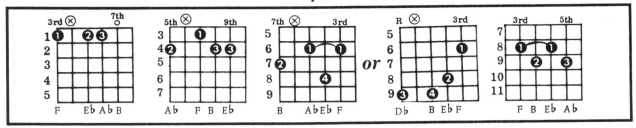

D♭ Minor 9th

Symbol (D♭m9)

Melody Chords

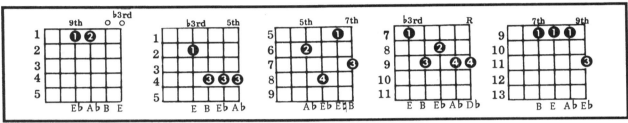

Inside & Rhythm Chords

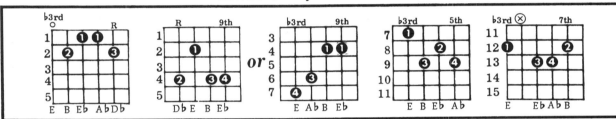

D♭ Major 9th

Symbol (D♭ma9)

Melody Chords

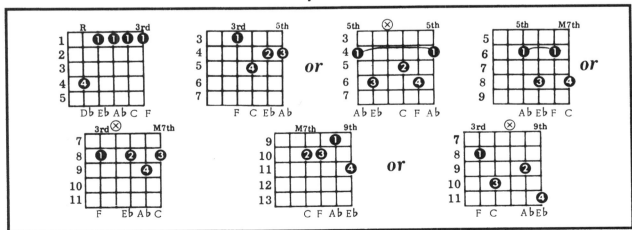

CHORDS

143

Db Major 9th Cont.

Inside Chords

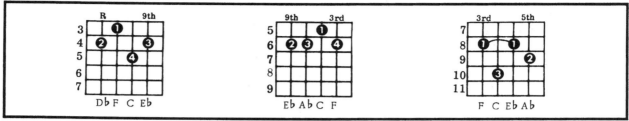

Rhythm Chords

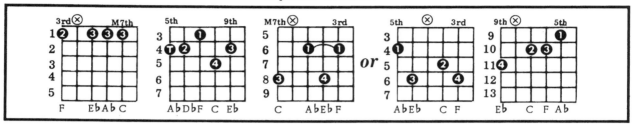

Db9 Sharp 5th

Symbols (Db9 + 5, Db9 #5)

Melody Chords

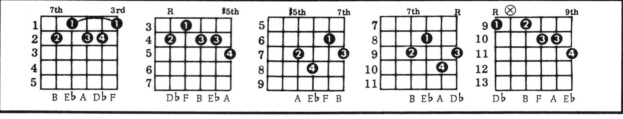

Inside & Rhythm Chords

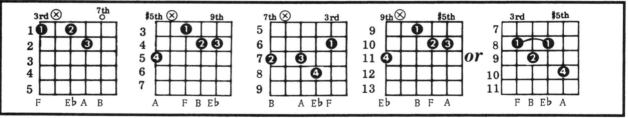

Db9 Flat 5th

Symbols (D9-5, D9b5)

Melody Chords

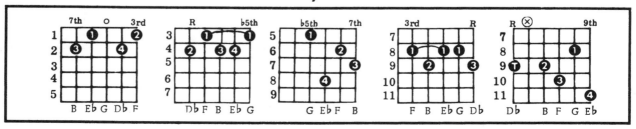

Inside & Rhythm Chords

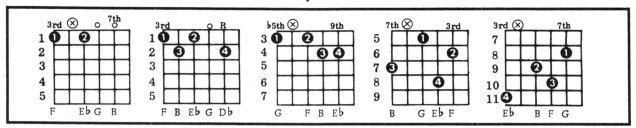

D♭7 Flat 9th

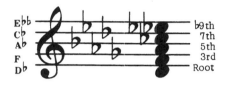

Symbol (D♭ -9)

Melody Chords

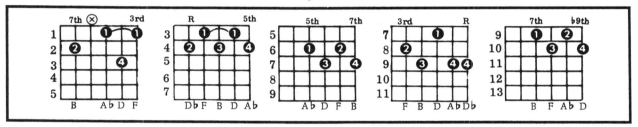

Inside & Rhythm Chords

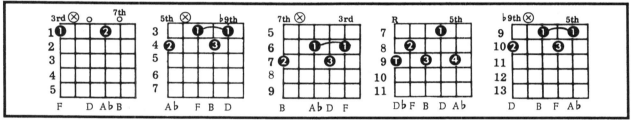

D♭7 Sharp 9th

Symbol (D♭9 +)

Melody Chords

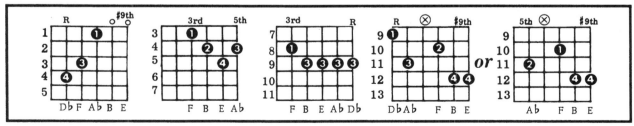

Inside & Rhythm Chords

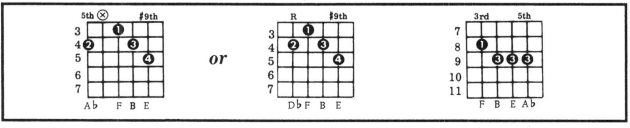

D♭6 Add 9th

Symbols
(D♭ 9/6, D♭6 add 9)

All Forms

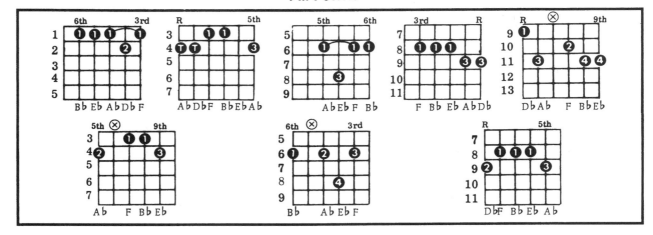

D♭ 11th

Symbol (D♭ 11)

Melody Chords

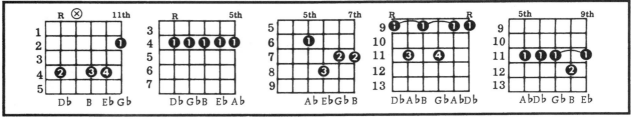

Inside & Rhythm Chords

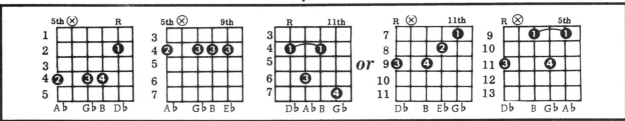

CHORDS

Db Aug. 11th

Symbol (Db 11 +)

All Forms

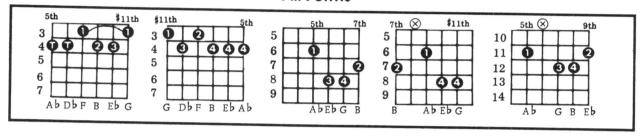

Db 13th

Symbol (Db13)

All Forms

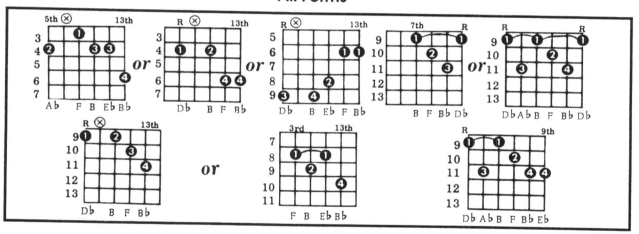

Db 13-9

Symbol (Db13-9)

All Forms

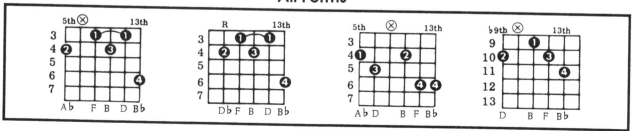

D♭ 13-9-5

Symbol(D♭13⁻⁹₋₅)

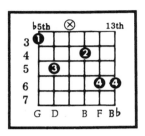

D Major

Symbol (D)

Melody Chords

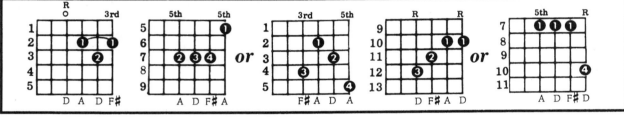

Inside Chords

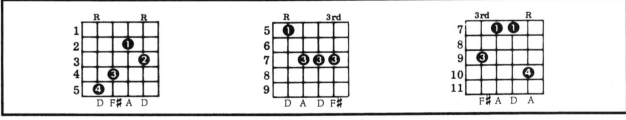

Rhythm Chords

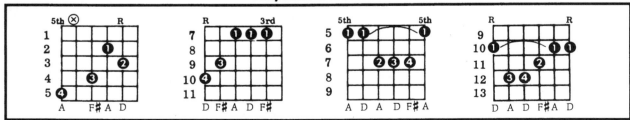

Bottom 4-String Chords

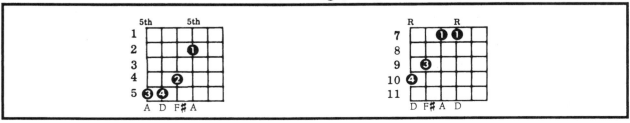

CHORDS

D Minor

Symbol (Dm)

Melody Chords

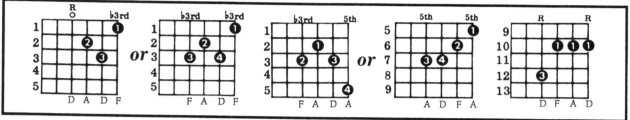

Inside Chords

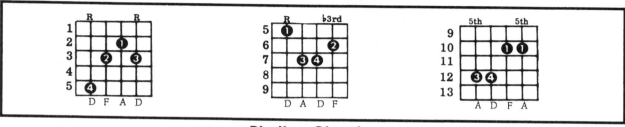

Rhythm Chords

Bottom 4-String Chords

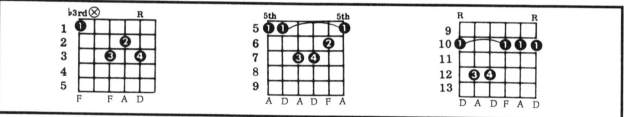

D Diminished

Symbols (D-, D⁰, Ddim)

Melody Chords

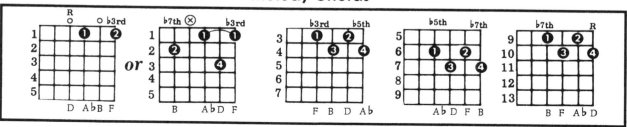

CHORDS

D Diminished Cont.

Inside Chords

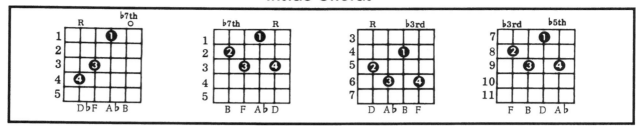

Rhythm Chords

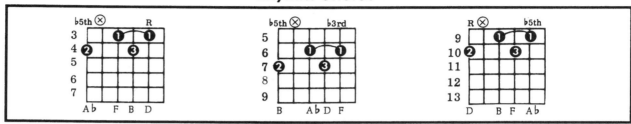

Bottom 4-String Chords

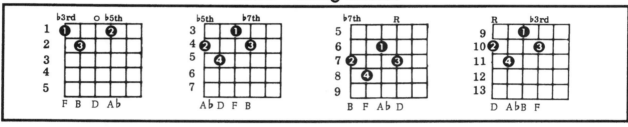

D Augmented

Symbol (D+)

Melody Chords

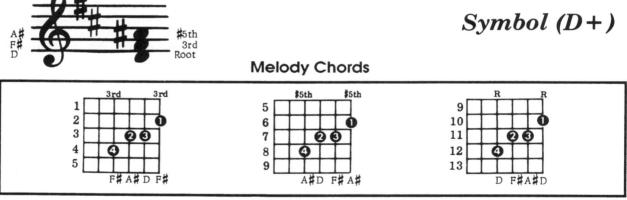

Inside & Rhythm Chords

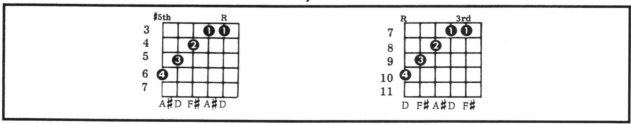

Bottom 4-String Chords

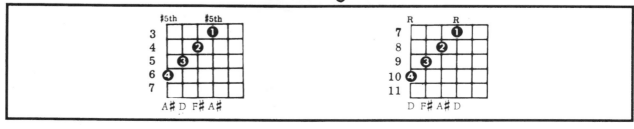

150

D 7th

Symbol (D7)

Melody Chords

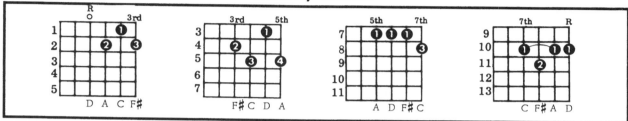

Inside Chords

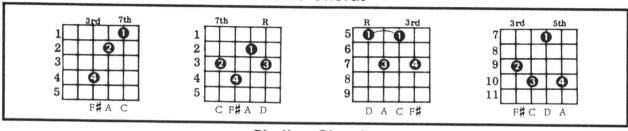

Rhythm Chords

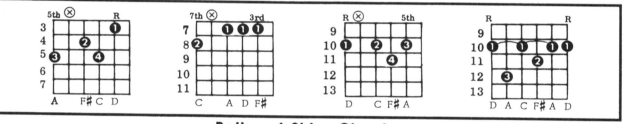

Bottom 4-String Chords

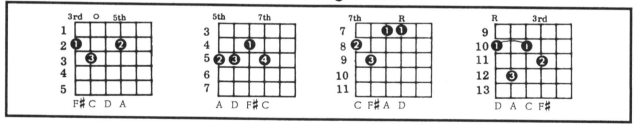

D Minor 7th

Symbol (Dm7)

Melody Chords

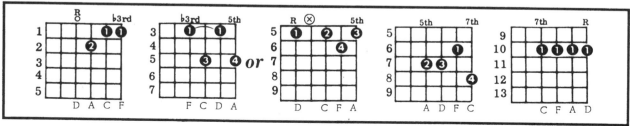

CHORDS

151

D Minor 7th Cont.

Inside Chords

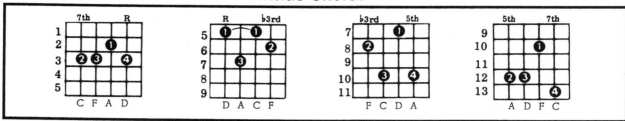

Rhythm Chords

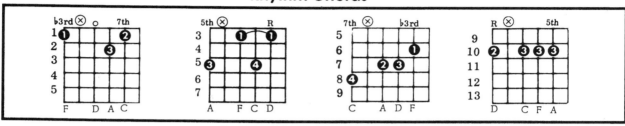

Bottom 4-String Chords

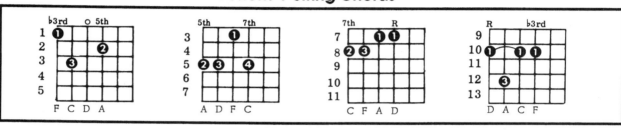

D 7th Aug. 5th

Symbol (D7+5)

Melody Chords

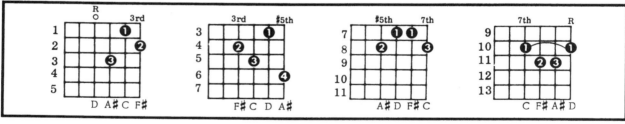

Inside Chords

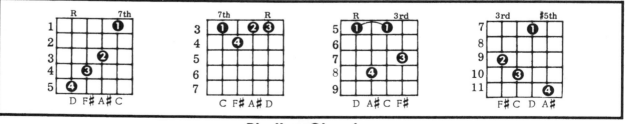

Rhythm Chords

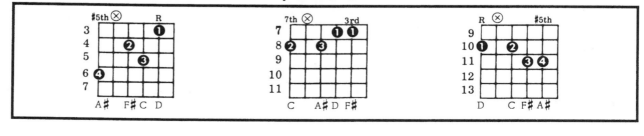

CHORDS

Bottom 4-String Chords

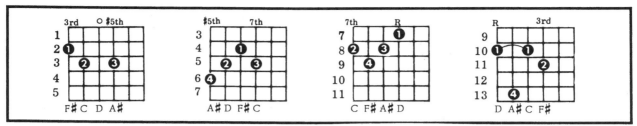

D 7th Flat 5th

Symbols
(D 7-5, D7♭5)

Melody Chords

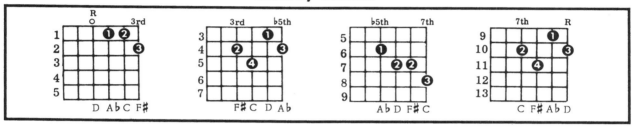

Inside Chords

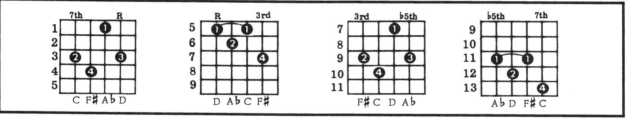

Rhythm Chords

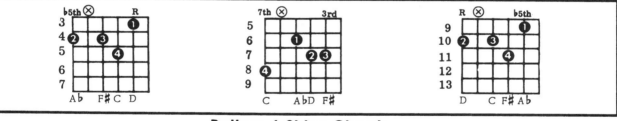

Bottom 4-String Chords

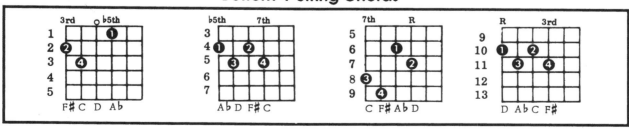

153

D Major 7th

Symbol (Dma7)

Melody Chords

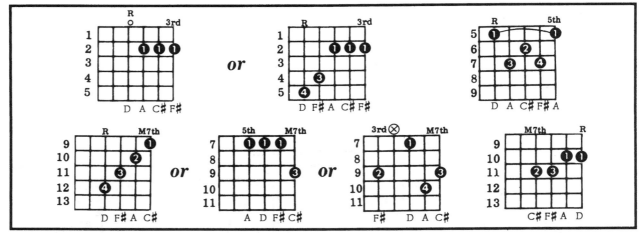

Inside & Rhythm Chords

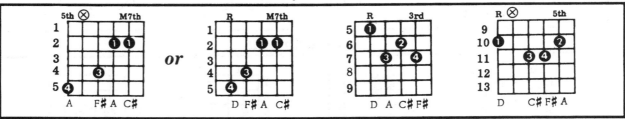

Bottom 4-String Chords

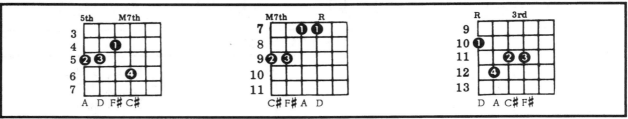

D Major 7th Flat 3rd

Symbols (D ma7♭3,
D min-maj7)

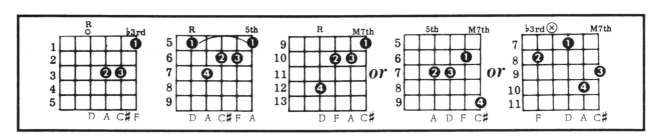

CHORDS

Inside & Rhythm Chords

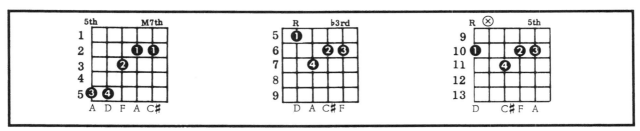

D Minor 7th Flat 5th

Symbol (Dm7♭5)

Melody Chords

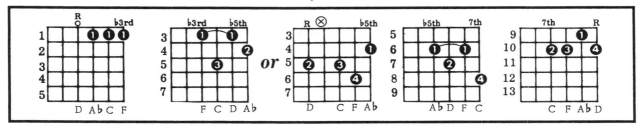

Inside Chords

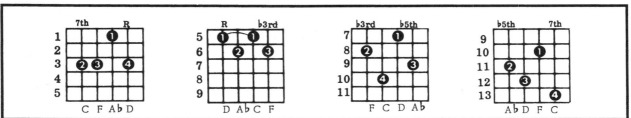

Rhythm Chords

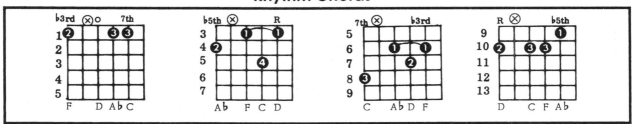

D7 Suspended 4th

Symbol (D7sus4)

Melody Chords

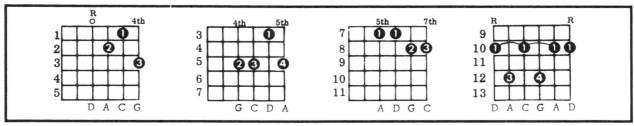

CHORDS

155

D7 Suspended 4th Cont.

Inside Chords

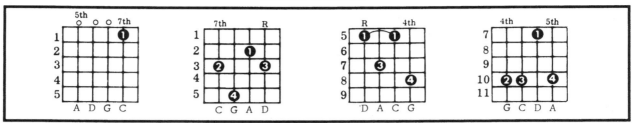

Rhythm Chords

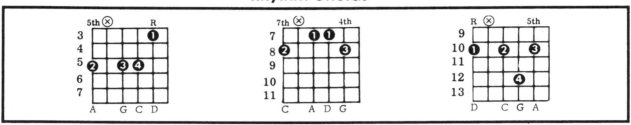

D 6th

B ♮ — 6th
A — 5th
F ♯ — 3rd
D — Root

Symbol (D6)

Melody Chords

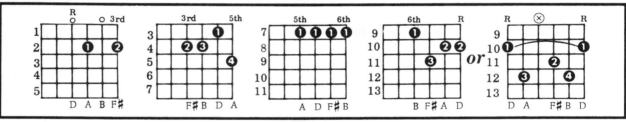

Inside Chords

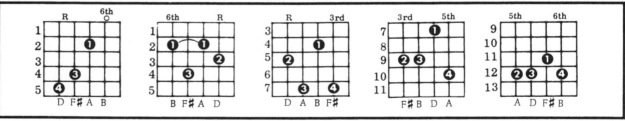

Rhythm Chords

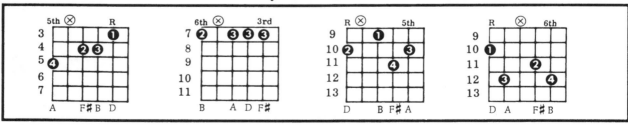

Bottom 4-String Chords

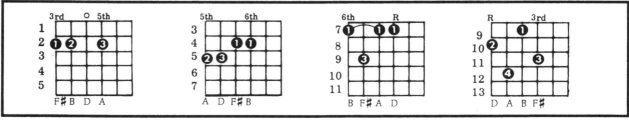

CHORDS

156

D Minor 6th

Symbol (D m6)

Melody Chords

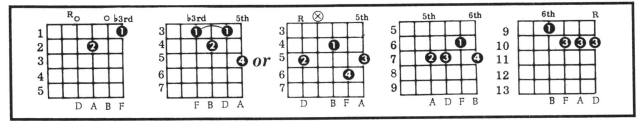

Inside Chords

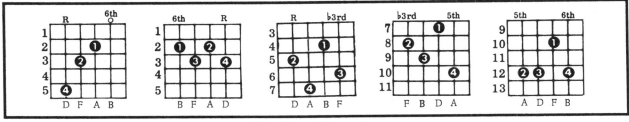

Rhythm Chords

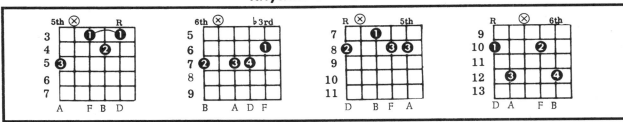

Bottom 4-String Chords

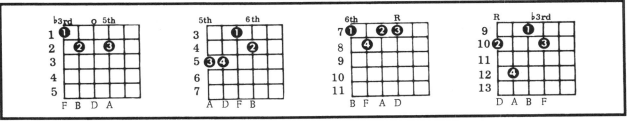

D 9th

Symbol (D 9)

Melody Chords

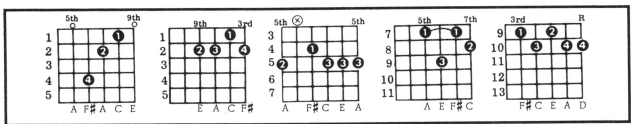

CHORDS

157

Inside & Rhythm Chords

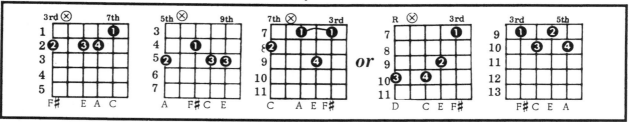

D Minor 9th

Symbol (Dm9)

Melody Chords

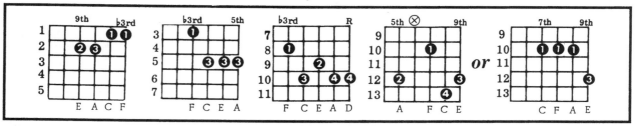

Inside & Rhythm Chords

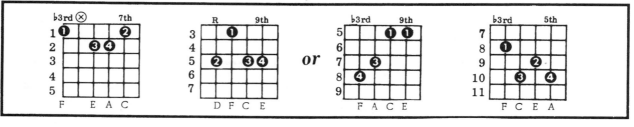

D Major 9th

Symbol (Dma9)

Melody Chords

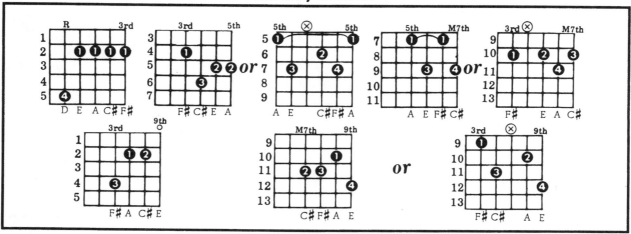

CHORDS

Inside Chords

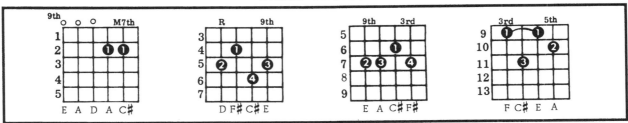

Rhythm Chords

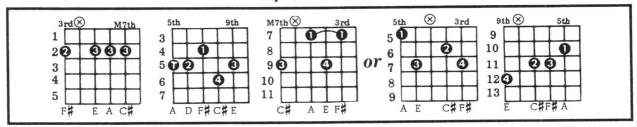

D9 Sharp 5th

Symbols
(D9 + 5, D9#5)

Melody Chords

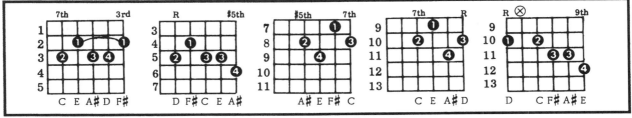

Inside & Rhythm Chords

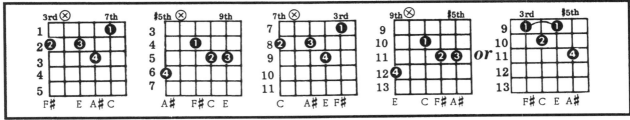

D9 Flat 5th

Symbol (D9-5)

Melody Chords

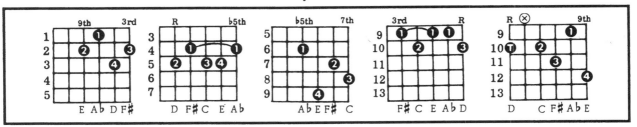

CHORDS

159

Inside & Rhythm Chords

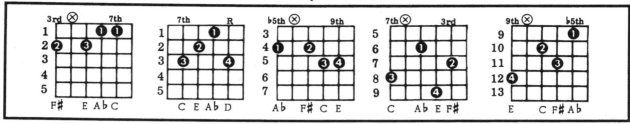

D7 Flat 9th

Symbol (D7-9)

Melody Chords

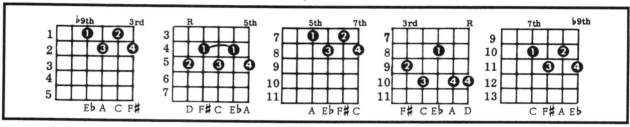

Inside & Rhythm Chords

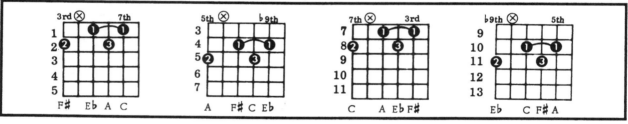

D7 Sharp 9th

*Symbols
(D9+, D7#9)*

Melody Chords

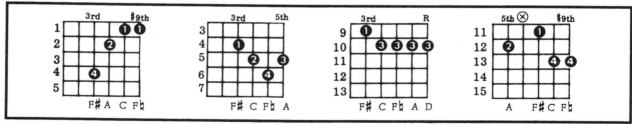

Inside & Rhythm Chords

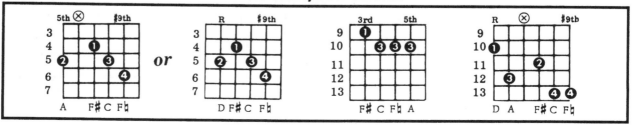

160

D6 Add 9th

E — 9th
B — 6th
A — 5th
F# — 3rd
D — Root

Symbols
(D 9/6, D6 add 9)

All Forms

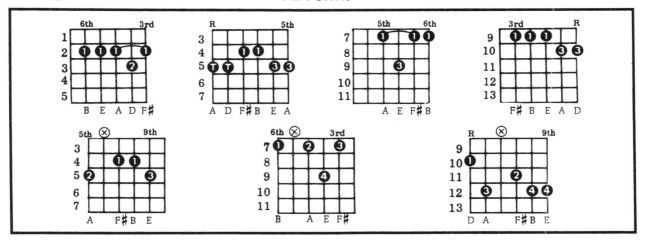

D 11th

G — 11th
E — 9th
C♮ — 7th
A — 5th
F# — 3rd
D — Root

Symbol (D 11)

Melody Chords

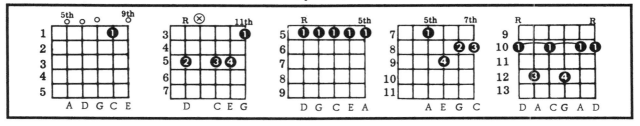

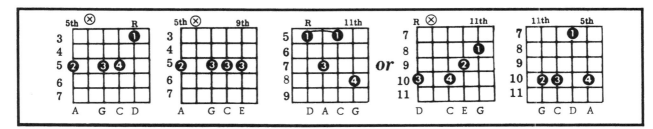

D Aug. 11th

G# — #11th
E — 9th
C♮ — 7th
A — 5th
F# — 3rd
D — Root

Symbol (D11 +)

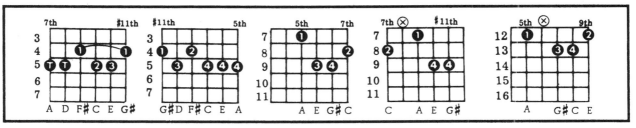

CHORDS

D 13th

Symbol (D 13)

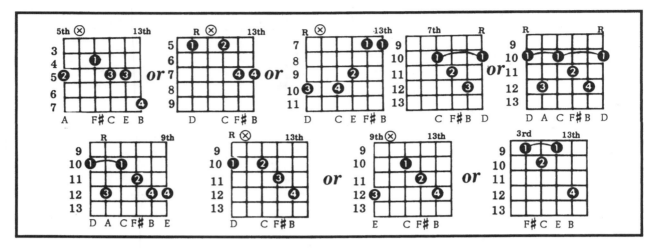

D 13-9

Symbol (D 13 - 9)

All Forms

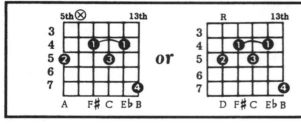 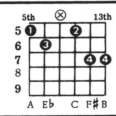 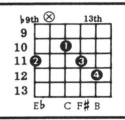

D 13-9-5

Symbol (D 13 $\begin{smallmatrix} -9 \\ -5 \end{smallmatrix}$)

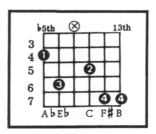

E♭ Major

Bb — 5th
G — 3rd
Eb — Root

Symbol (E♭)

Melody Chords

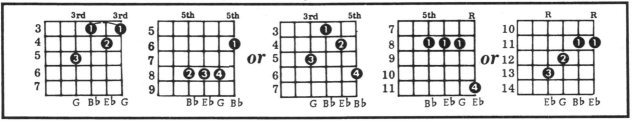

Inside Chords

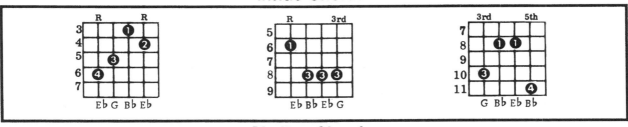

Rhythm Chords

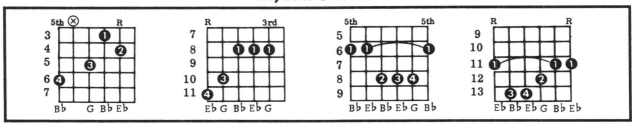

Bottom 4-String Chords

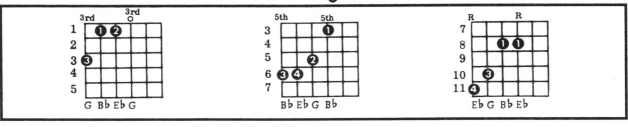

E♭ Minor

Bb — 5th
Gb — b3rd
Eb — Root

Symbol (E♭m)

Melody Chords

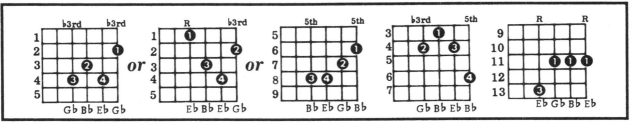

CHORDS

163

Eb Minor Cont.

Inside Chords

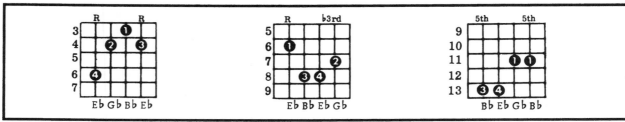

Rhythm Chords

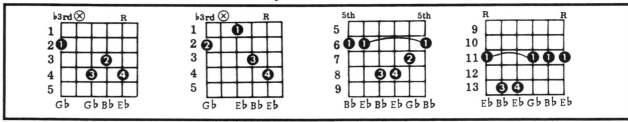

Bottom 4-String Chords

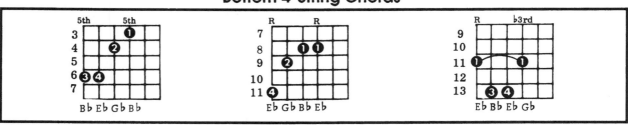

Eb Diminished

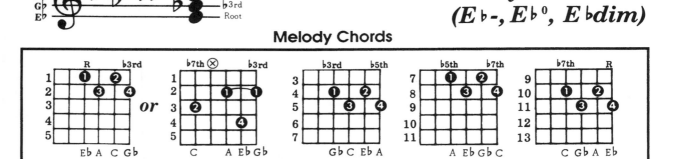

Symbols
(Eb-, Eb⁰, Ebdim)

Melody Chords

Inside Chords

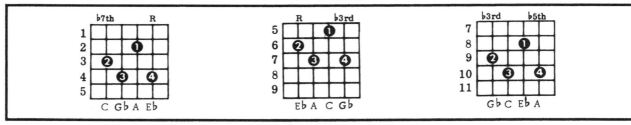

Rhythm Chords

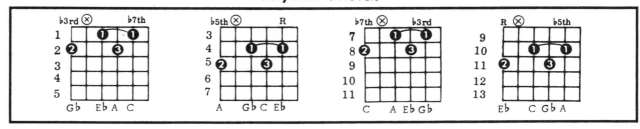

CHORDS

Bottom 4-String Chords

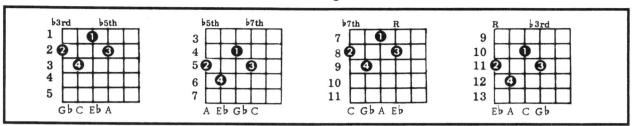

E♭ Augmented

Symbol (E♭+)

Melody Chords

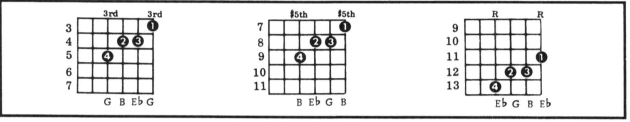

Inside & Rhythm Chords

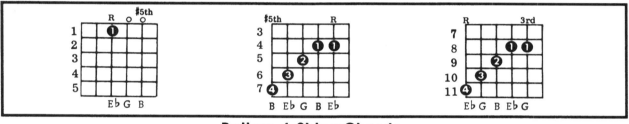

Bottom 4-String Chords

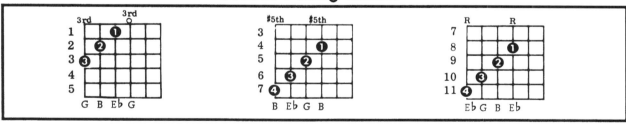

E♭ 7th

Symbol (E♭7)

Melody Chords

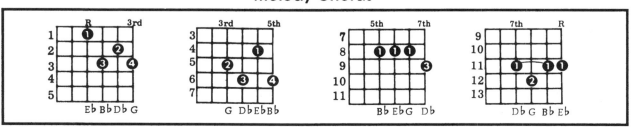

165

Inside Chords

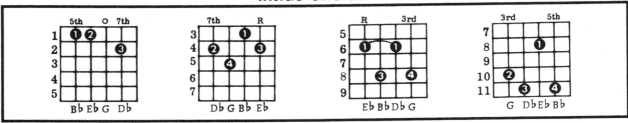

Rhythm Chords

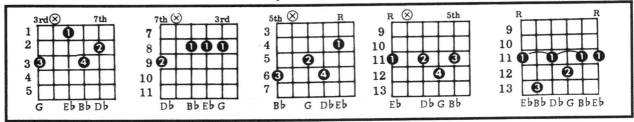

Bottom 4-String Chords

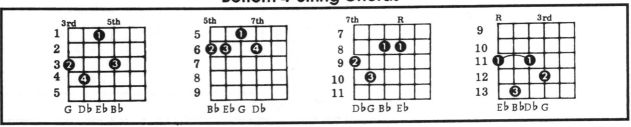

Eb Minor 7th

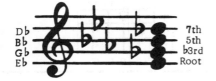

Symbol (Ebm7)

Melody Chords

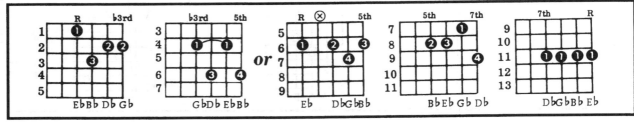

Inside Chords

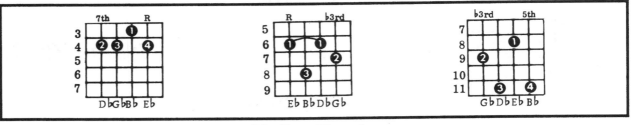

Rhythm Chords

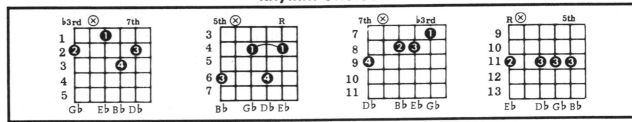

166

Bottom 4-String Chords

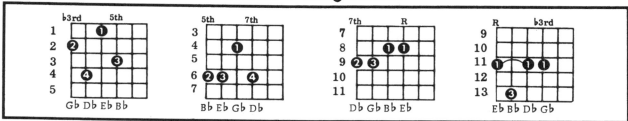

E♭ 7th Aug. 5th

Symbol (E♭7+5)

Melody Chords

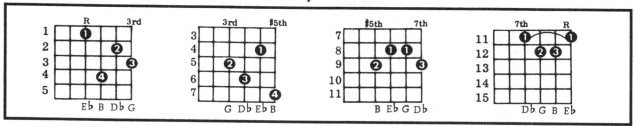

Inside Chords

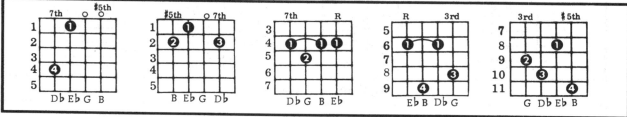

Rhythm Chords

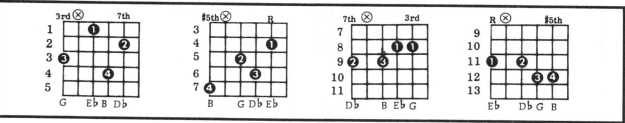

Bottom 4-String Chords

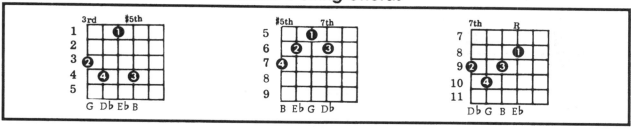

CHORDS

Eb 7th Flat 5th

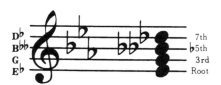

Db
Bbb
G
Eb
7th
b5th
3rd
Root

Symbols
(Eb7-5, Eb7b5)

Melody Chords

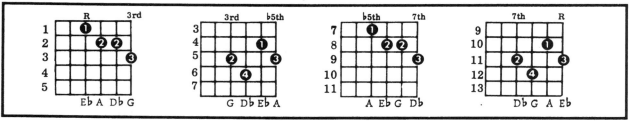

Inside Chords

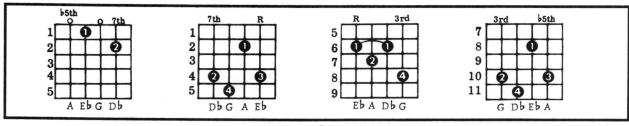

Rhythm Chords

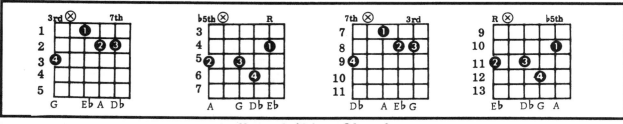

Bottom 4-String Chords

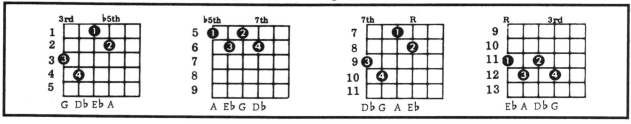

Eb Major 7th

D
Bb
G
Eb
maj7th
5th
3rd
Root

Symbol (Ebma7)

Melody Chords

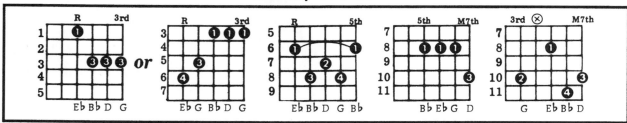

168

Inside & Rhythm Chords

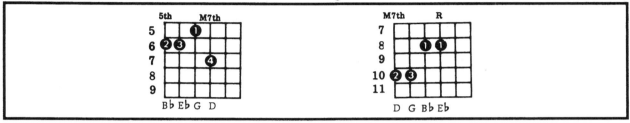

Bottom 4-String Chords

E♭ Major 7th Flat 3rd

Symbols (E♭ ma7♭3, E♭ min-maj7)

Melody Chords

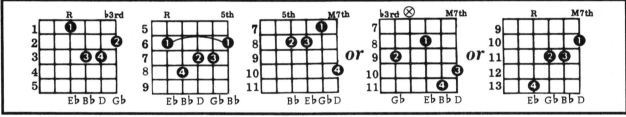

Inside & Rhythm Chords

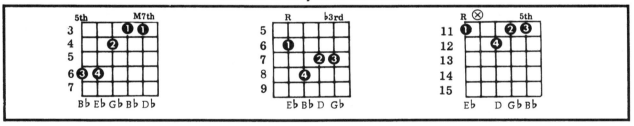

E♭ Minor 7th Flat 5th

Symbol (E♭m7♭5)

Melody Chords

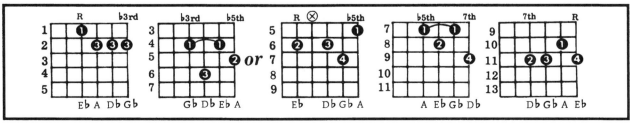

E♭ Minor 7th Flat 5th Cont.

Inside Chords

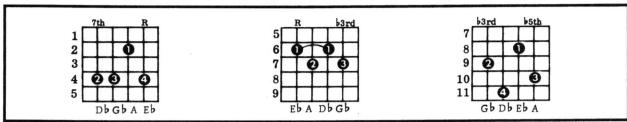

Rhythm Chords

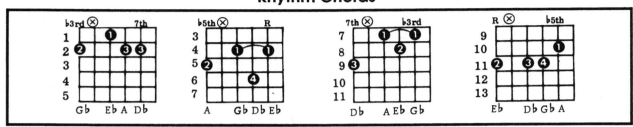

E♭7 Suspended 4th

Symbol (E♭7sus4)

Melody Chords

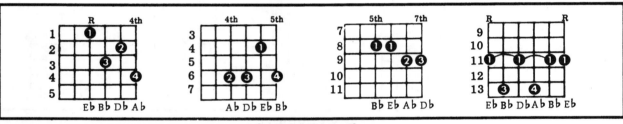

Inside Chords

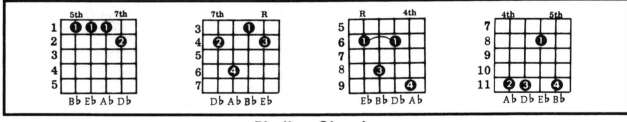

Rhythm Chords

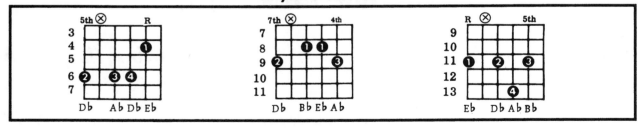

CHORDS

E♭ 6th

Symbol (E♭6)

Melody Chords

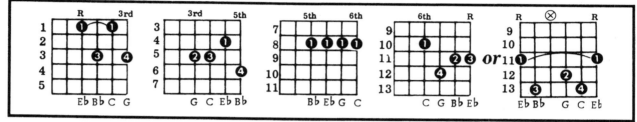

Inside Chords

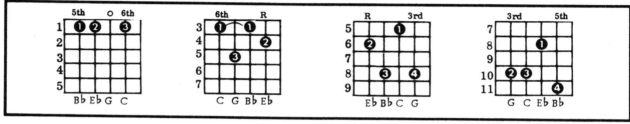

Rhythm Chords

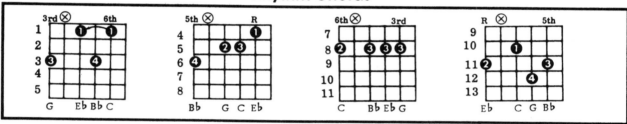

Bottom 4-String Chords

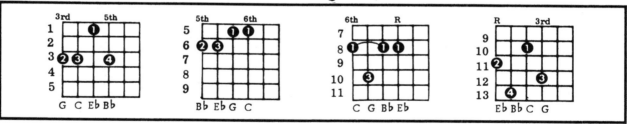

E♭ Minor 6th

Symbol (E♭m6)

Melody Chords

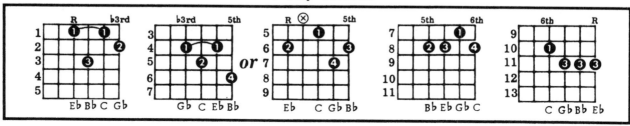

171

Inside Chords

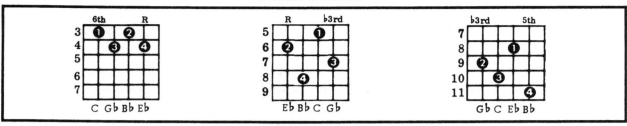

Rhythm Chords

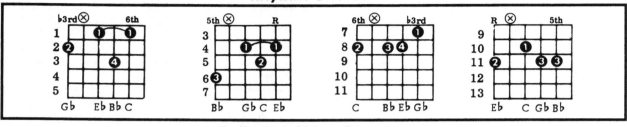

Bottom 4-String Chords

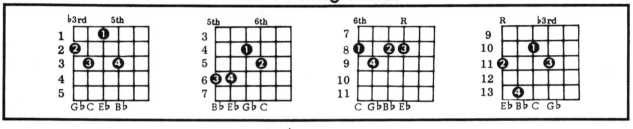

E♭ 9th

Symbol (E♭9)

Melody Chords

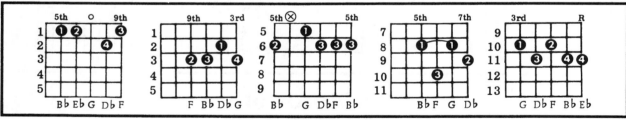

Inside & Rhythm Chords

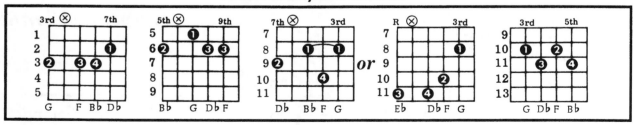

172

E♭ Minor 9th

Symbol (E♭m9)

Melody Chords

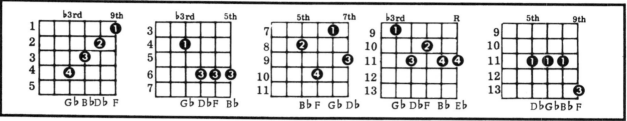

Inside & Rhythm Chords

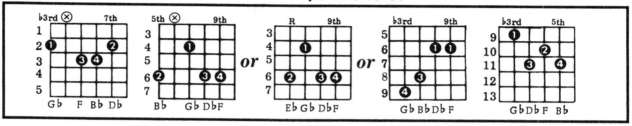

E♭ Major 9th

Symbol (E♭ma 9th)

Melody Chords

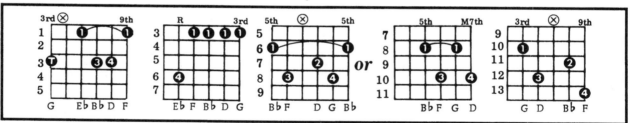

Inside Chords

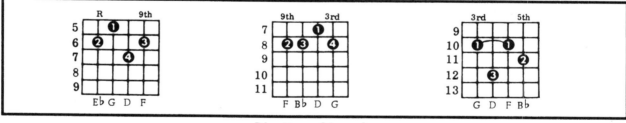

Rhythm Chords

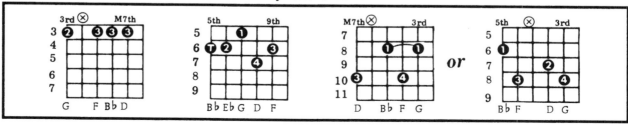

CHORDS

173

Eb9 Sharp 5th

Symbols
(Eb 9#5, Eb 9 + 5)

Melody Chords

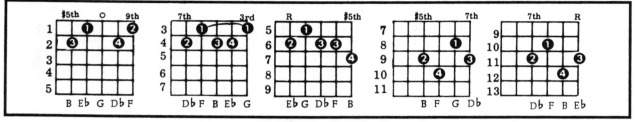

Rhythm Chords

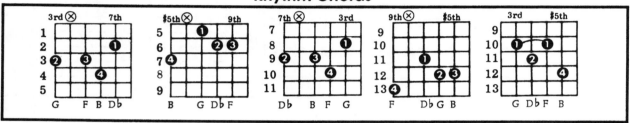

Eb9 Flat 5th

Symbol (Eb9-5)

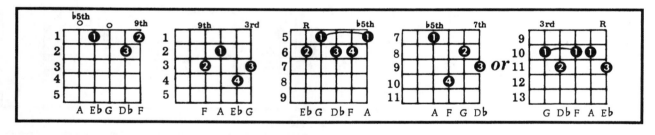

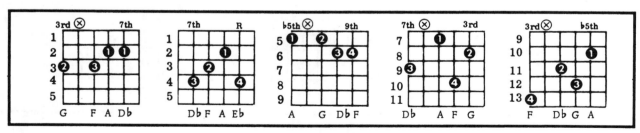

CHORDS

174

E♭7 Flat 9th

Symbol (E♭7-9)

Melody Chords

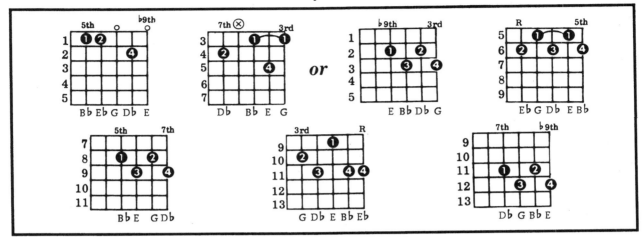

Inside & Rhythm Chords

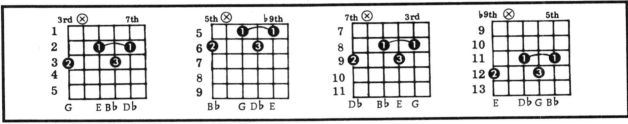

E♭7 Sharp 9th

Symbols
(E♭9+, E♭7#9)

All Forms

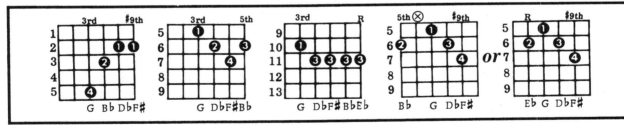

E♭6 Add 9th

Symbols
(E♭ 9/6, E♭6add9)

All Forms

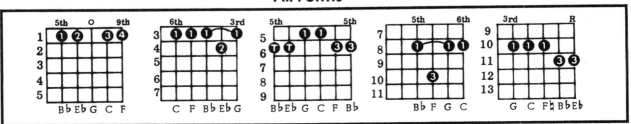

175

E♭ 11th

Symbol (E♭ 11)

Melody Chords

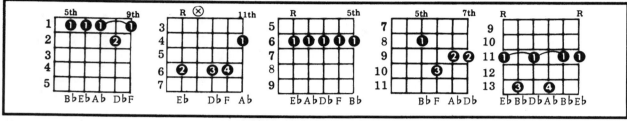

Inside & Rhythm Chords

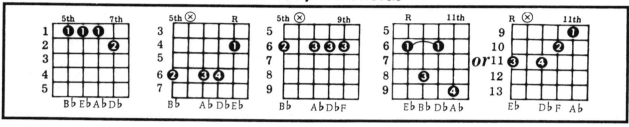

E♭ Aug. 11th

Symbol (E♭ 11 +)

All Forms

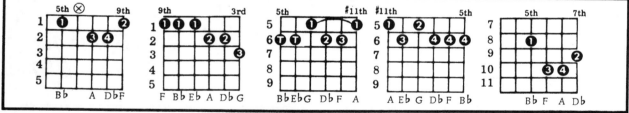

E♭ 13th

Symbol (E♭ 13)

All Forms

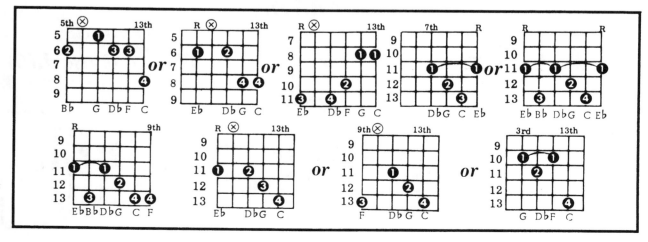

E♭ 13-9

Symbol (E♭13-9)

All Forms

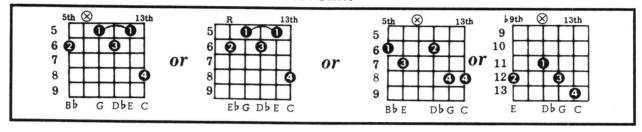

E♭ 13-9-5

Symbol (E♭13 ⁻⁹₋₅)

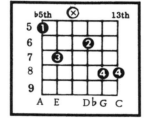

CHORDS

177

E Major

Symbol (E)

Melody Chords

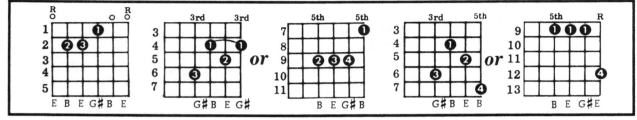

Inside Chords

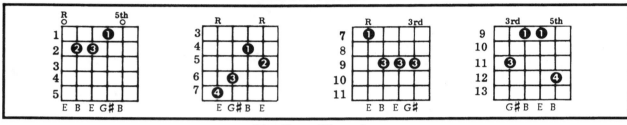

Rhythm Chords

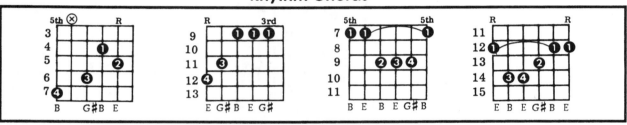

Bottom 4-String Chords

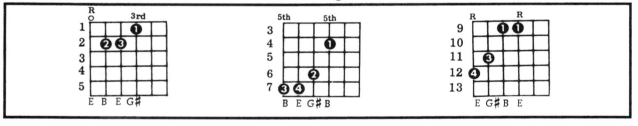

E Minor

Symbol (Em)

Melody Chords

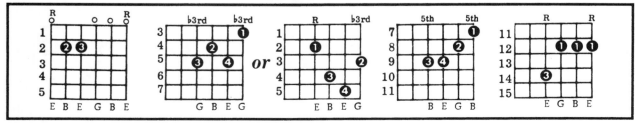

CHORDS

178

Inside Chords

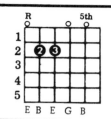 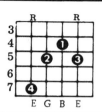 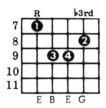

Rhythm Chords

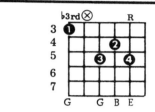 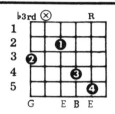 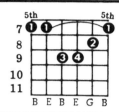

Bottom 4-String Chords

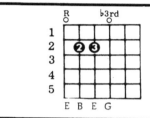 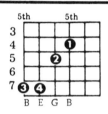 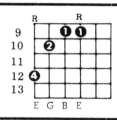

E Diminished

*Symbols (E-,
E⁰, Edim)*

Melody Chords

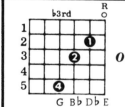 *or*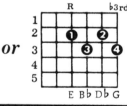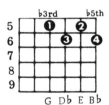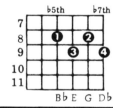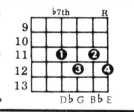

Inside Chords

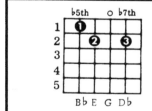 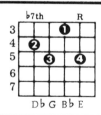 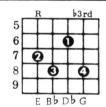 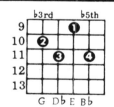

Rhythm Chords

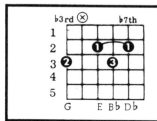 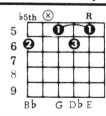 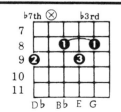 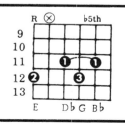

CHORDS

E Diminished Cont.

Bottom 4-String Chords

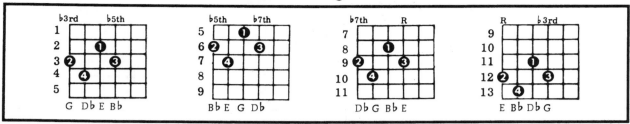

E Augmented

Symbol (E +)

Melody Chords

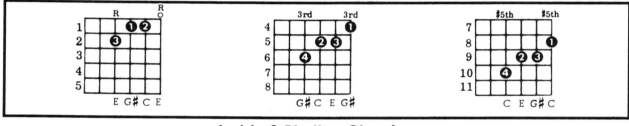

Inside & Rhythm Chords

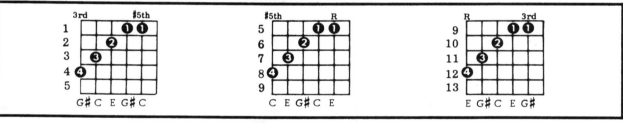

Bottom 4-String Chords

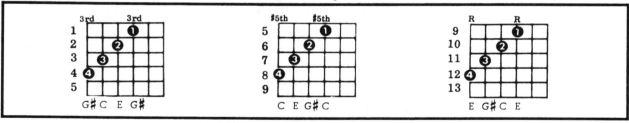

E 7th

Symbol (E 7)

Melody Chords

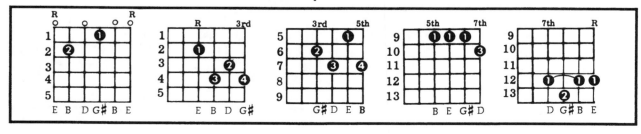

Inside Chords

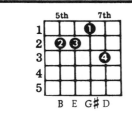 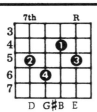 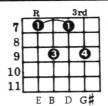 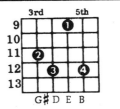

Rhythm Chords

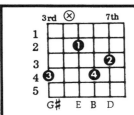 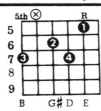 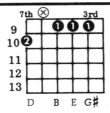 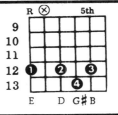

Bottom 4-String Chords

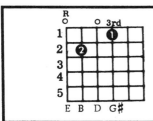 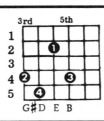 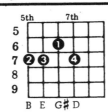 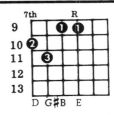

E Minor 7th

D♭ — 7th
B — 5th
G♭ — ♭3rd
E — Root

Symbol (E m7)

Melody Chords

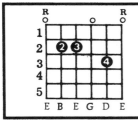 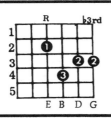 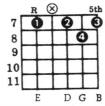 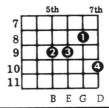 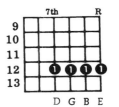

Inside Chords

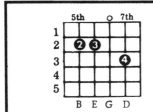 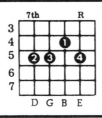 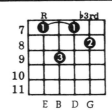 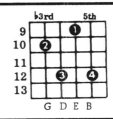

Rhythm Chords

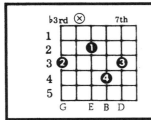 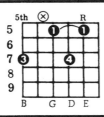 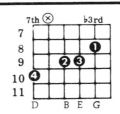 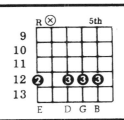

CHORDS

Bottom 4-String Chords

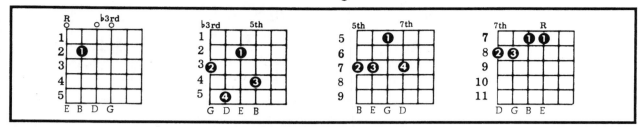

E 7th Aug. 5th

Symbol (E7 + 5)

Melody Chords

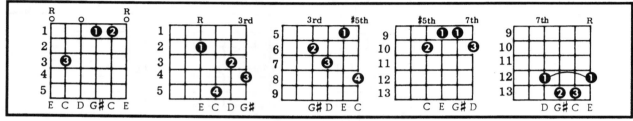

Inside Chords

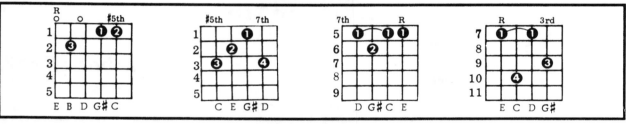

Rhythm Chords

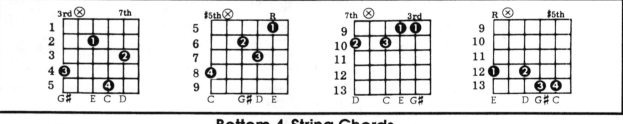

Bottom 4-String Chords

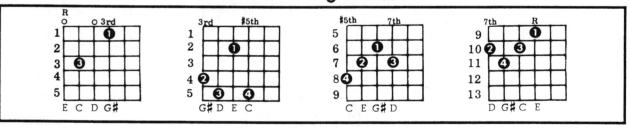

CHORDS

E 7th Flat 5th

D♯ — 7th
B♭ — b5th
G♯ — 3rd
E — Root

Symbols
(E7♭5, E7-5)

Melody Chords

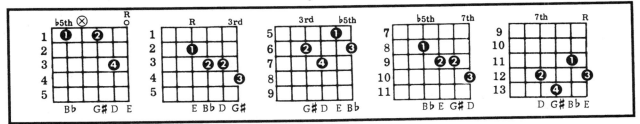

Inside Chords

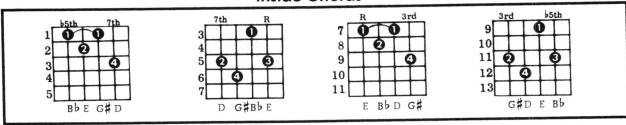

Rhythm Chords

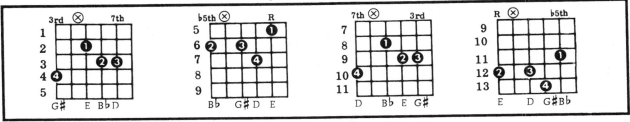

Bottom 4-String Chords

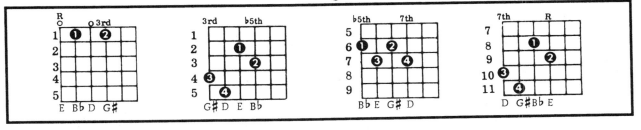

E Major 7th

D♯ — maj7th
B — 5th
G♯ — 3rd
E — Root

Symbol (Ema7)

Melody Chords

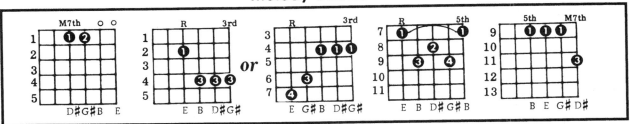

CHORDS

E Major 7th Cont.

Inside & Rhythm Chords

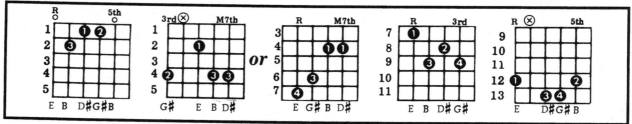

Bottom 4-String Chords

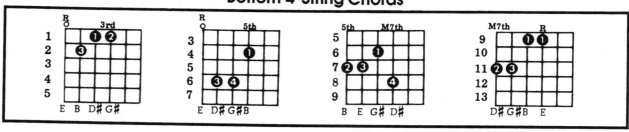

E Major 7th Flat 3rd

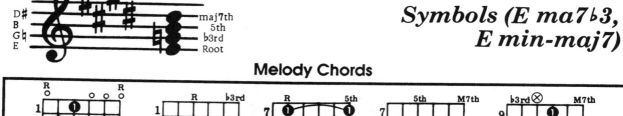

Symbols (E ma7♭3, E min-maj7)

Melody Chords

Inside & Rhythm Chords

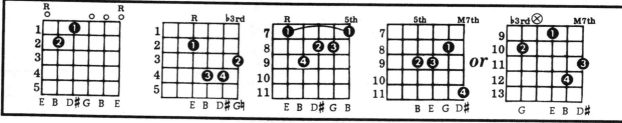

E Minor 7th Flat 5th

Symbol (E m7♭5)

Melody Chords

CHORDS

Inside Chords

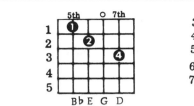 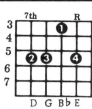 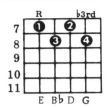 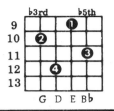

Rhythm Chords

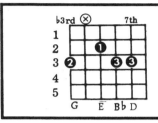 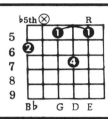 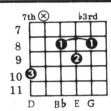 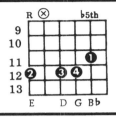

E7 Suspended 4th

Symbol (E 7sus4)

Melody Chords

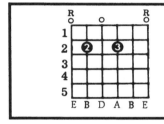 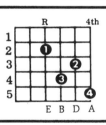 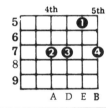 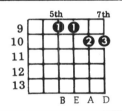

Inside Chords

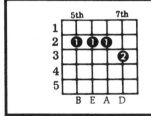 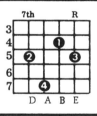 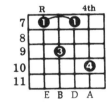 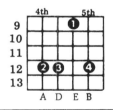

Rhythm Chords

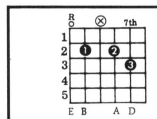 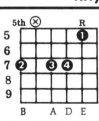 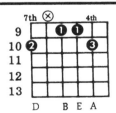 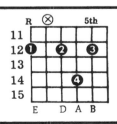

CHORDS

185

E 6th

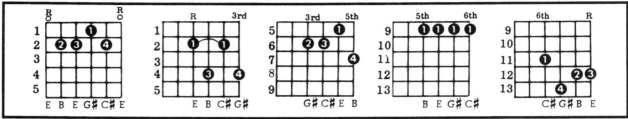

Symbol (E 6)

Melody Chords

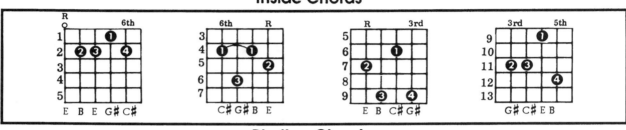

Inside Chords

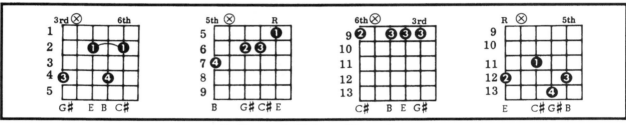

Rhythm Chords

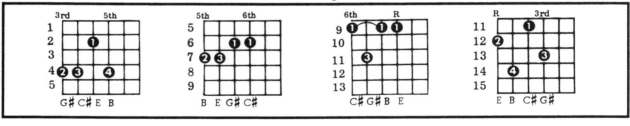

Bottom 4-String Chords

E Minor 6th

Symbol (E m6)

Melody Chords

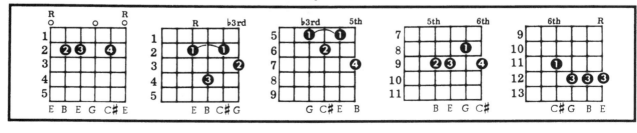

CHORDS

186

Inside Chords

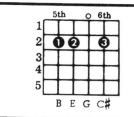 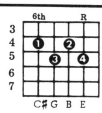 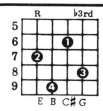 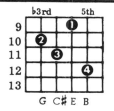

Rhythm Chords

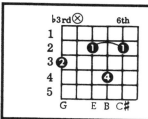 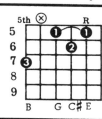 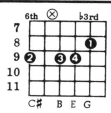 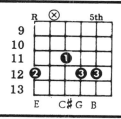

Bottom 4-String Chords

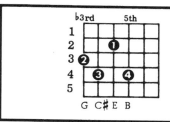 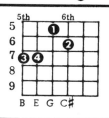 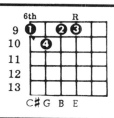

E 9th

Symbol (E 9)

Melody Chords

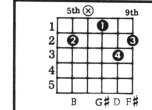 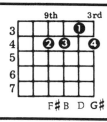 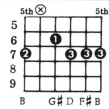 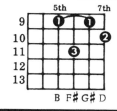 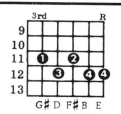

Inside & Rhythm Chords

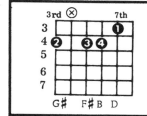 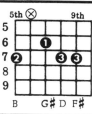 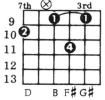 *or*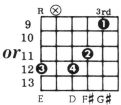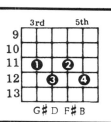

187

CHORDS

E Minor 9th

Symbol (E m9)

Melody Chords

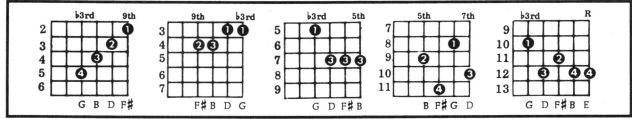

Inside & Rhythm Chords

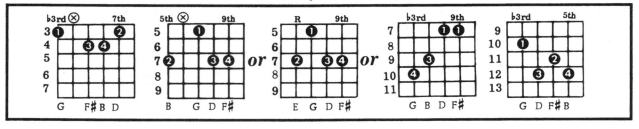

E Major 9th

Symbol (Ema 9th)

Melody Chords

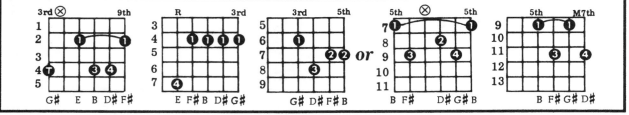

Inside Chords

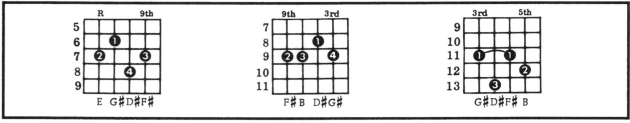

Rhythm Chords

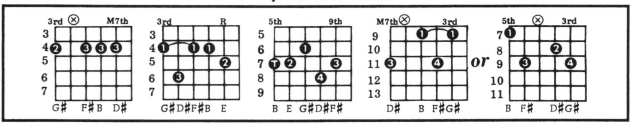

CHORDS

188

E9 Sharp 5th

Symbols
(E9+5, E9#5)

Melody Chords

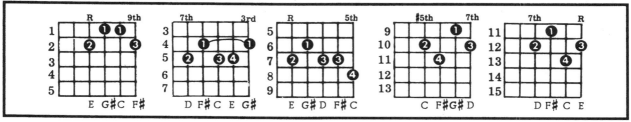

Inside & Rhythm Chords

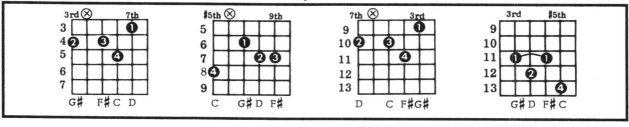

E9 Flat 5th

Symbol (E9-5)

Melody Chords

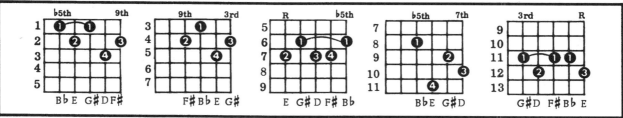

Inside & Rhythm Chords

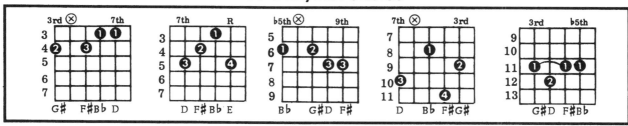

CHORDS

189

E7 Flat 9th

Symbol (E 7-9)

Melody Chords

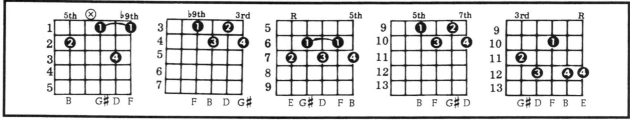

Inside & Rhythm Chords

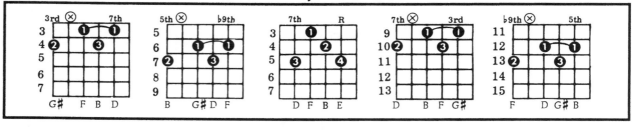

E7 Sharp 9th

*Symbols
(E 9+, E 7#9)*

All Forms

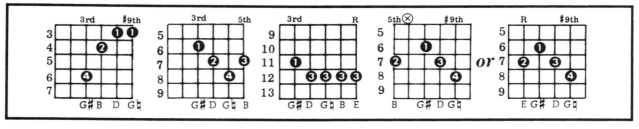

E6 Add 9th

*Symbols
(E $\frac{9}{6}$, E6add9)*

All Forms

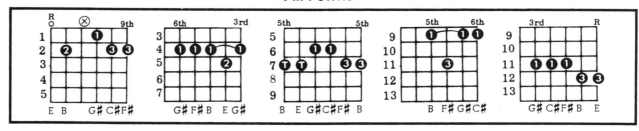

190

E 11th

Symbol (E 11)

Melody Chords

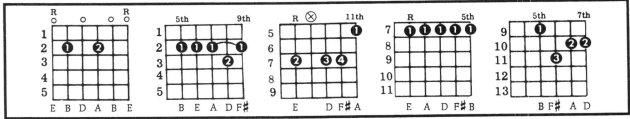

Inside & Rhythm Chords

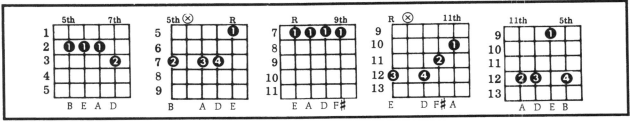

E Aug. 11th

Symbol (E 11 +)

All Forms

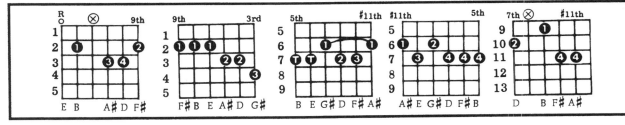

E 13th

Symbol (E 13)

All Forms

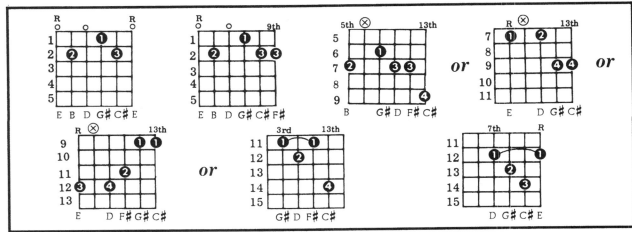

CHORDS

E 13-9

Symbol (E13-9)

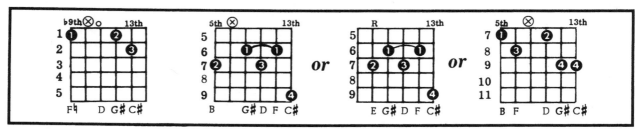

E 13-9-5

Symbol
(E 13⁻⁹₋₅)

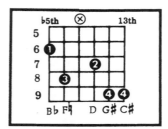

192

F Major

Symbol (F)

Melody Chords

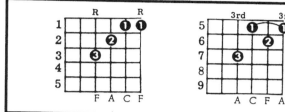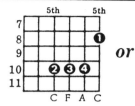 *or*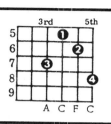

Inside Chords

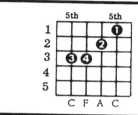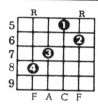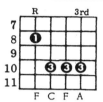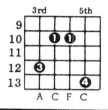

Rhythm Chords

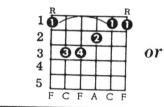 *or*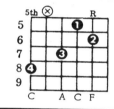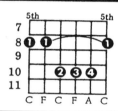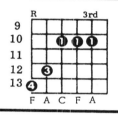

Bottom 4-String Chords

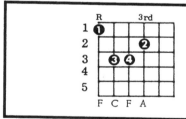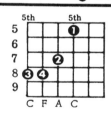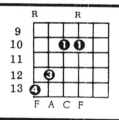

F Minor

Symbol (F m)

Melody Chords

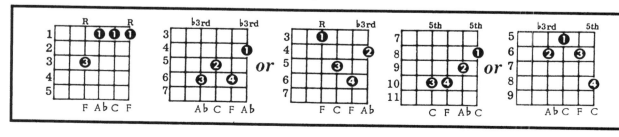

193

F Minor Cont.

Inside Chords

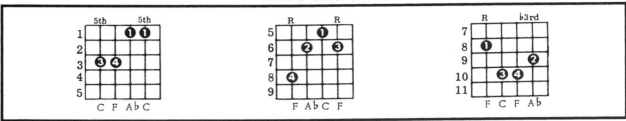

Rhythm Chords

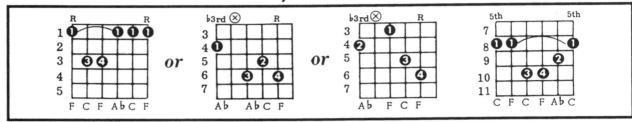

Bottom 4-String Chords

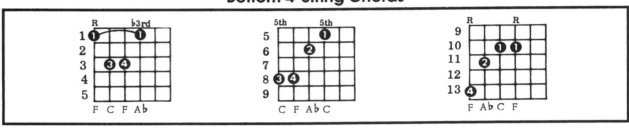

F Diminished

Symbols (F -, F⁰, F dim)

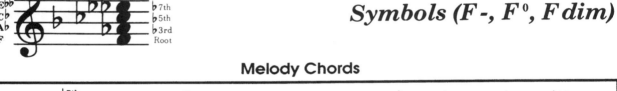

Melody Chords

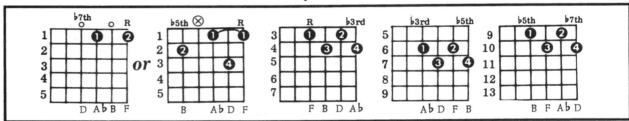

Inside Chords

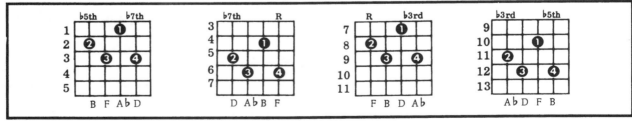

Rhythm Chords

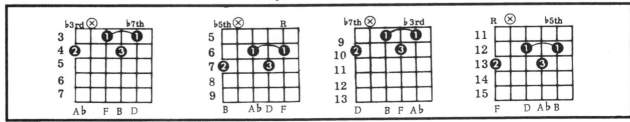

Bottom 4-String Chords

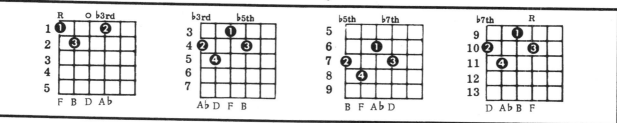

F Augmented

Symbol   (F +)

Melody Chords

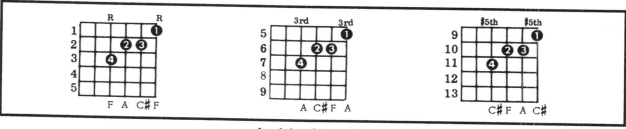

Inside Chords

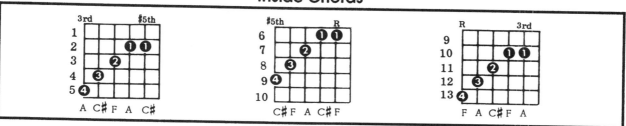

Bottom 4-String Chords

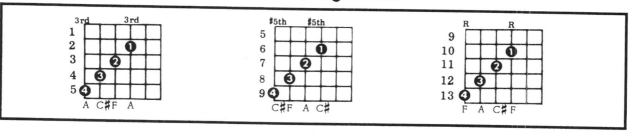

F 7th

Symbol (F 7)

Melody Chords

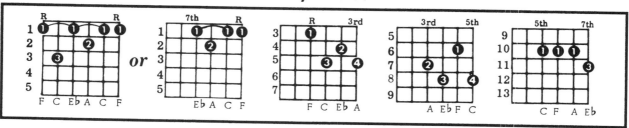

CHORDS

195

Inside Chords

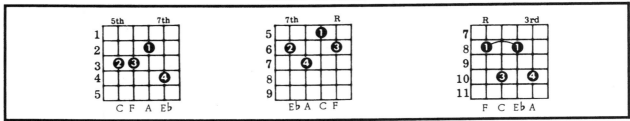

Rhythm Chords

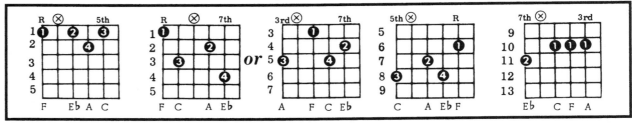

Bottom 4-String Chords

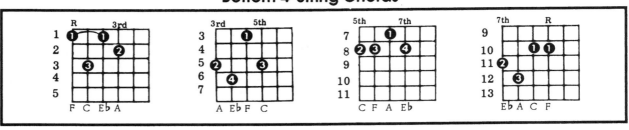

F Minor 7th

Symbol (Fm7)

Melody Chords

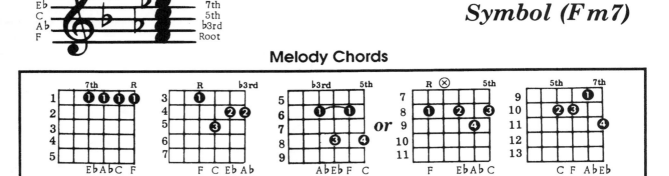

Inside Chords

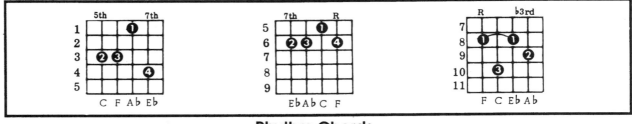

Rhythm Chords

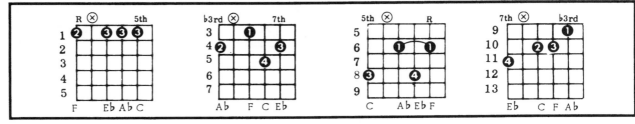

CHORDS

Bottom 4-String Chords

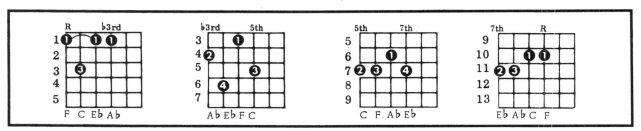

F 7th Aug. 5th

Symbol (F 7+5)

Melody Chords

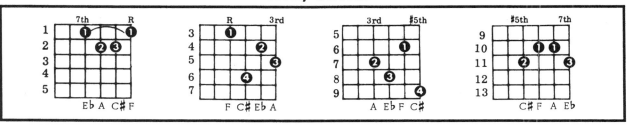

Inside Chords

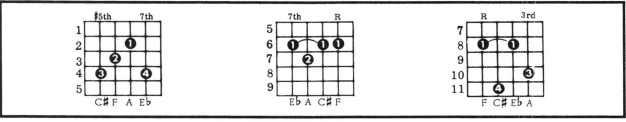

Rhythm Chords

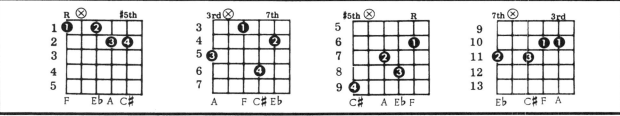

Bottom 4-String Chords

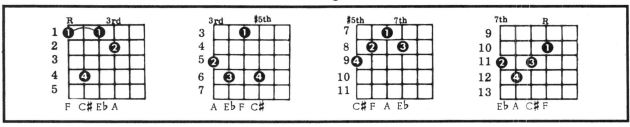

F 7th Flat 5th

Symbols
(F 7-5, F 7♭5)

Melody Chords

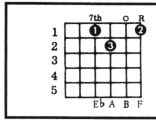
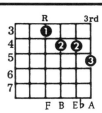
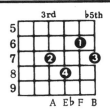
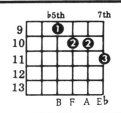

Inside Chords

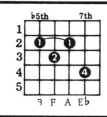
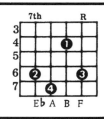
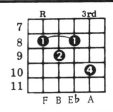
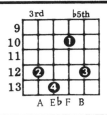

Rhythm Chords

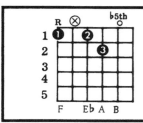
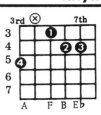
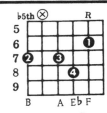
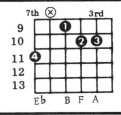

Bottom 4-String Chords

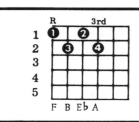
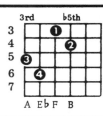
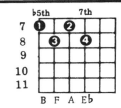
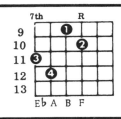

F Major 7th

Symbol (Fma7)

Melody Chords

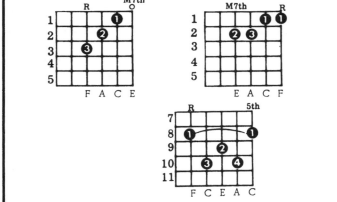
or
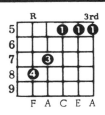

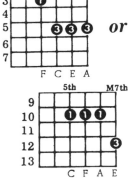

198

Inside & Rhythm Chords

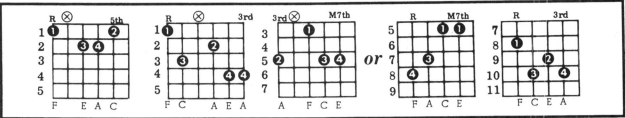

Bottom 4-String Chords

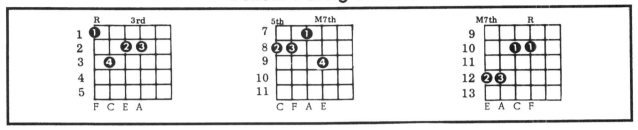

F Major 7th Flat 3rd

Symbols (Fma7♭3, Fmin-maj7)

Melody Chords

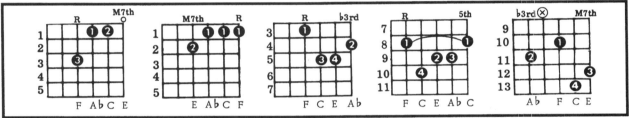

Inside & Rhythm Chords

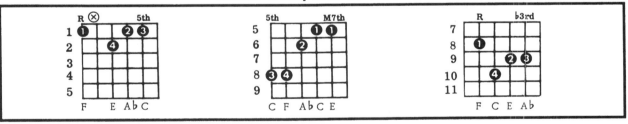

F Minor 7th Flat 5th

Symbol (Fm7♭5)

Melody Chords

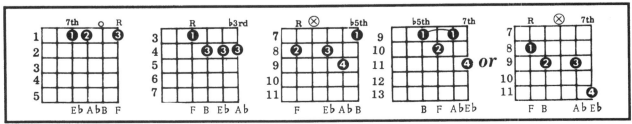

CHORDS

199

F Minor 7th Flat 5th Cont.

Inside Chords

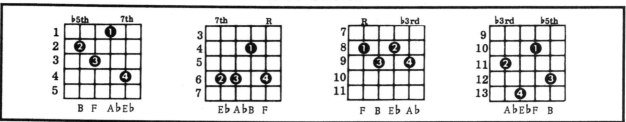

Rhythm Chords

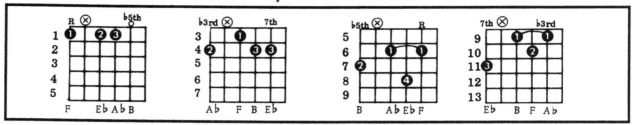

F7 Suspended 4th

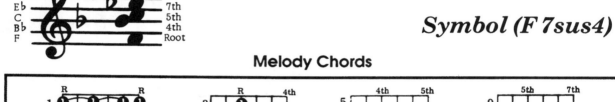

Symbol (F 7sus4)

Melody Chords

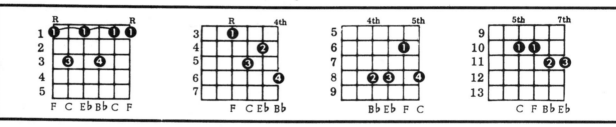

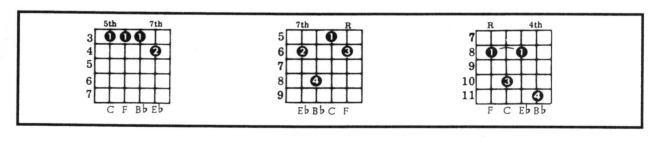

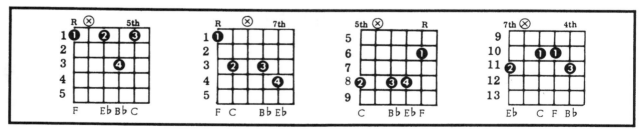

CHORDS

200

F 6th

Symbol (F6)

Melody Chords

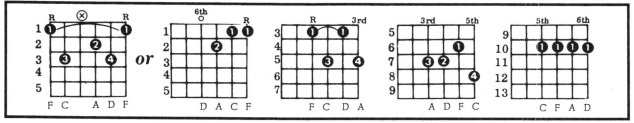

Inside Chords

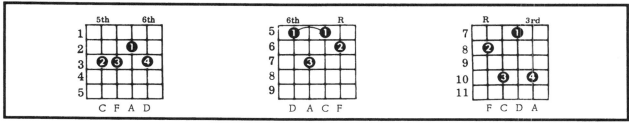

Rhythm Chords

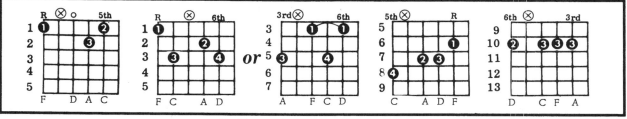

Bottom 4-String Chords

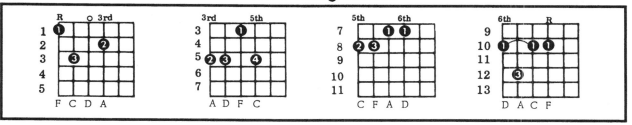

F Minor 6th

Symbol (F m6)

Melody Chords

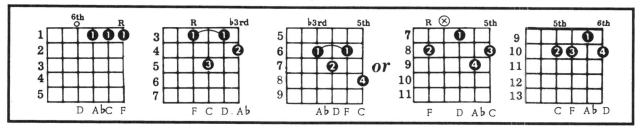

CHORDS

201

Inside Chords

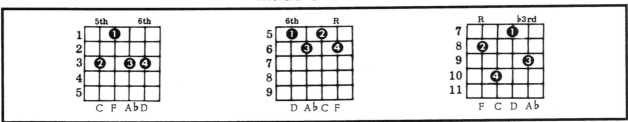

Rhythm Chords

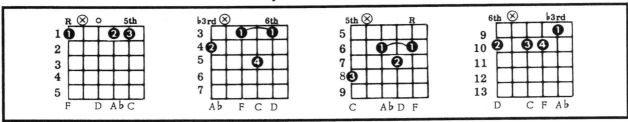

Bottom 4-String Chords

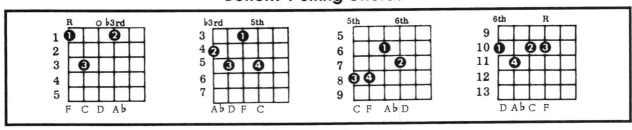

F 9th

Symbol (F 9)

Melody Chords

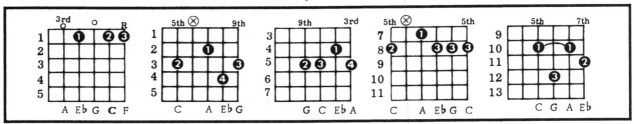

Inside & Rhythm Chords

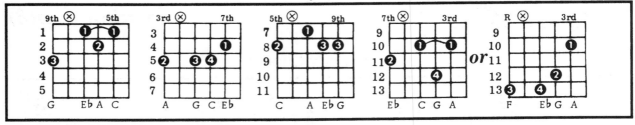

F Minor 9th

Symbol (F m9)

Melody Chords

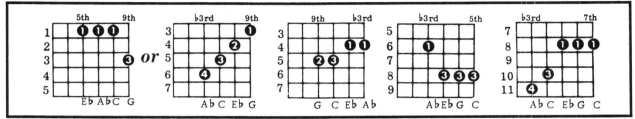

Inside & Rhythm Chords

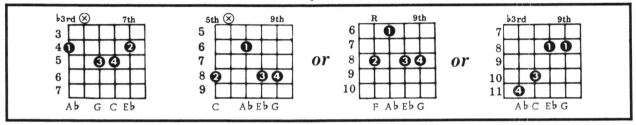

F Major 9th

Symbol (F ma9)

Melody Chords

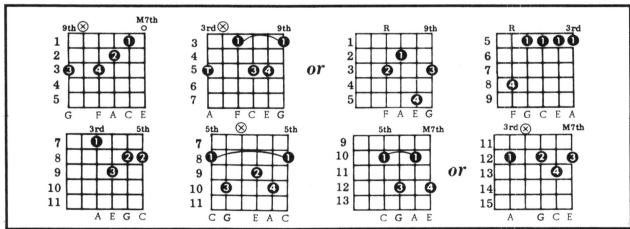

Inside Chords

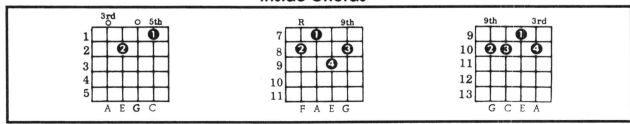

CHORDS

203

Rhythm Chords

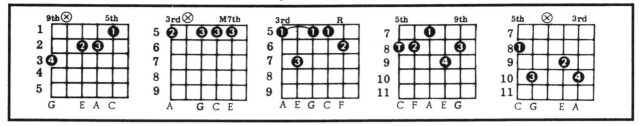

F9 Sharp 5th

Symbols (F 9 + 5, F 9 # 5)

Melody Chords

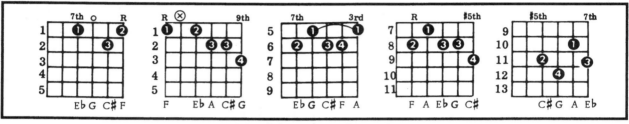

Inside & Rhythm Chords

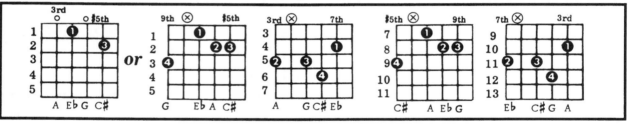

F9 Flat 5th

Symbol (F 9-5)

Melody Chords

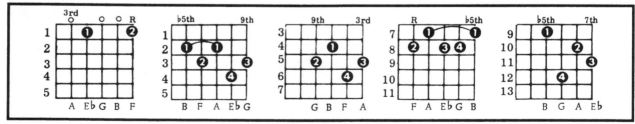

Inside & Rhythm Chords

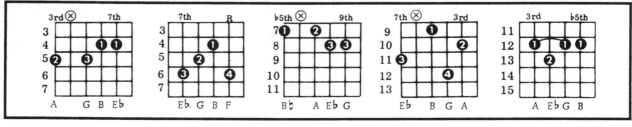

CHORDS

F7 Flat 9th

Symbol (F 7-9)

Melody Chords

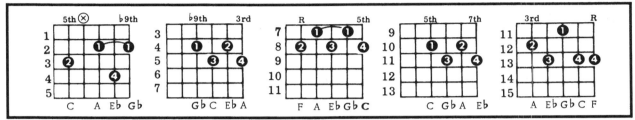

Inside & Rhythm Chords

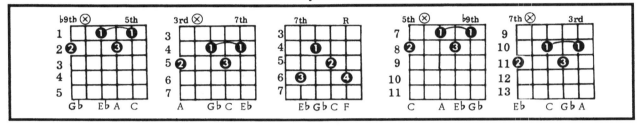

F7 Sharp 9th

*Symbols (F 9 + ,
F 7 # 9)*

All Forms

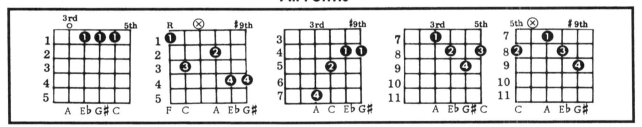

F6 Add 9th

Symbols (F $\frac{9}{6}$, F 6add9)

All Forms

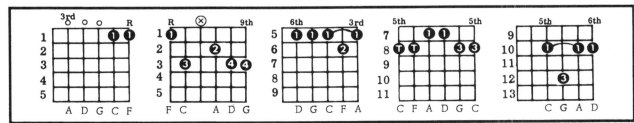

F 11th

Symbol (F 11)

All Forms

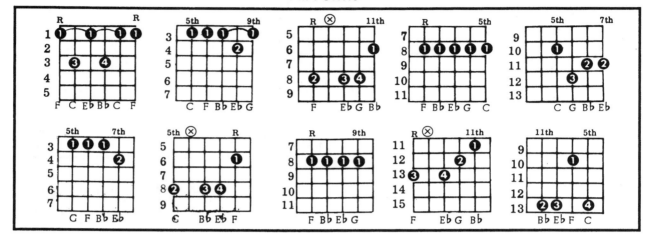

F Aug. 11th

Symbol (F 11+)

All Forms

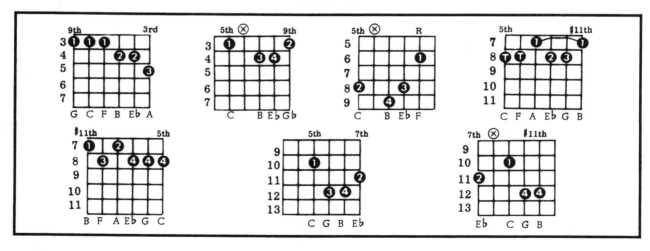

F 13th

Symbol (F 13)

All Forms

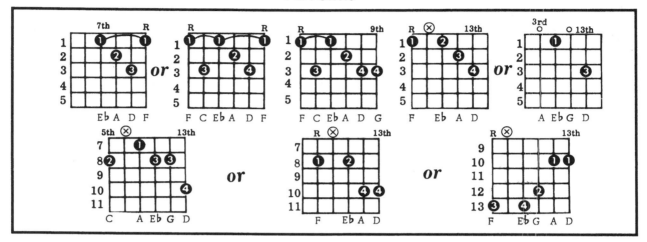

F 13-9

Symbol (F 13-9)

All Forms

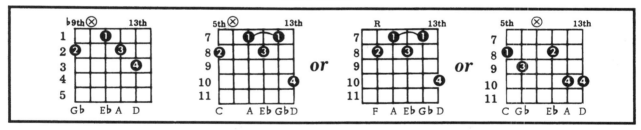

CHORDS

F 13-9-5

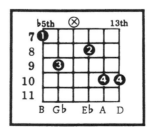

Symbol (F 13$_{-5}^{-9}$)

G♭ Major

Db
Bb
Gb

5th
3rd
Root

Symbol (G♭)

Melody Chords

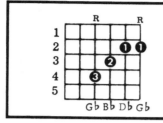
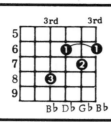
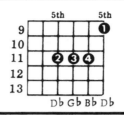

or

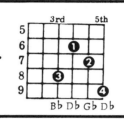

Inside Chords

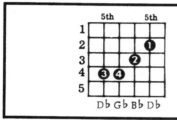
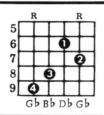
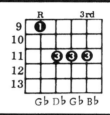

Rhythm Chords

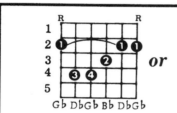

or

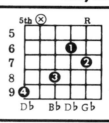
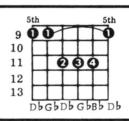
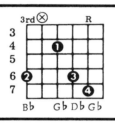

Bottom 4-String Chords

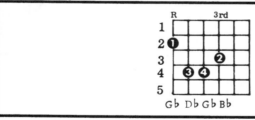
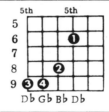

G♭ Minor

Db
Bbb
Gb

5th
♭3rd
Root

Symbol (G♭m)

Melody Chords

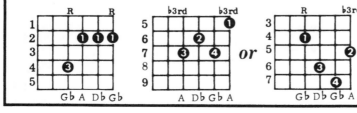

or

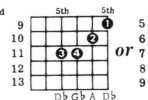

or

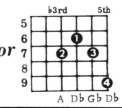

CHORDS

208

Inside Chords

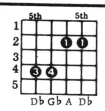 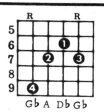 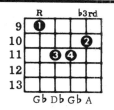

Rhythm Chords

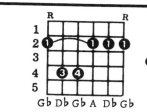 *or* 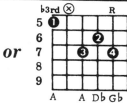 *or*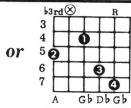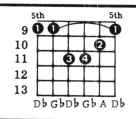

Bottom 4-String Chords

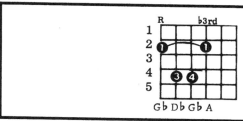 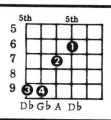

G♭ Diminished

Symbols (G♭-,
G♭⁰, G♭dim)

Melody Chords

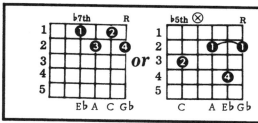 *or*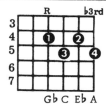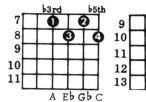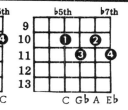

Inside Chords

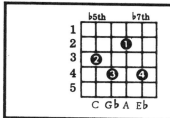 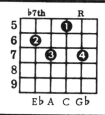 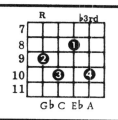

Rhythm Chords

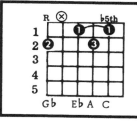 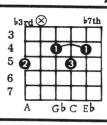 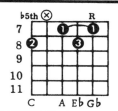 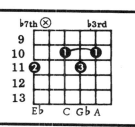

Gb Diminished Cont.

Bottom 4-String Chords

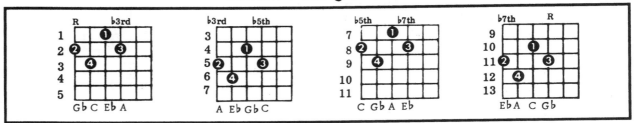

Gb Augmented

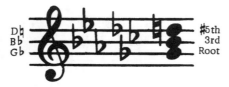

Symbol (Gb+)

Melody Chords

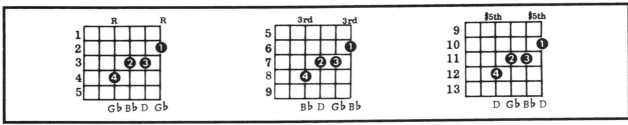

Inside Chords

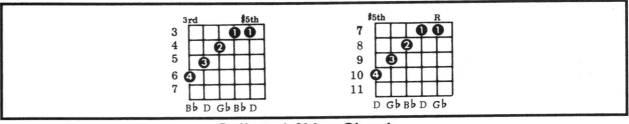

Bottom 4-String Chords

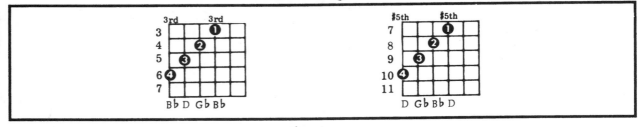

Gb 7th

Symbol (Gb7)

Melody Chords

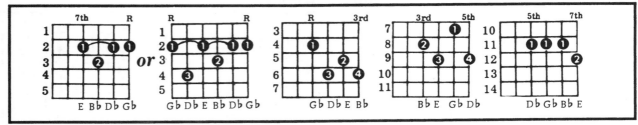

Inside Chords

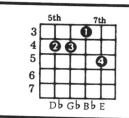 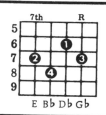 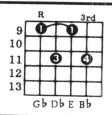

Rhythm Chords

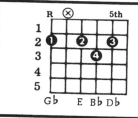 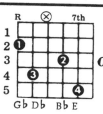 *or*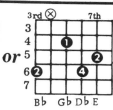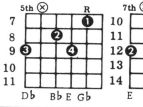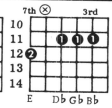

Bottom 4-String Chords

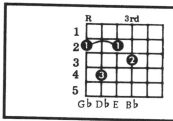 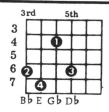 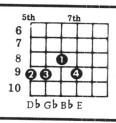

G♭ Minor 7th

Symbol (G♭m7)

Melody Chords

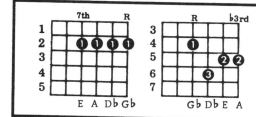 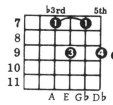 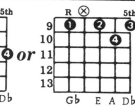 *or*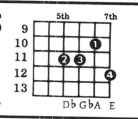

Inside Chords

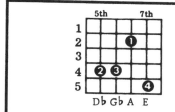 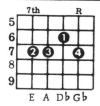 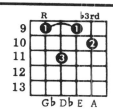

Rhythm Chords

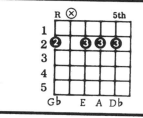 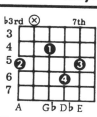 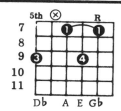 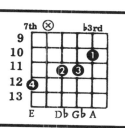

CHORDS

211

Bottom 4-String Chords

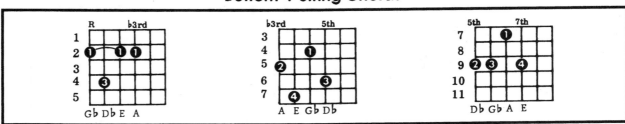

Gb 7th Aug. 5th

Symbol (Gb7 + 5)

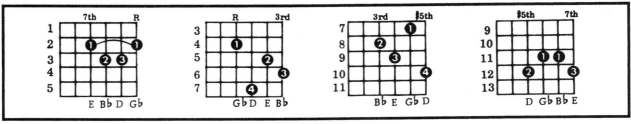

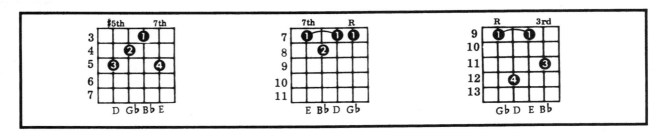

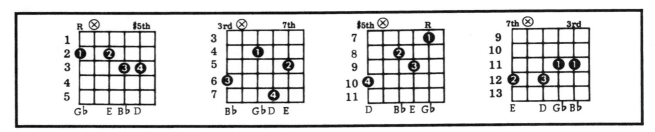

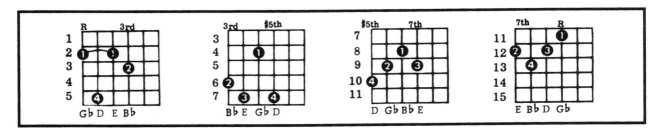

CHORDS

G♭ 7th Flat 5th

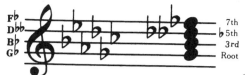

Symbols
(G♭7-5, G♭7♭5)

Melody Chords

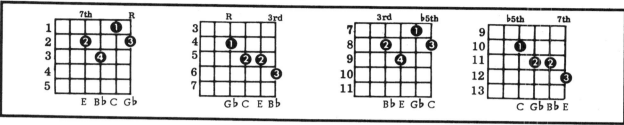

Inside Chords

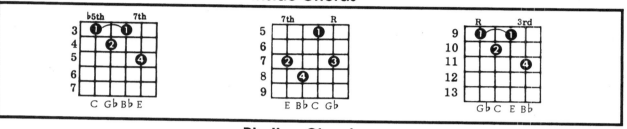

Rhythm Chords

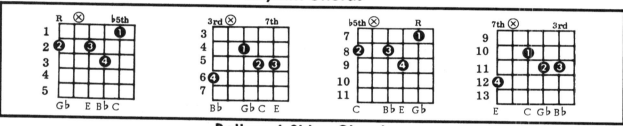

Bottom 4-String Chords

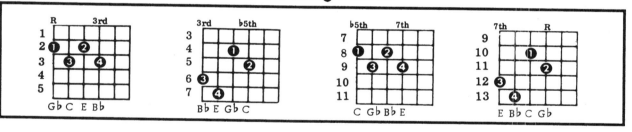

G♭ Major 7th

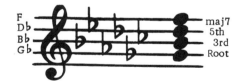

Symbol (G♭ma7)

Melody Chords

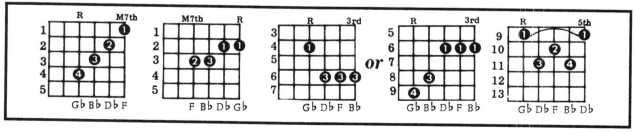

213

CHORDS

Gb Major 7th Cont.

Inside & Rhythm Chords

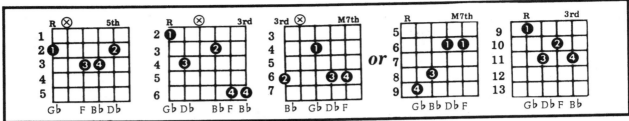

Bottom 4-String Chords

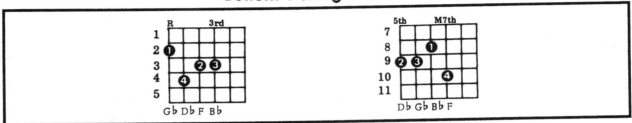

Gb Major 7th Flat 3rd

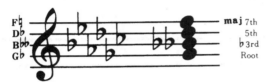

Symbols
(Gbma7b3,
Gbmin-maj7)

Melody Chords

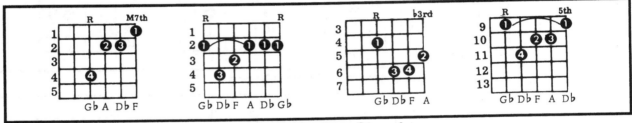

Inside & Rhythm Chords

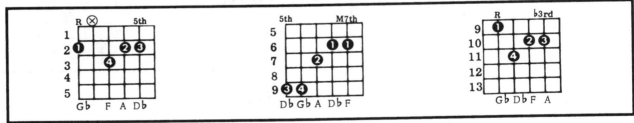

Gb Minor 7th Flat 5th

Symbol (Gbm7b5)

Melody Chords

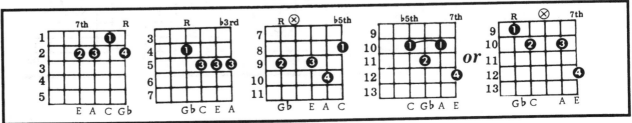

214

Inside Chords

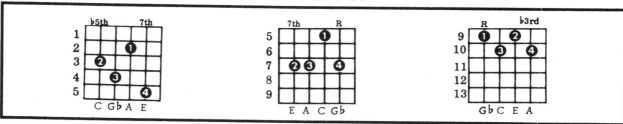

Rhythm Chords

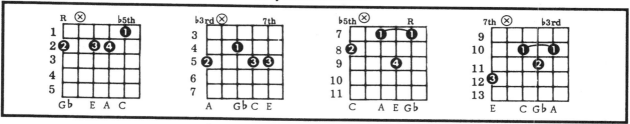

G♭7 Suspended 4th

Symbol (G♭7sus4)

Melody Chords

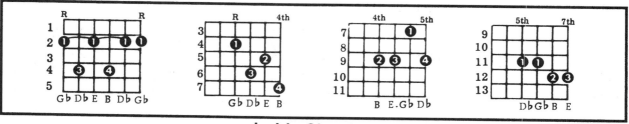

Inside Chords

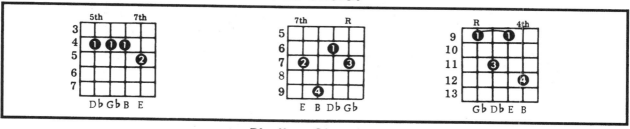

Rhythm Chords

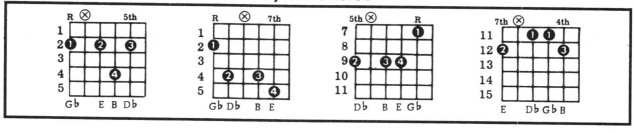

G♭ 6th

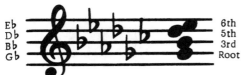

Symbol (G♭6)

Melody Chords

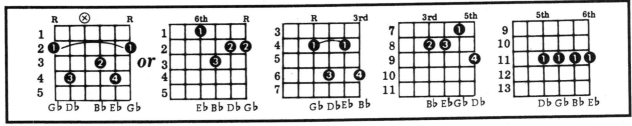

Inside Chords

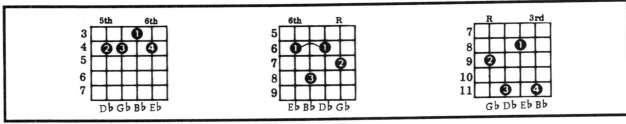

Rhythm Chords

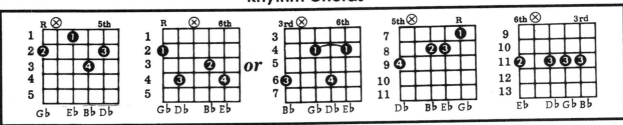

Bottom 4-String Chords

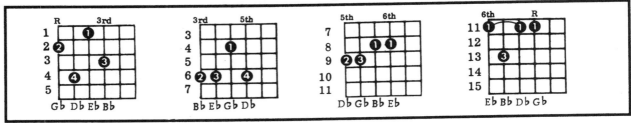

G♭ Minor 6th

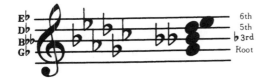

Symbol (G♭m6)

Melody Chords

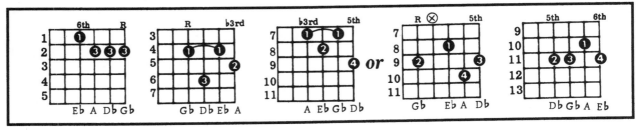

CHORDS

216

Inside Chords

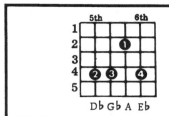
Db Gb A Eb

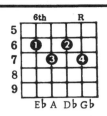
Eb A Db Gb

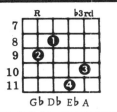
Gb Db Eb A

Rhythm Chords

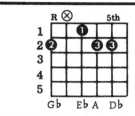
Gb Eb A Db

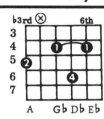
A Gb Db Eb

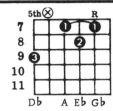
Db A Eb Gb

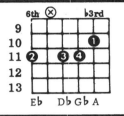
Eb Db Gb A

Bottom 4-String Chords

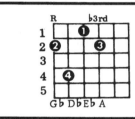
Gb Db Eb A

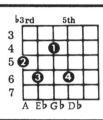
A Eb Gb Db

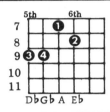
Db Gb A Eb

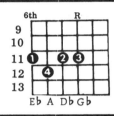
Eb A Db Gb

Gb 9th

Symbol (Gb 9)

Melody Chords

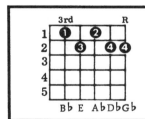
Bb E Ab Db Gb

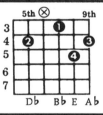
Db Bb E Ab

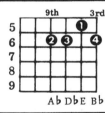
Ab Db E Bb

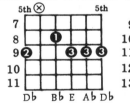
Db Bb E Ab Db

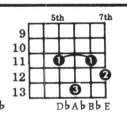
Db Ab Bb E

Inside & Rhythm Chords

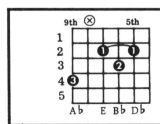
Ab E Bb Db

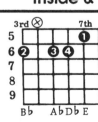
Bb Ab Db E

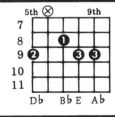
Db Bb E Ab

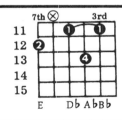
E Db Ab Bb

CHORDS

G♭ Minor 9th

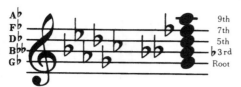

Symbol (G♭m9)

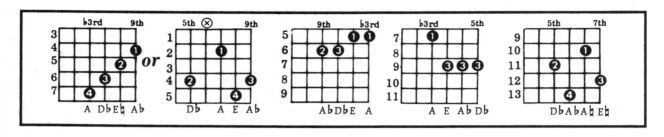

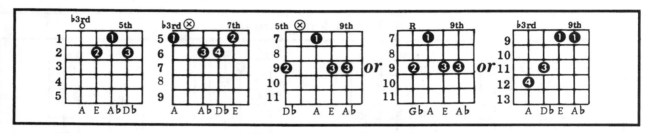

G♭ Major 9th

Symbol (G♭ma9th)

Melody Chords

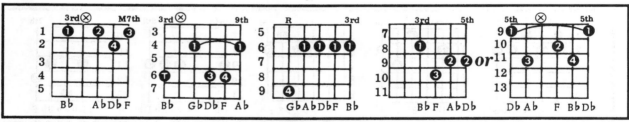

Inside Chords

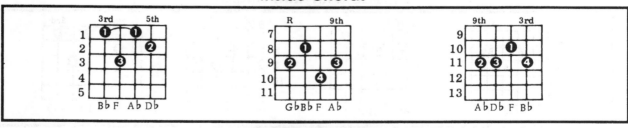

Rhythm Chords

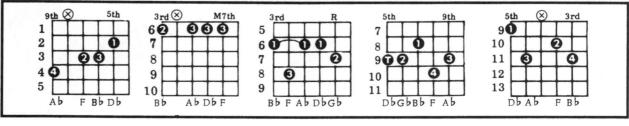

G♭9 Sharp 5th

Symbols
(G♭9 + 5, G♭9#5)

Melody Chords

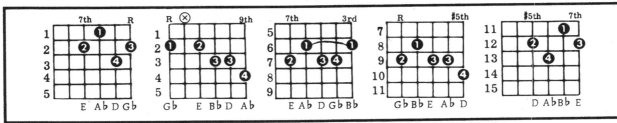

Inside & Rhythm Chords

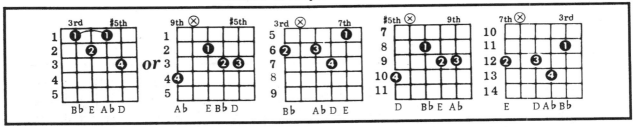

G♭9 Flat 5th

Symbol (G♭ 9-5)

Melody Chords

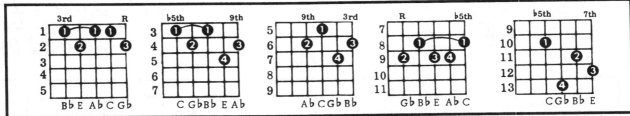

Inside & Rhythm Chords

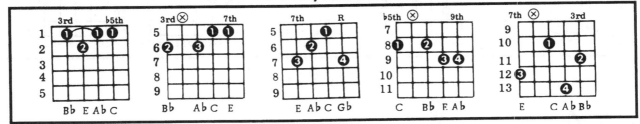

G♭7 Flat 9th

Symbol (G♭7-9)

Melody Chords

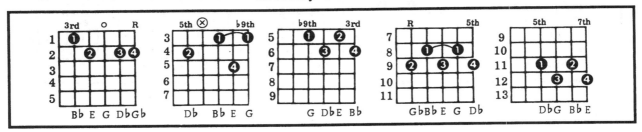

CHORDS

219

Inside & Rhythm Chords

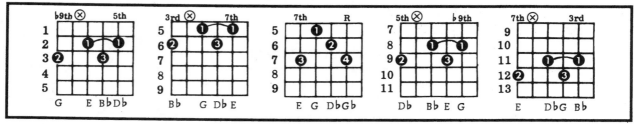

Gb7 Sharp 9th

Symbols (Gb9 +,
Gb7# 9)

All Forms

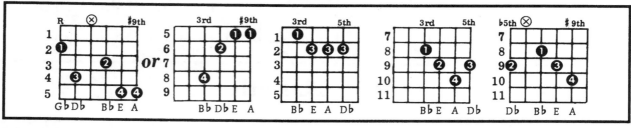

Gb6 Add 9th

Symbols (Gb 9/6,
Gb6 add 9)

All Forms

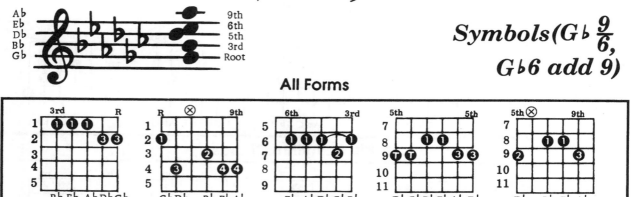

Gb 11th

Symbol (Gb11)

Melody Chords

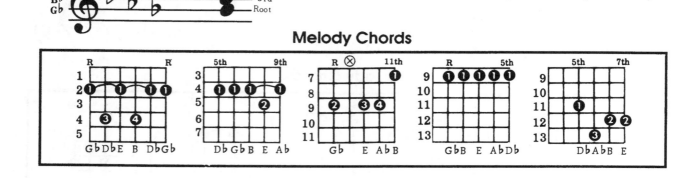

220

Inside & Rhythm Chords

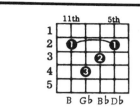 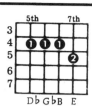 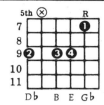 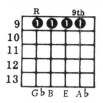

G♭ Aug. 11th

Symbol (G♭11 +)

All Forms

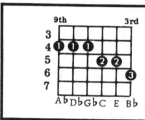 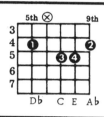 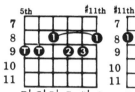 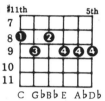 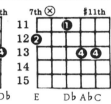

G♭ 13th

Symbol (G♭13)

All Forms

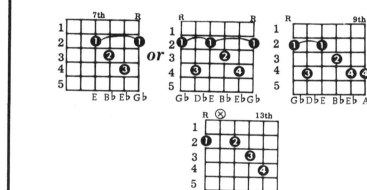 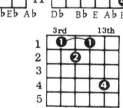

G♭ 13-9

Symbol (G♭13-9)

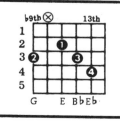 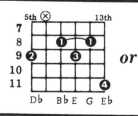 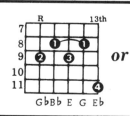 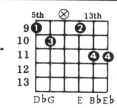

CHORDS

221

Gb 13-9-5

Symbol (Gb13$\begin{smallmatrix}-9\\-5\end{smallmatrix}$)

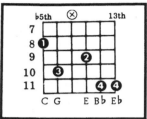

G Major

Symbol (G)

Melody Chords

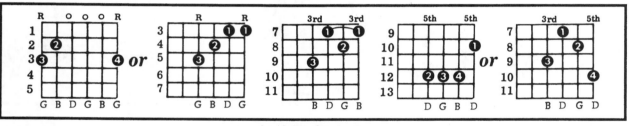

Inside Chords

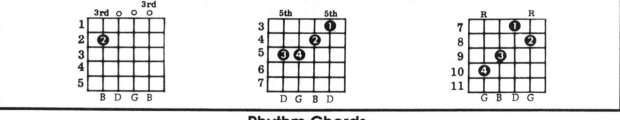

Rhythm Chords

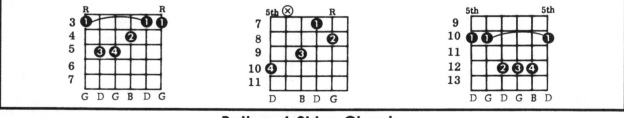

Bottom 4-String Chords

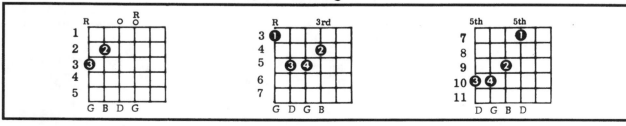

CHORDS

G Minor

Symbol (Gm)

Melody Chords

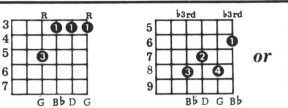 *or*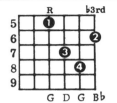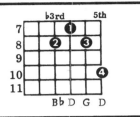

Inside Chords

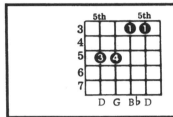 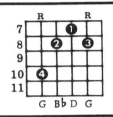 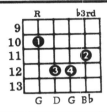

Rhythm Chords

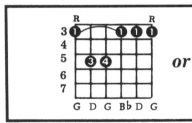 *or* 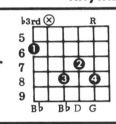 *or*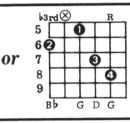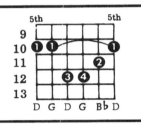

Bottom 4-String Chords

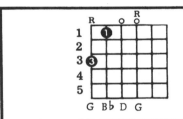 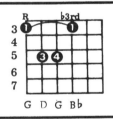 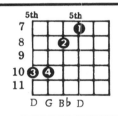

G Diminished

Symbols (G-, G⁰, Gdim)

Melody Chords

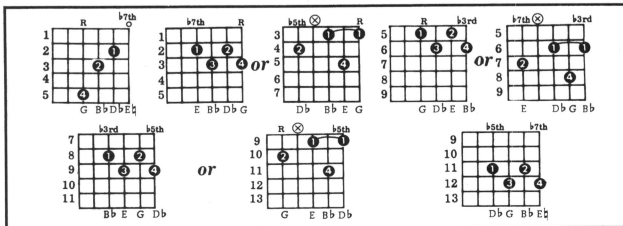

223

G Diminished Cont.

Inside Chords

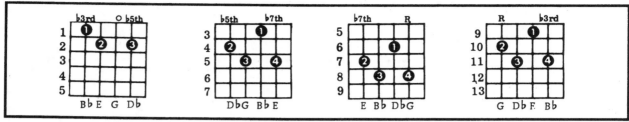

Rhythm Chords

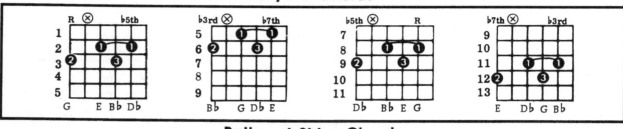

Bottom 4-String Chords

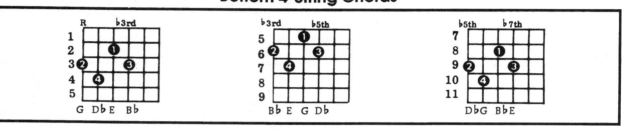

G Augmented

Symbol (G +)

Melody Chords

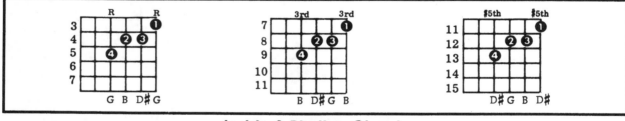

Inside & Rhythm Chords

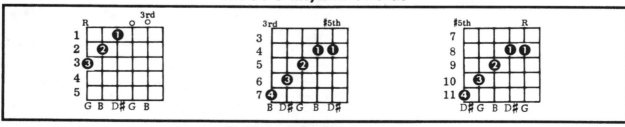

Bottom 4-String Chords

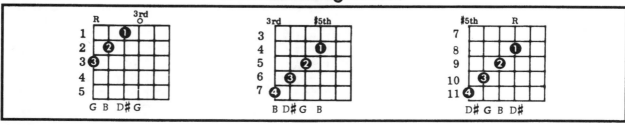

CHORDS

224

G 7th

Symbol (G7)

Melody Chords

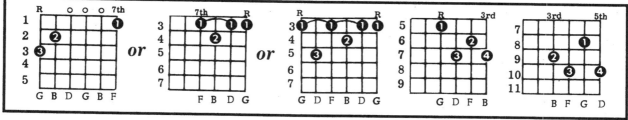

Inside Chords

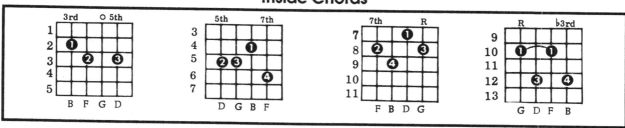

Rhythm Chords

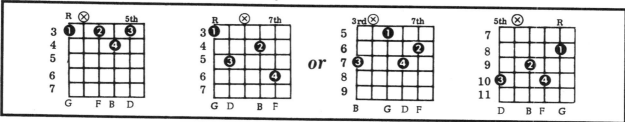

Bottom 4-String Chords

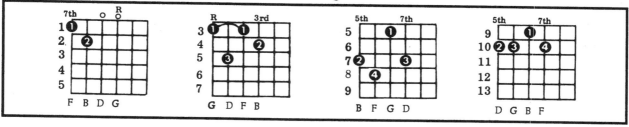

G Minor 7th

Symbol (G m7)

Melody Chords

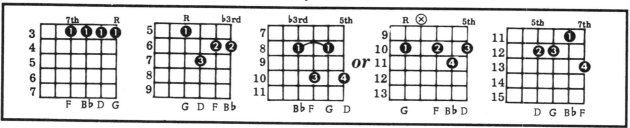

CHORDS

225

Inside Chords

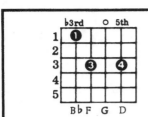
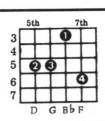
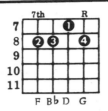
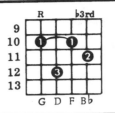

Rhythm Chords

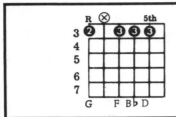
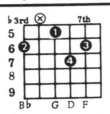
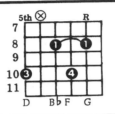

Bottom 4-String Chords

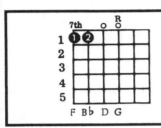
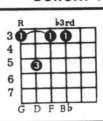
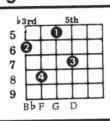
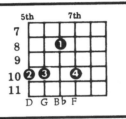

G 7th Aug. 5th

Symbol (G7 + 5)

Melody Chords

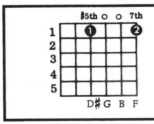

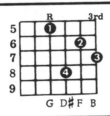
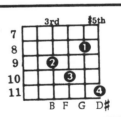

Inside Chords

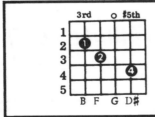
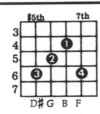
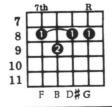
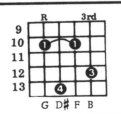

Rhythm Chords

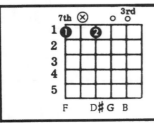
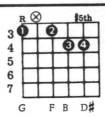
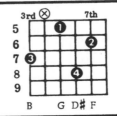
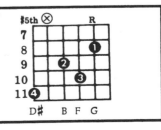

CHORDS

Bottom 4-String Chords

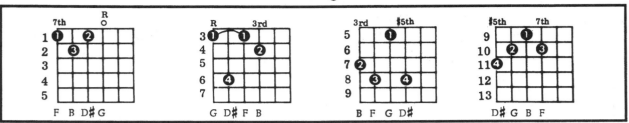

G 7th Flat 5th

Symbols
(G 7-5, G 7♭5)

Melody Chords

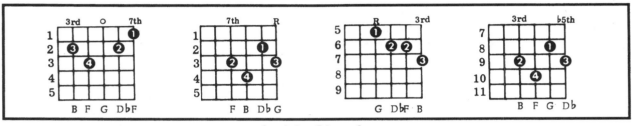

Inside Chords

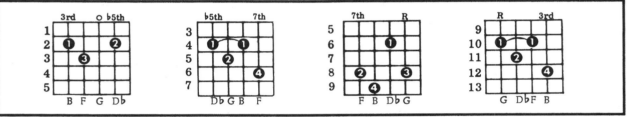

Rhythm Chords

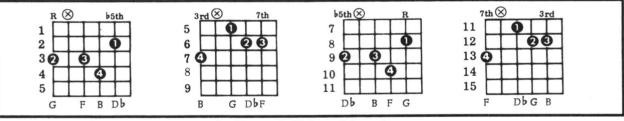

Bottom 4-String Chords

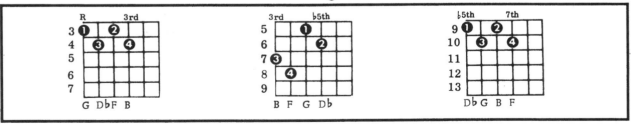

CHORDS

227

G Major 7th

Symbol (G ma7)

Melody Chords

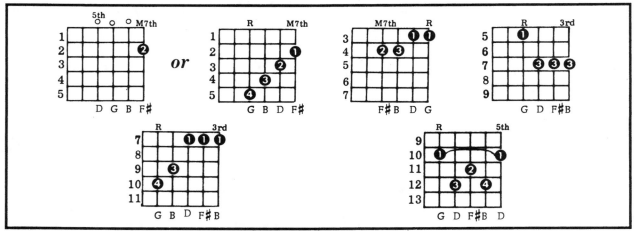

Inside & Rhythm Chords

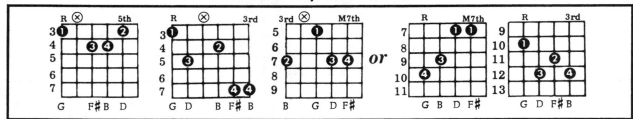

Bottom 4-String Chords

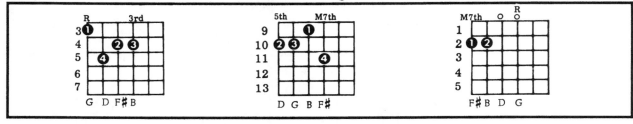

G Major 7th Flat 3rd

Symbols (G ma7♭3, G min-maj7)

Melody Chords

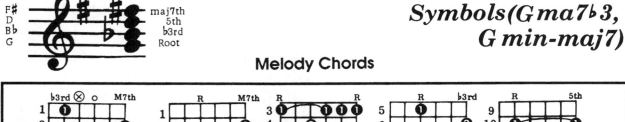

Inside & Rhythm Chords

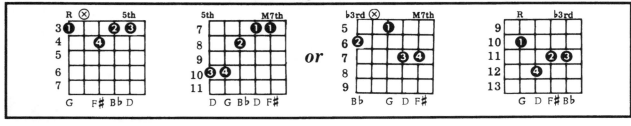

CHORDS

G Minor 7th Flat 5th

Symbol (Gm7♭5)

Melody Chords

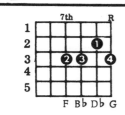 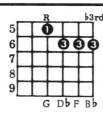 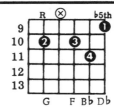 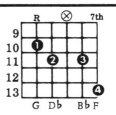

Inside Chords

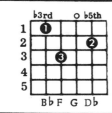 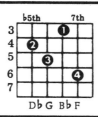 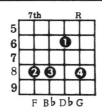 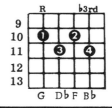

Rhythm Chords

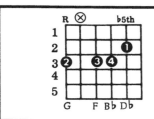 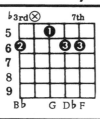 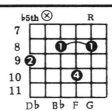 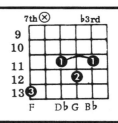

G7 Suspended 4th

Symbol (G 7sus4)

Melody Chords

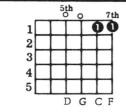 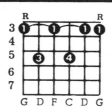 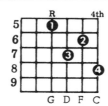 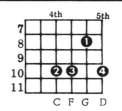

Inside Chords

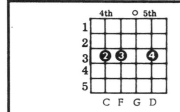 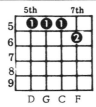 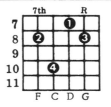

Rhythm Chords

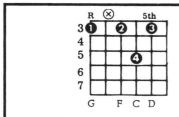 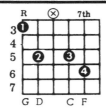 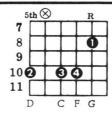

CHORDS

229

G 6th

Symbol (G 6)

Melody Chords

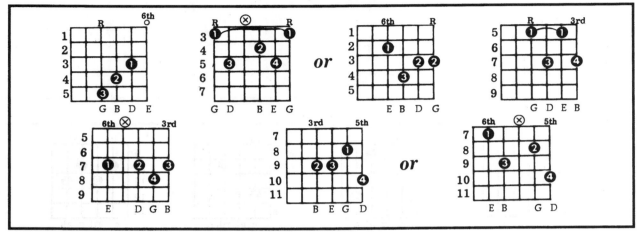

or

or

Inside Chords

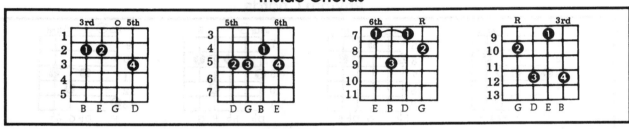

Rhythm Chords

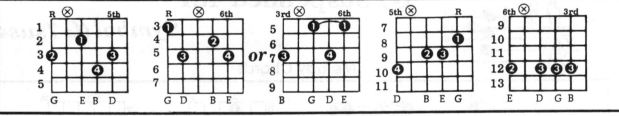

or

Bottom 4-String Chords

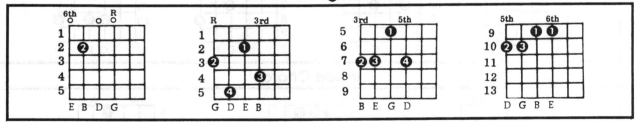

G Minor 6th

Symbol (Gm6)

Melody Chords

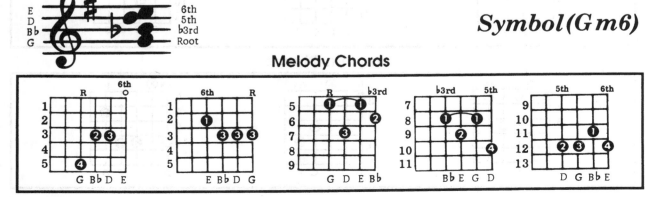

230

Inside Chords

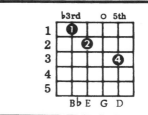 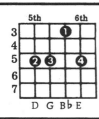 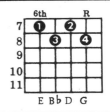 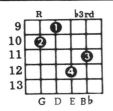

Rhythm Chords

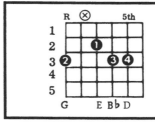 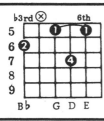 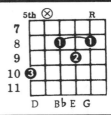 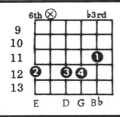

Bottom 4-String Chords

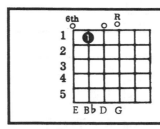 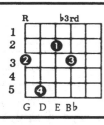 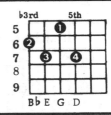 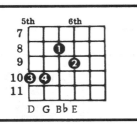

G 9th

Symbol (G9)

Melody Chords

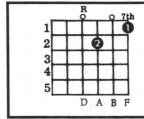 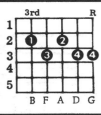 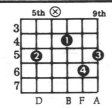 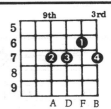 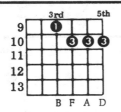

Inside & Rhythm Chords

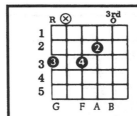 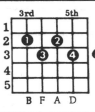 *or*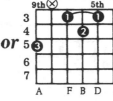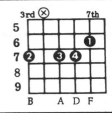

231

G Minor 9th

Symbol (G m9)

Melody Chords

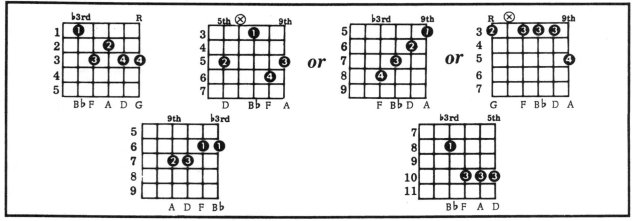

Inside & Rhythm Chords

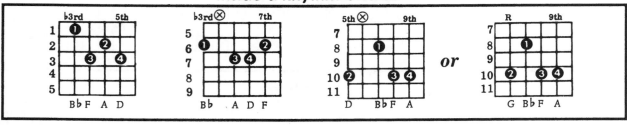

G Major 9th

Symbol (G ma 9)

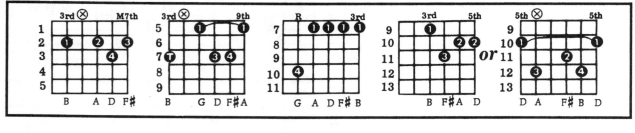

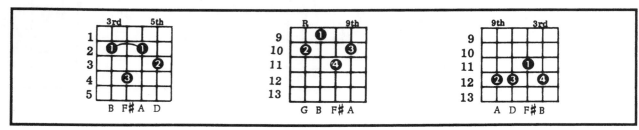

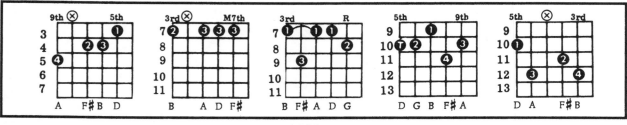

G9 Sharp 5th

Melody Chords

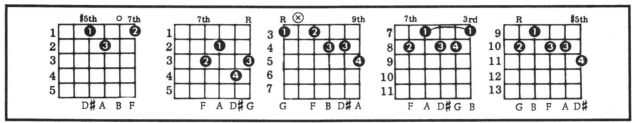

Inside & Rhythm Chords

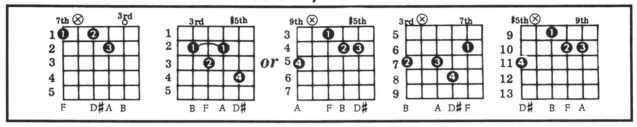

G9 Flat 5th

Symbol (G 9-5)

Melody Chords

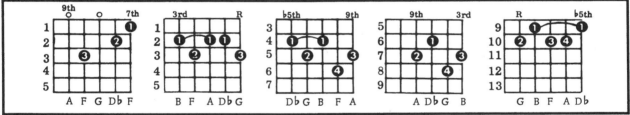

Inside & Rhythm Chords

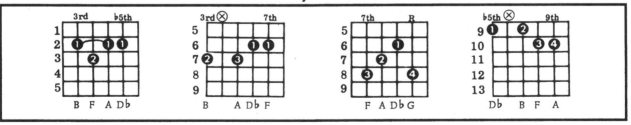

CHORDS

233

G7 Flat 9th

Symbol (G7-9)

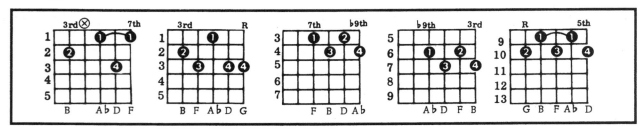

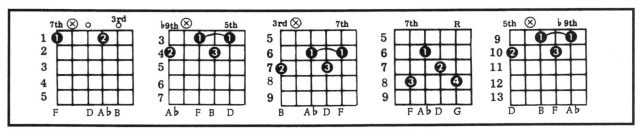

G7 Sharp 9th

Symbols (G 9 +, G 7 ♯ 9)

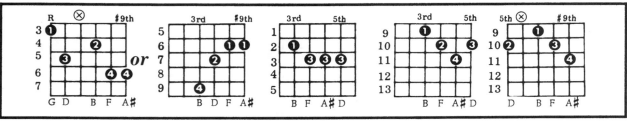

G6 Add 9th

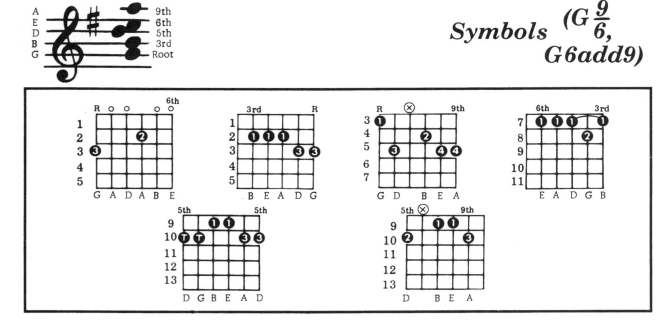

Symbols (G 9/6, G6add9)

CHORDS

G 11th

Symbol (G 11)

Melody Chords

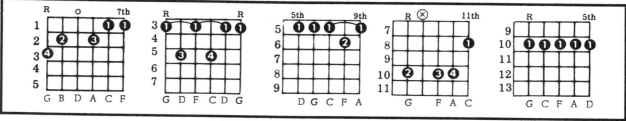

Inside & Rhythm Chords

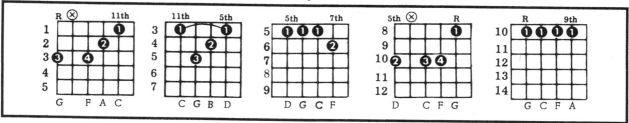

G Aug. 11th

Symbol (G 11 +)

All Forms

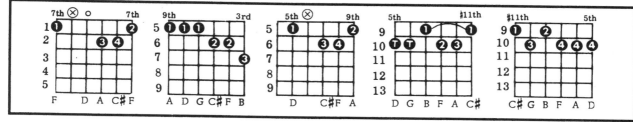

G 13th

Symbol (G 13)

All Forms

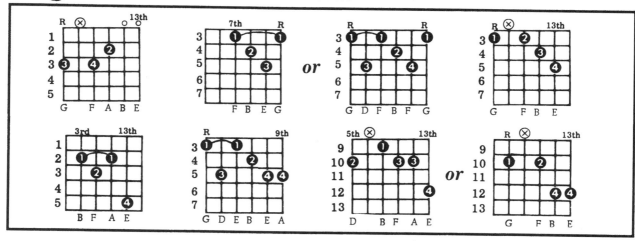

235

G 13-9

Symbol (G 13-9)

All Forms

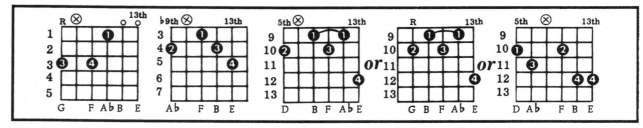

G 13-9-5

Symbol (G 13 -9 -5)

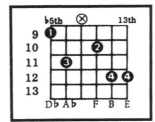

A♭ Major

Symbol (A♭maj)

Melody Chords

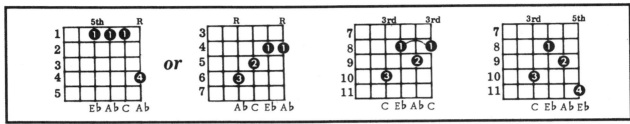

Inside Chords

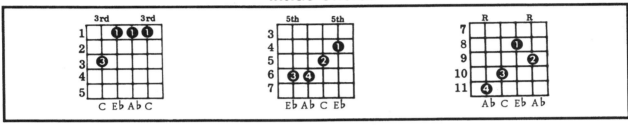

Rhythm Chords

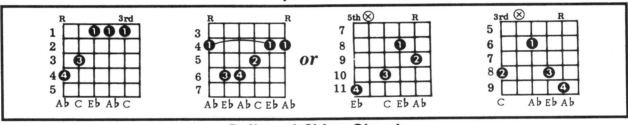

Bottom 4-String Chords

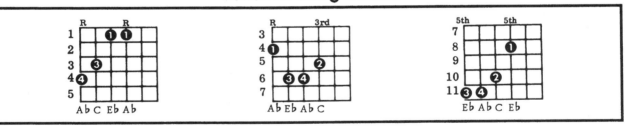

A♭ Minor

Symbol (A♭m)

Melody Chords

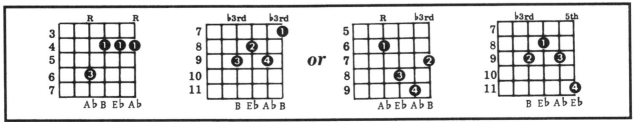

CHORDS

237

Inside Chords

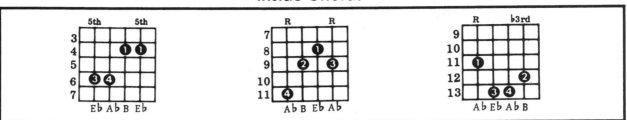

Rhythm Chords

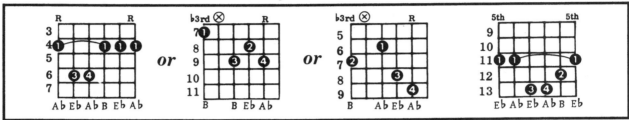

Bottom 4-String Chords

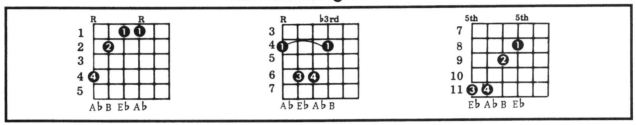

A♭ Diminished

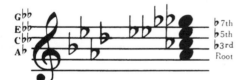

*Symbols (A♭-,
A♭⁰, A♭dim)*

Melody Chords

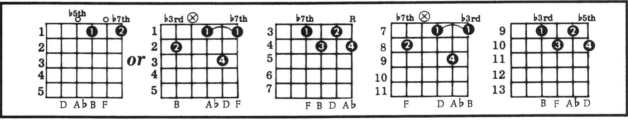

Inside Chords

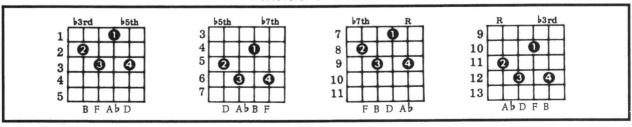

Rhythm Chords

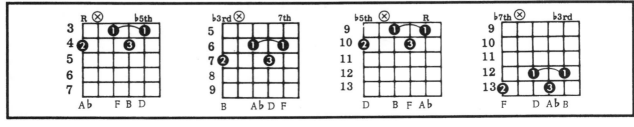

CHORDS

Bottom 4-String Chords

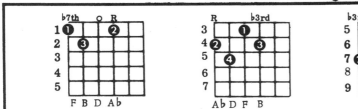
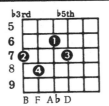
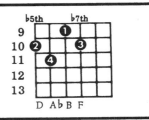

A♭ Augmented

Symbol (A♭ +)

Melody Chords

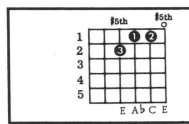
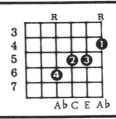
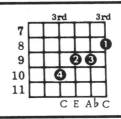

Inside & Rhythm Chords

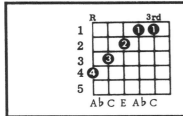
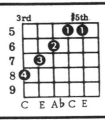
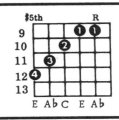

Bottom 4-String Chords

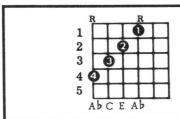
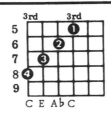
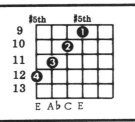

A♭ 7th

Symbol (A♭ 7)

Melody Chords

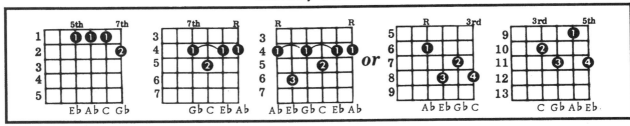

239

Inside Chords

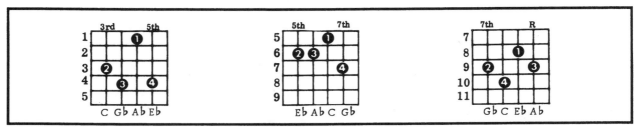

Rhythm Chords

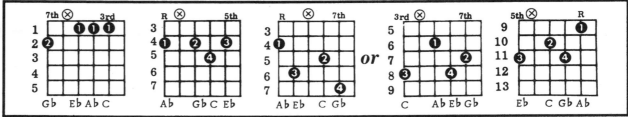

Bottom 4-String Chords

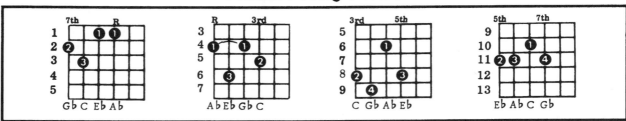

Ab Minor 7th

Symbol (Abm7)

Melody Chords

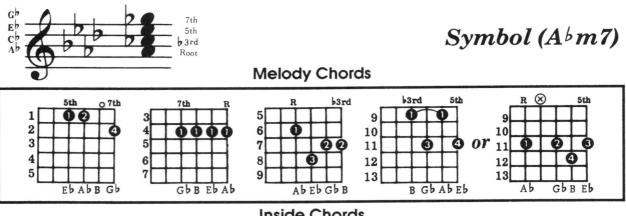

Inside Chords

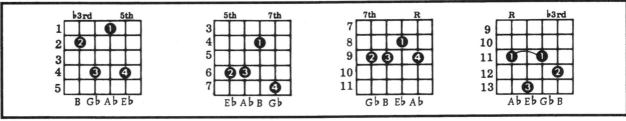

Rhythm Chords

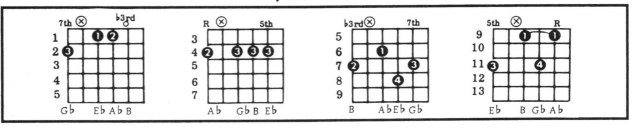

CHORDS

240

Bottom 4-String Chords

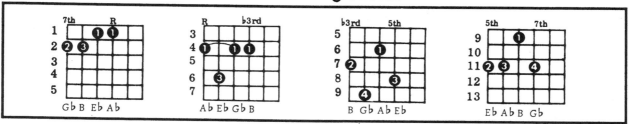

A♭ 7th Aug. 5th

Symbol (A♭7 + 5)

Melody Chords

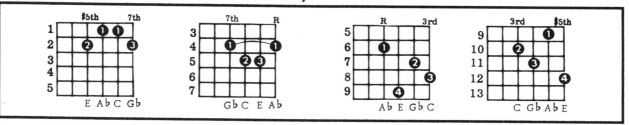

Inside Chords

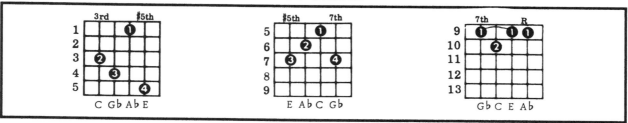

Rhythm Chords

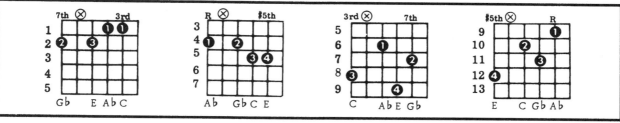

Bottom 4-String Chords

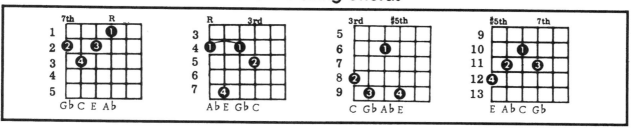

CHORDS

241

A♭ 7th Flat 5th

Symbols (A♭7-5, A♭7♭5)

Melody Chords

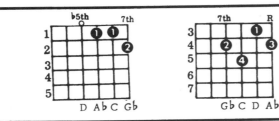
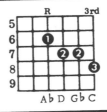
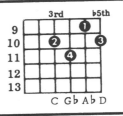

Inside Chords

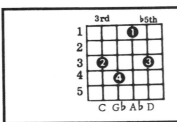
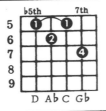
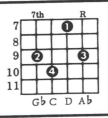

Rhythm Chords

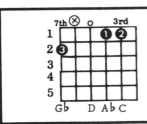
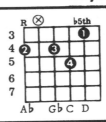
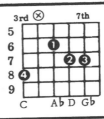
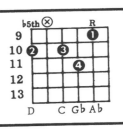

Bottom 4-String Chords

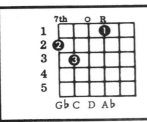
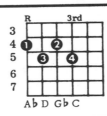
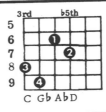
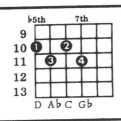

A♭ Major 7th

Symbol (A♭ma7)

Melody Chords

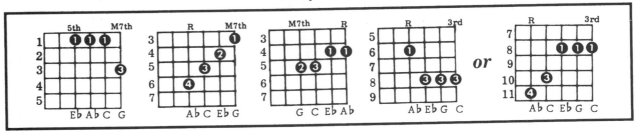

Inside & Rhythm Chords

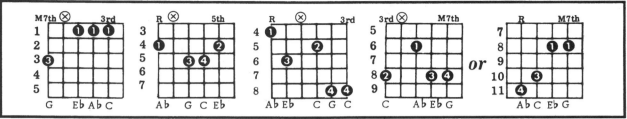

Bottom 4-String Chords

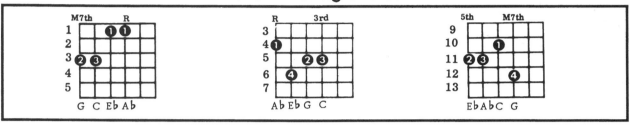

A♭ Major 7th Flat 3rd

Symbols (A♭ma7♭3, A♭min-maj7)

Melody Chords

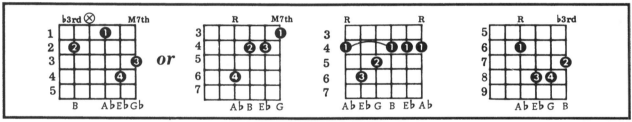

Inside & Rhythm Chords

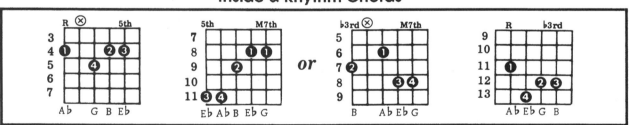

A♭ Minor 7th Flat 5th

Symbol (A♭m7♭5)

Melody Chords

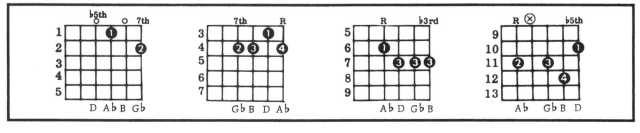

CHORDS

243

Inside Chords

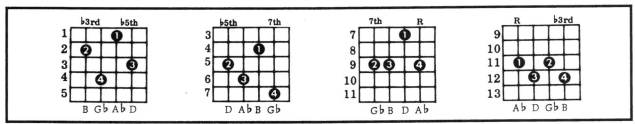

Rhythm Chords

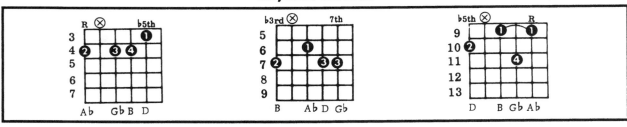

Ab 7 Suspended 4th

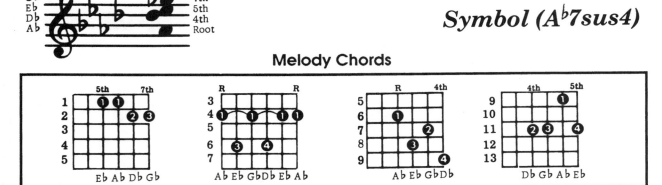

Symbol (Ab7sus4)

Melody Chords

Inside Chords

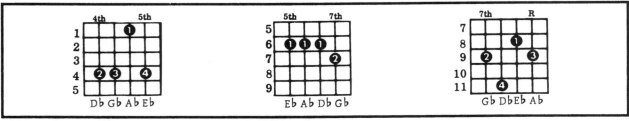

Rhythm Chords

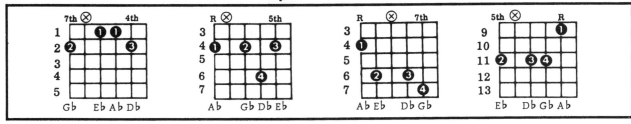

A♭ 6th

F
E♭
C
A♭

6th
5th
3rd
Root

Symbol (A♭6)

Melody Chords

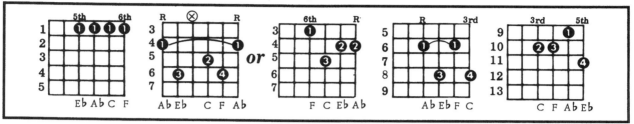

Inside Chords

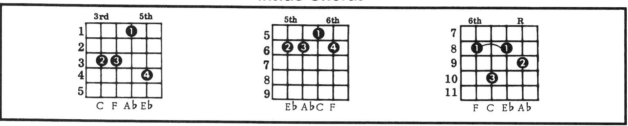

Rhythm Chords

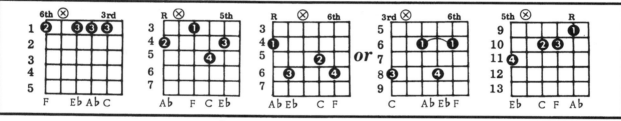

Bottom 4-String Chords

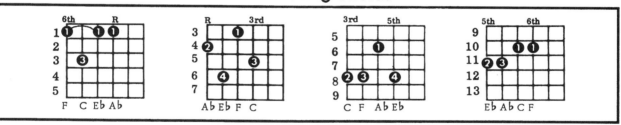

A♭ Minor 6th

F
E♭
C♭
A♭

6th
5th
♭3rd
Root

Symbol (A♭m6)

Melody Chords

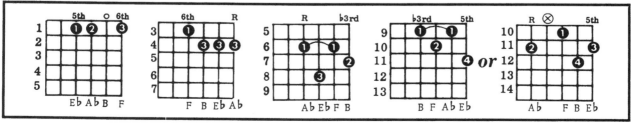

CHORDS

Inside Chords

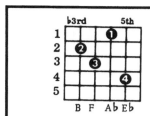
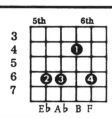
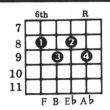
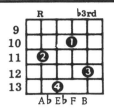

Rhythm Chords

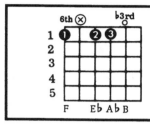
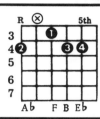
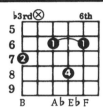
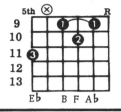

Bottom 4-String Chords

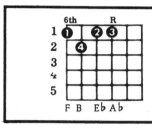
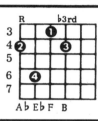
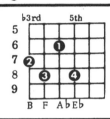
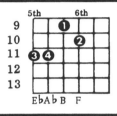

Ab 9th

Symbol (Ab 9)

Melody Chords

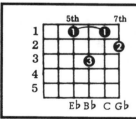
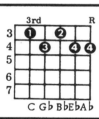
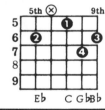
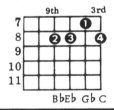
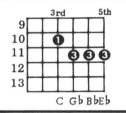

Inside & Rhythm Chords

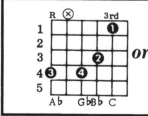
or
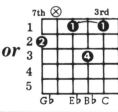
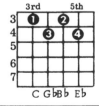
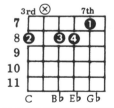
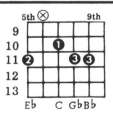

CHORDS

A♭ Minor 9th

Symbol (A♭ m9)

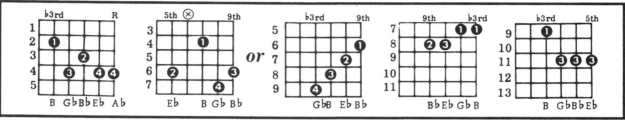

Melody Chords

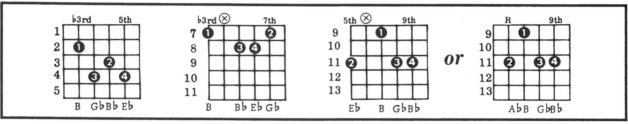

Inside & Rhythm Chords

A♭ Major 9th

Symbol (A♭ ma 9th)

Melody Chords

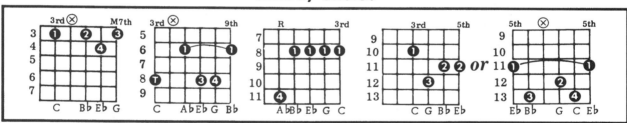

Inside Chords

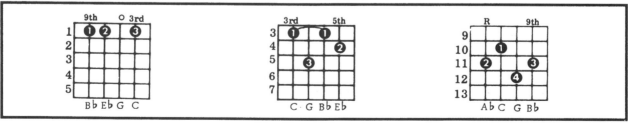

Rhythm Chords

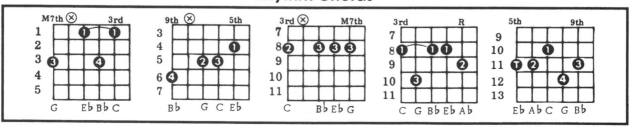

CHORDS

247

A♭9 Sharp 5th

Symbols
(A♭9 + 5, A♭9#5)

Melody Chords

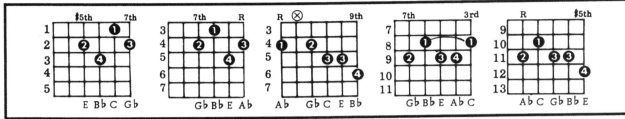

Inside & Rhythm Chords

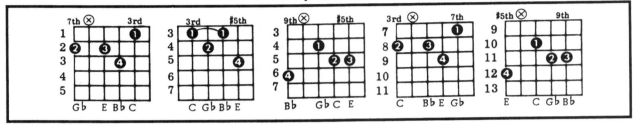

A♭9 Flat 5th

Symbol (A♭9-5)

Melody Chords

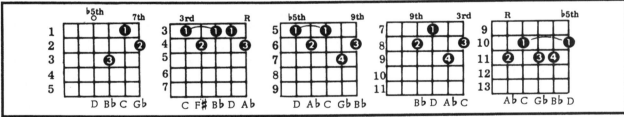

Inside & Rhythm Chords

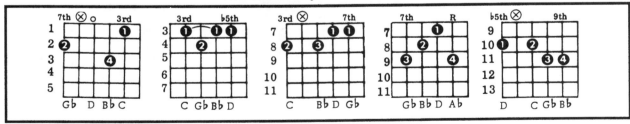

CHORDS

A♭7 Flat 9th

Symbol (A♭7-9)

Melody Chords

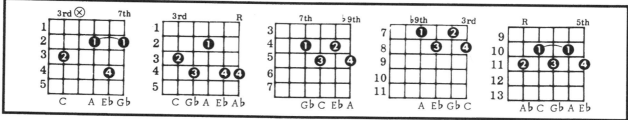

Inside & Rhythm Chords

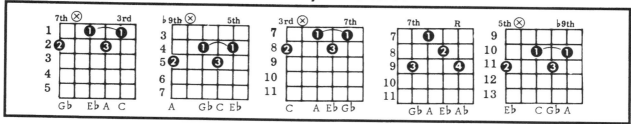

A♭7 Sharp 9th

Symbols (A♭9 +, A♭7 #9)

All Forms

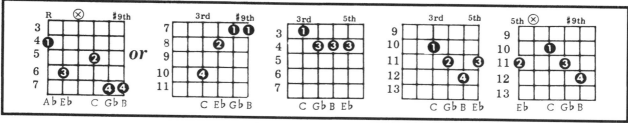

A♭6 Add 9th

Symbols (A♭$\frac{9}{6}$, A♭6 add 9)

All Forms

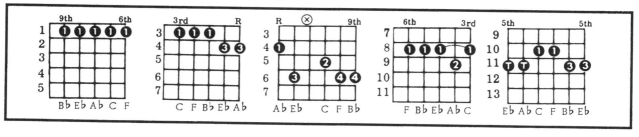

A♭ 11th

Symbol (A♭11)

Melody Chords

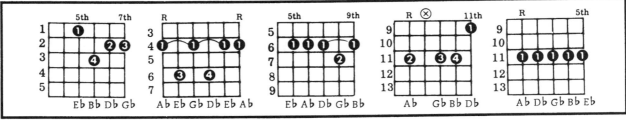

Inside & Rhythm Chords

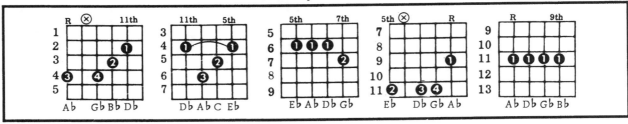

A♭ Aug. 11th

Symbol (A♭ 11 +)

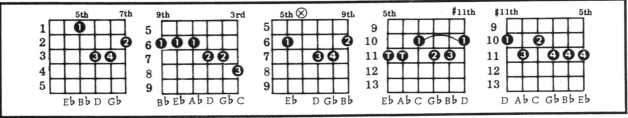

A♭ 13th

Symbol (A♭ 13)

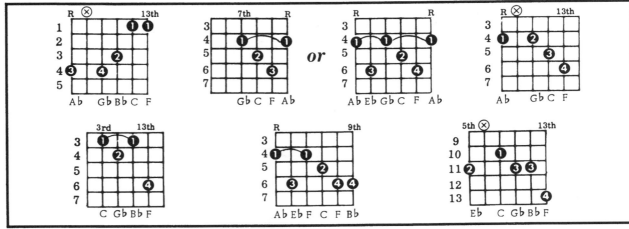

CHORDS

A♭ 13-9

Symbol (A♭ 13-9)

All Forms

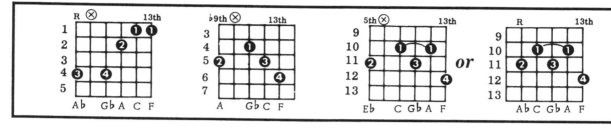

A Major

Symbol (A)

Melody Chords

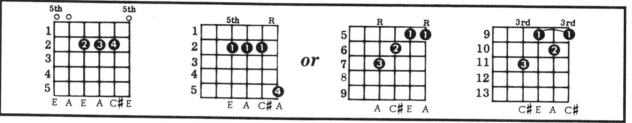

Inside Chords

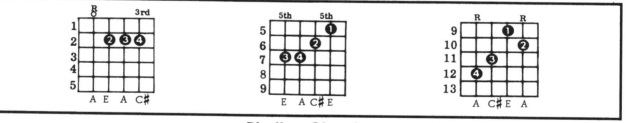

Rhythm Chords

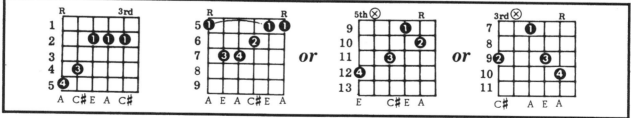

Bottom 4-String Chords

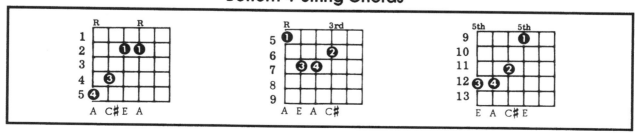

CHORDS

A Minor

Symbol (Am)

Melody Chords

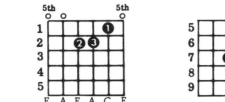 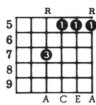 *or*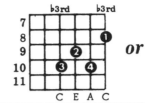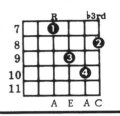

Inside Chords

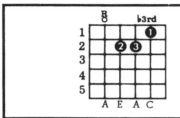 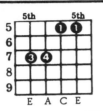 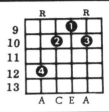

Rhythm Chords

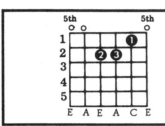 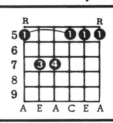 *or*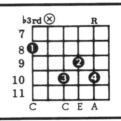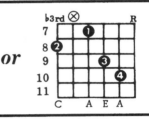

Bottom 4-String Chords

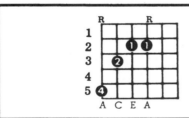 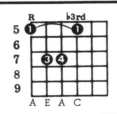 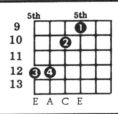

A Diminished

Symbols
(A-, A⁰, Adim)

Melody Chords

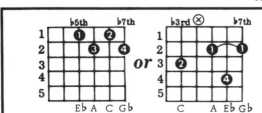 *or*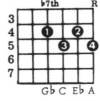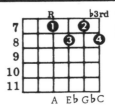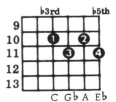

252

Inside Chords

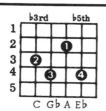 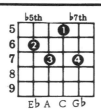 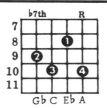

Rhythm Chords

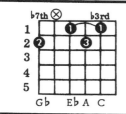 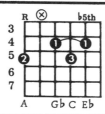 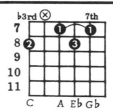 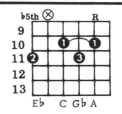

Bottom 4-String Chords

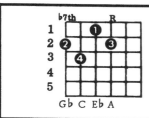 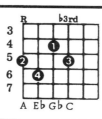 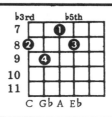 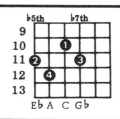

A Augmented

Symbol (A +)

Melody Chords

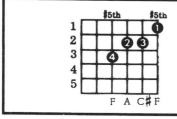 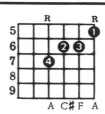 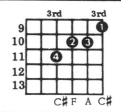

Inside & Rhythm Chords

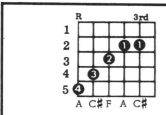 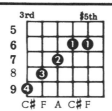 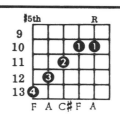

Bottom 4-String Chords

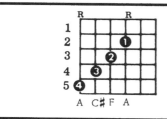 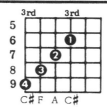 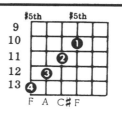

CHORDS

253

A 7th

Symbol (A7)

Melody Chords

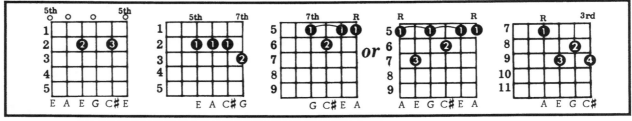

Inside Chords

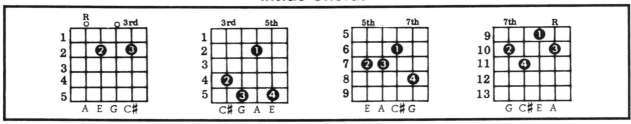

Rhythm Chords

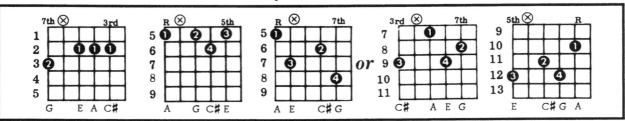

Bottom 4-String Chords

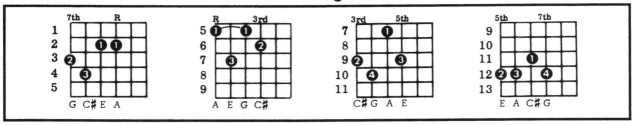

A Minor 7th

Symbol (A m7)

Melody Chords

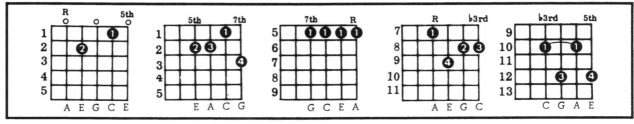

254

Inside Chords

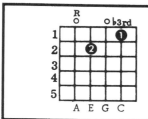 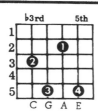 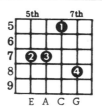 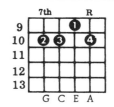

Rhythm Chords

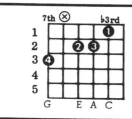 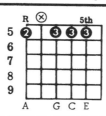 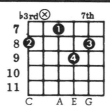 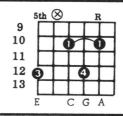

Bottom 4-String Chords

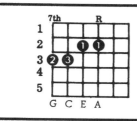 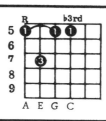 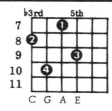 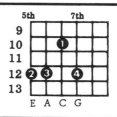

A 7th Aug. 5th

Symbol (A7 + 5)

Melody Chords

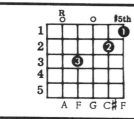 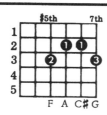 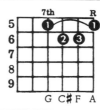 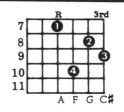

Inside Chords

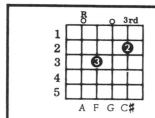 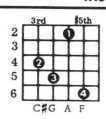 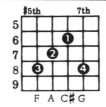 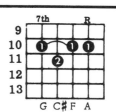

Rhythm Chords

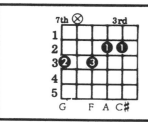 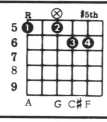 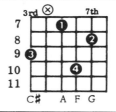 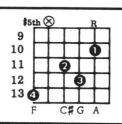

CHORDS

Bottom 4-String Chords

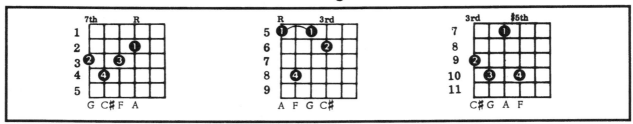

A 7th Flat 5th

Symbols(A7-5, A7♭5)

Melody Chords

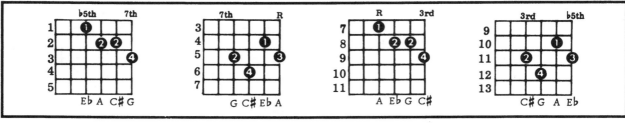

Inside Chords

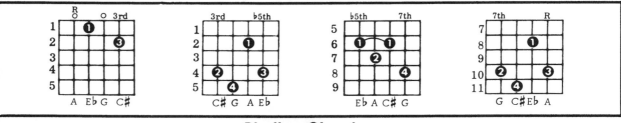

Rhythm Chords

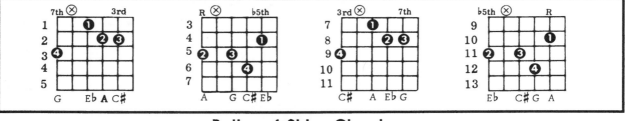

Bottom 4-String Chords

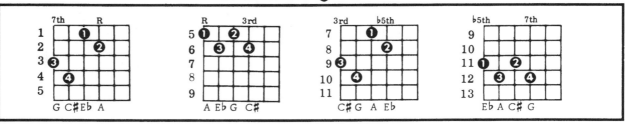

CHORDS

256

A Major 7th

Symbol (Ama7)

Melody Chords

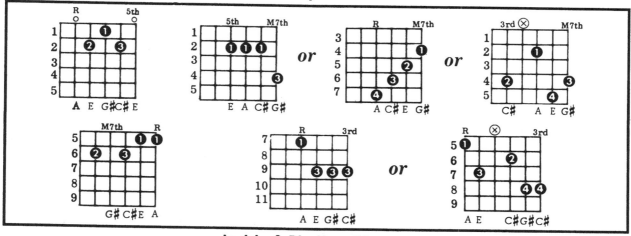

Inside & Rhythm Chords

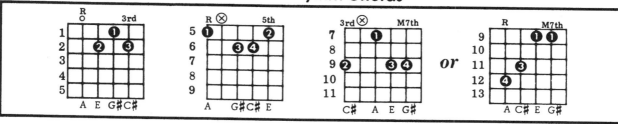

Bottom 4-String Chords

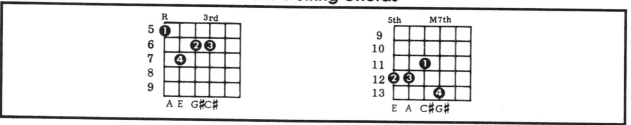

A Major 7th Flat 3rd

Symbols (Ama7♭3, Amin-maj7)

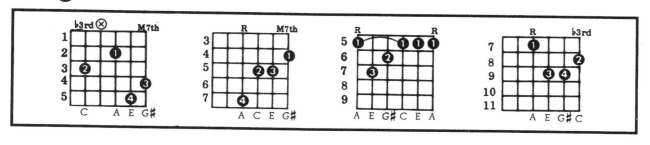

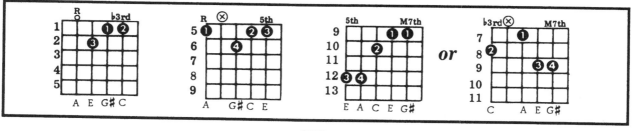

CHORDS

257

A Minor 7th Flat 5th

G♮ 7th
E♭ ♭5th
C♮ ♭3rd
A   Root

Symbol (Am7♭5)

Melody Chords

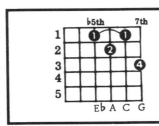 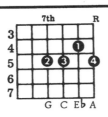 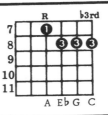 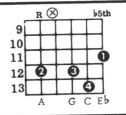

Inside Chords

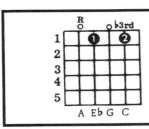 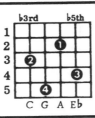 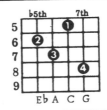 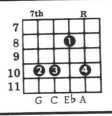

Rhythm Chords

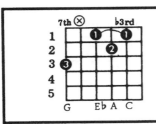 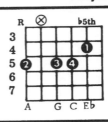 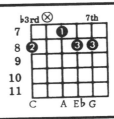 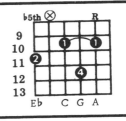

A7 Suspended 4th

G♯ 7th
E   5th
D   4th
A   Root

Symbol (A7sus4)

Melody Chords

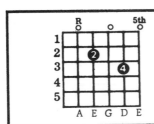 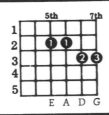  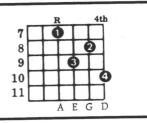

Inside Chords

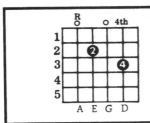 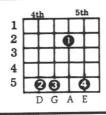 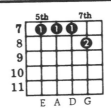 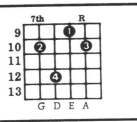

CHORDS

258

Rhythm Chords

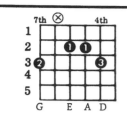 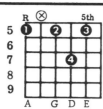 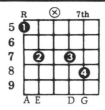 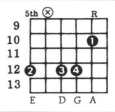

A 6th

Symbol (A6)

Melody Chords

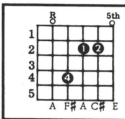 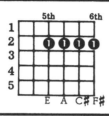 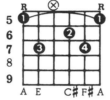 *or*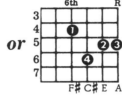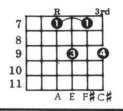

Inside Chords

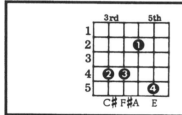 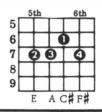 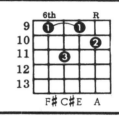

Rhythm Chords

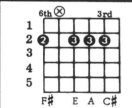 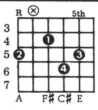 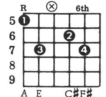 *or*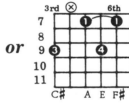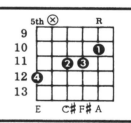

Bottom 4-String Chords

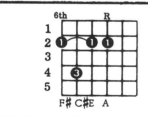 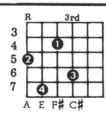 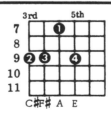 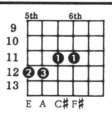

CHORDS

259

A Minor 6th

Symbol (Am6)

Melody Chords

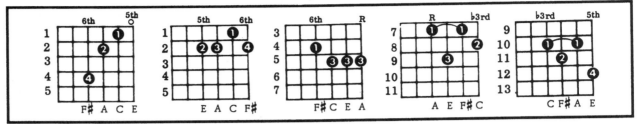

Inside Chords

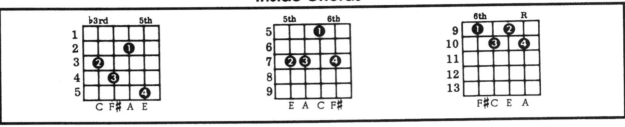

Rhythm Chords

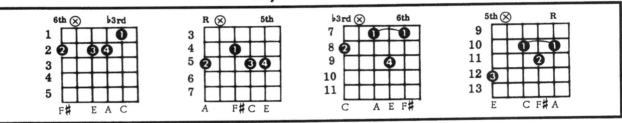

Bottom 4-String Chords

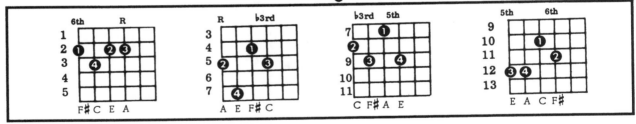

A 9th

Symbol (A9)

Melody Chords

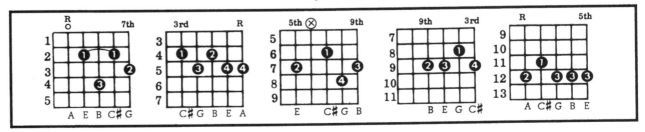

CHORDS

260

Inside & Rhythm Chords

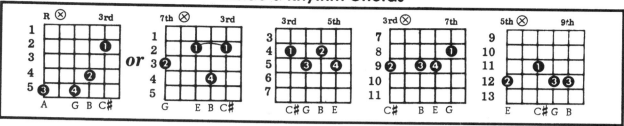

A Minor 9th

Symbol (Am9)

Melody Chords

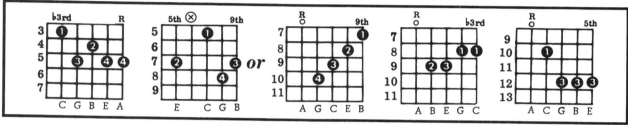

Inside & Rhythm Chords

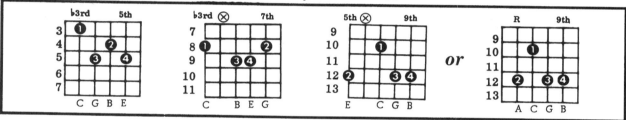

A Major 9th

Symbol (Ama9)

Melody Chords

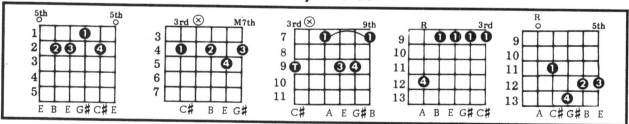

Inside Chords

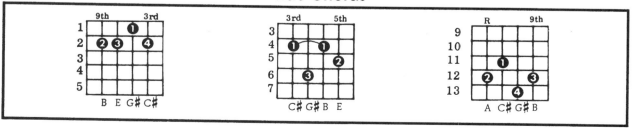

CHORDS

261

A Major 9th Cont.

Rhythm Chords

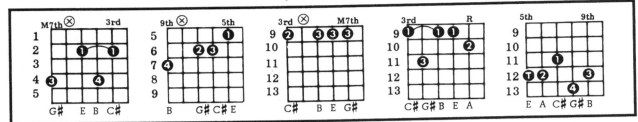

A9 Sharp 5th

Symbols (A9 + 5, A9 #5)

Melody Chords

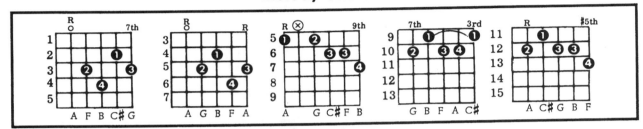

Inside & Rhythm Chords

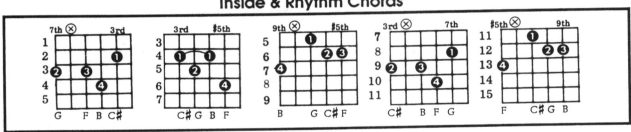

A9 Flat 5th

Symbol (A9-5)

Melody Chords

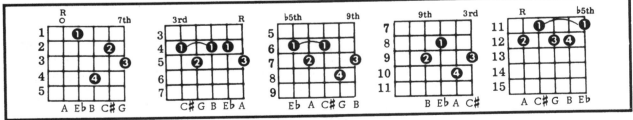

Inside & Rhythm Chords

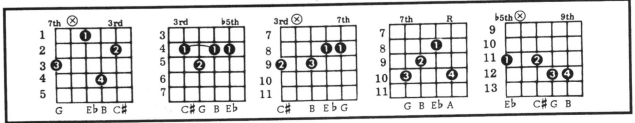

CHORDS

A7 Flat 9th

Symbol (A7-9)

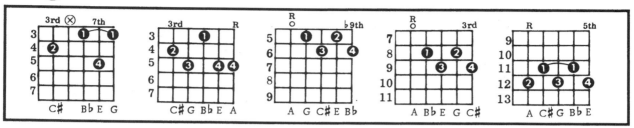

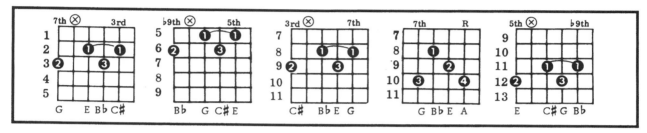

A7 Sharp 9th

Symbols (A + 9, A7 #9)

All Forms

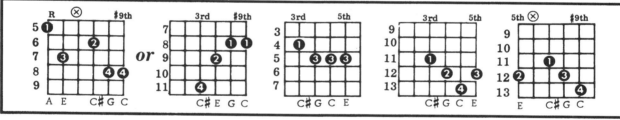

A6 Add 9th

Symbol (A 9/6, A6add9)

All Forms

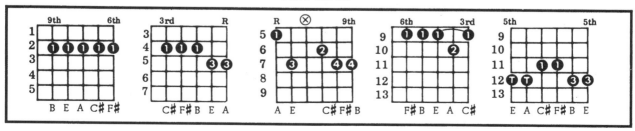

A 11th

Symbol (A11)

Melody Chords

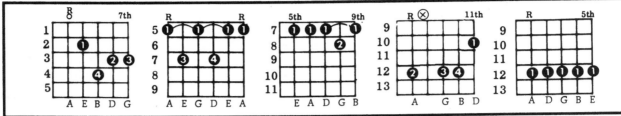

Inside & Rhythm Chords

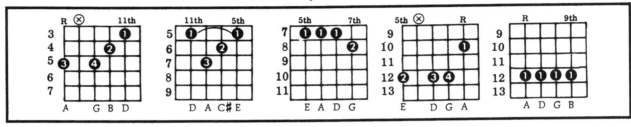

A Aug. 11th

Symbol (A 11 +)

All Forms

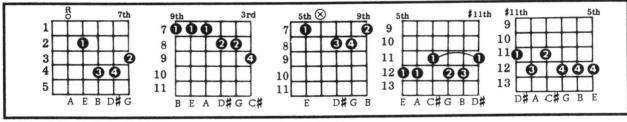

A 13th

Symbol (A 13)

All Forms

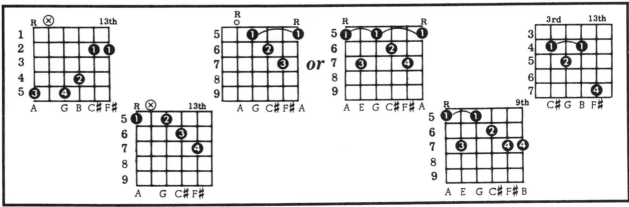

264

A 13-9

Symbol (A 13-9)

All Forms

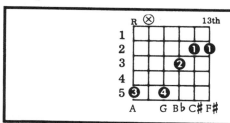

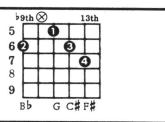

B♭ Major

Symbol (B♭)

Melody Chords

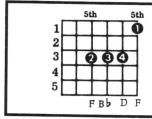

or

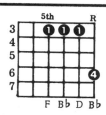

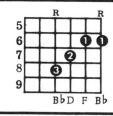

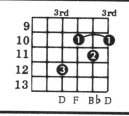

Inside Chords

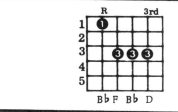

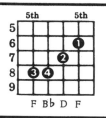

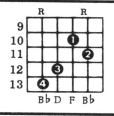

Rhythm Chords

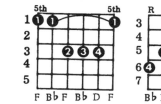

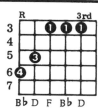

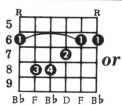

or

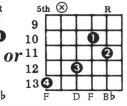

or

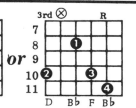

Bottom 4-String Chords

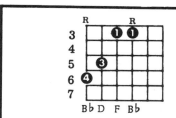

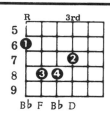

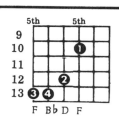

CHORDS

265

B♭ Minor

Symbol (B♭m)

Melody Chords

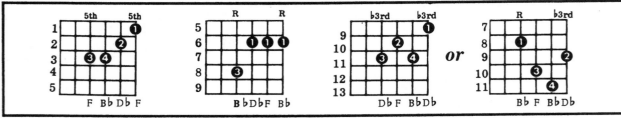

Inside Chords

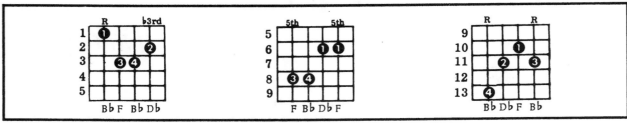

Rhythm Chords

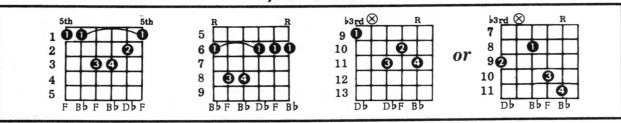

Bottom 4-String Chords

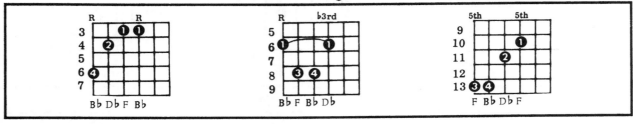

B♭ Diminished

Symbols (B♭-, B♭⁰, B♭dim)

Melody Chords

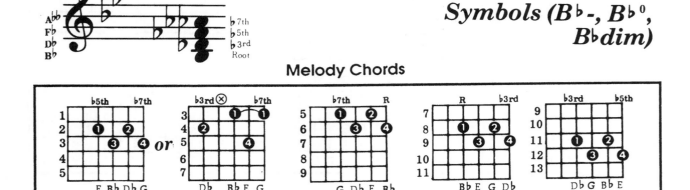

CHORDS

266

Inside Chords

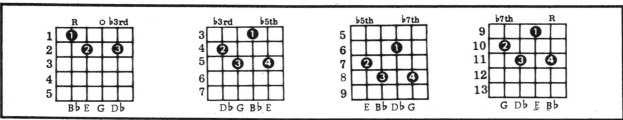

Rhythm Chords

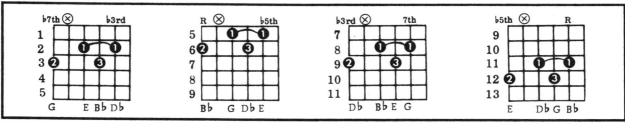

Bottom 4-String Chords

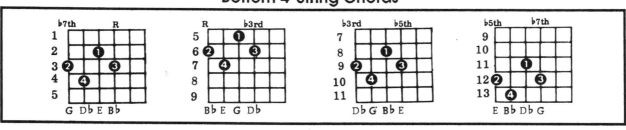

B♭ Augmented

Symbol (B♭+)

Melody Chords

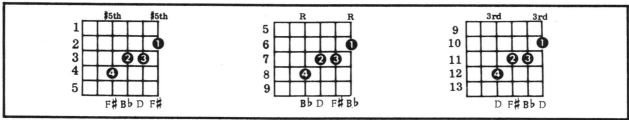

Inside & Rhythm Chords

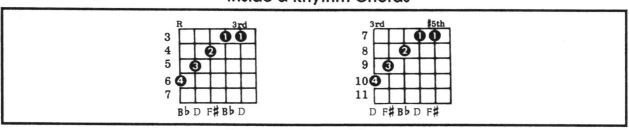

Bottom 4-String Chords

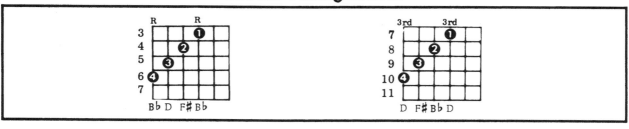

Bb 7th

Ab
F
D
Bb

7th
5th
3rd
Root

Symbol (Bb7)

Melody Chords

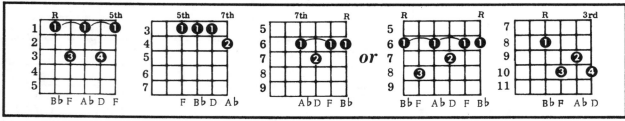

Inside Chords

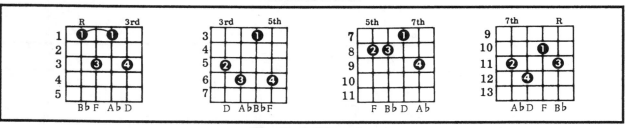

Rhythm Chords

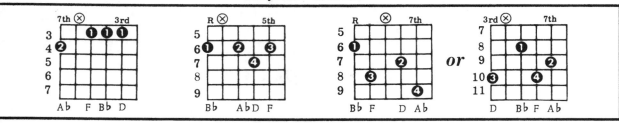

Bottom 4-String Chords

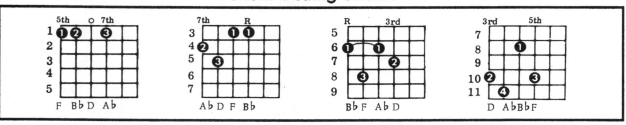

Bb Minor 7th

Ab
F
Db
Bb

7th
5th
b3rd
Root

Symbol (Bbm7)

Melody Chords

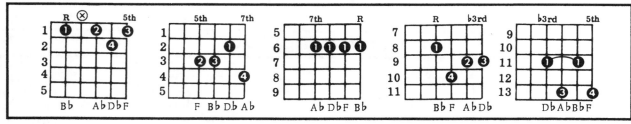

Inside Chords

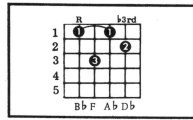 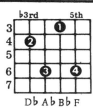 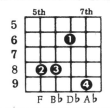 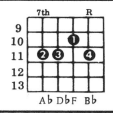

Rhythm Chords

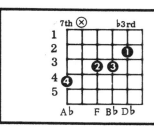 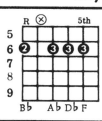 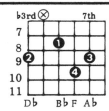 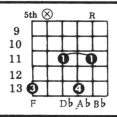

Bottom 4-String Chords

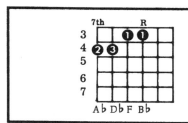 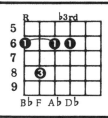 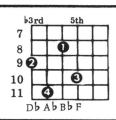

B♭ 7th Aug. 5th

Symbol (B♭7+5)

Melody Chords

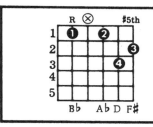 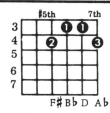 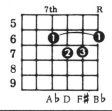 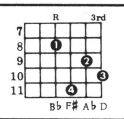

Inside Chords

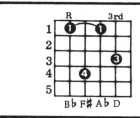 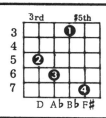 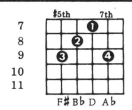 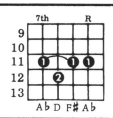

Rhythm Chords

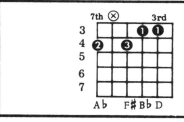 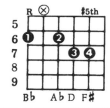 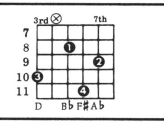

CHORDS

Bb 7th Aug. 5th Cont.

Bottom 4-String Chords

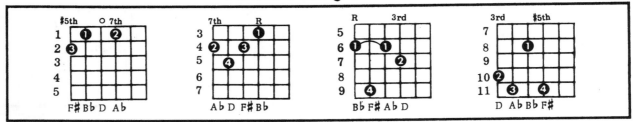

Bb 7th Flat 5th

Symbols
(Bb7-5, Bb7b5)

Melody Chords

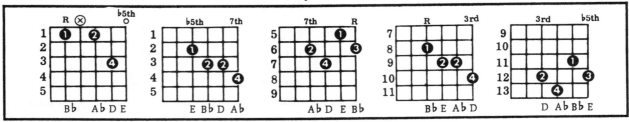

Inside Chords

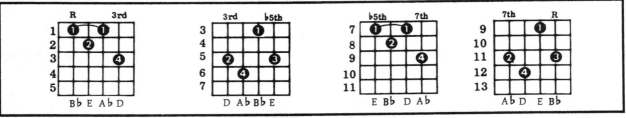

Rhythm Chords

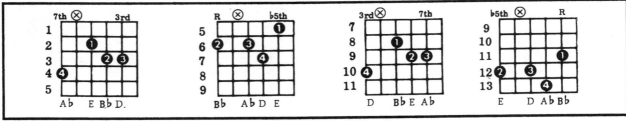

Bottom 4-String Chords

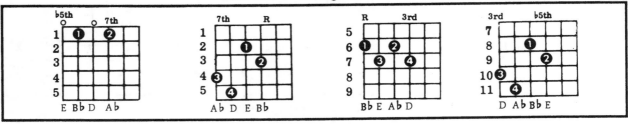

CHORDS

270

B♭ Major 7th

A
F
D
B♭

maj7th
5th
3rd
Root

Symbol (B♭ma7)

Melody Chords

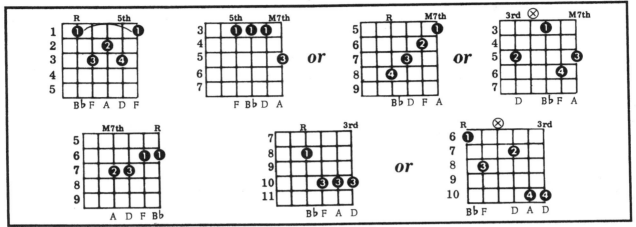

Inside & Rhythm Chords

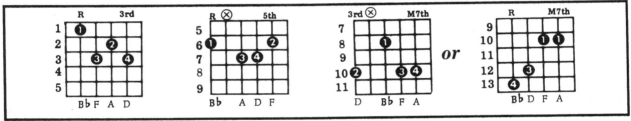

Bottom 4-String Chords

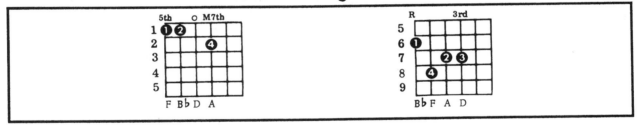

B♭ Major 7th Flat 3rd

A
F
D♭
B♭

maj7th
5th
♭3rd
Root

*Symbols (B♭ma7♭3,
B♭min-maj7)*

Melody Chords

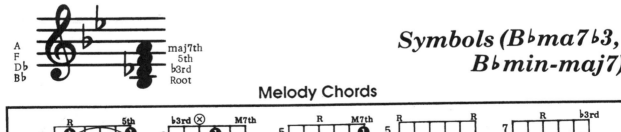
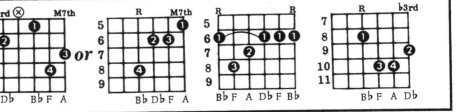

CHORDS

271

Inside & Rhythm Chords

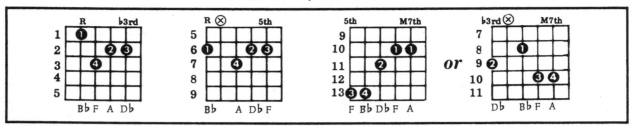

B♭ Minor 7th Flat 5th

Symbol (B♭m7♭5)

Melody Chords

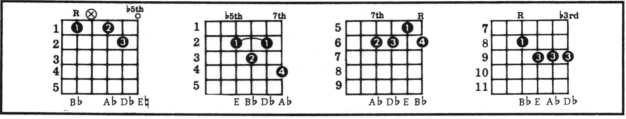

Inside & Rhythm Chords

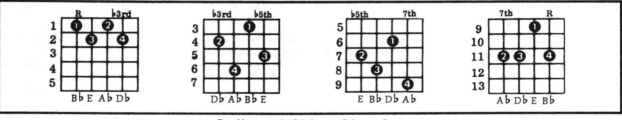

Bottom 4-String Chords

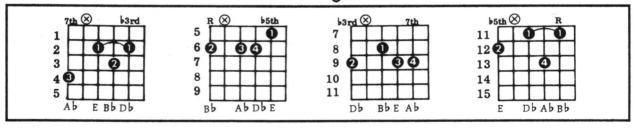

B♭7 Suspended 4th

Symbol (B♭7sus4)

Melody Chords

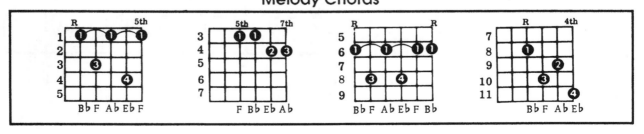

CHORDS

Inside Chords

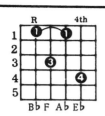 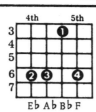 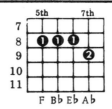 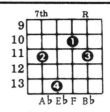

Rhythm Chords

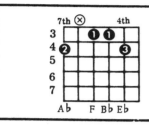 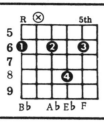 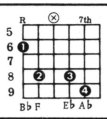 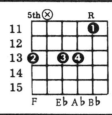

B♭ 6th

G
F
D
B♭

6th
5th
3rd
Root

Symbol (B♭6)

Melody Chords

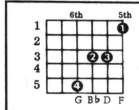 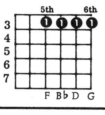 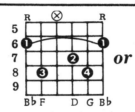 *or*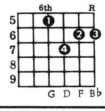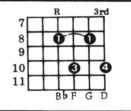

Inside Chords

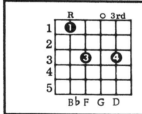 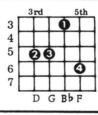 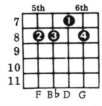 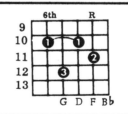

Rhythm Chords

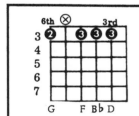 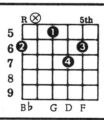 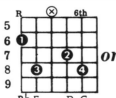 *or*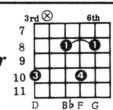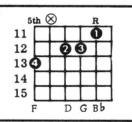

Bottom 4-String Chords

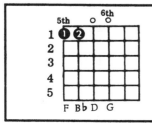 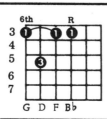 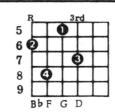 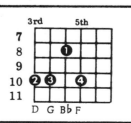

CHORDS

B♭ Minor 6th

G
F
D♭
B♭

6th
5th
♭3rd
Root

Symbol (B♭m6)

Melody Chords

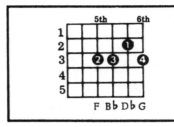
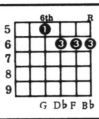
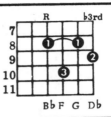
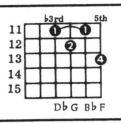

Inside Chords

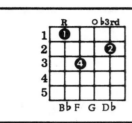
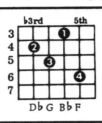
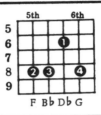
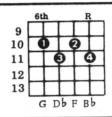

Rhythm Chords

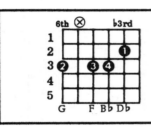
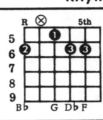
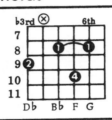
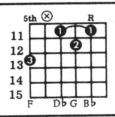

Bottom 4-String Chords

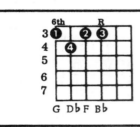
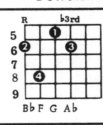
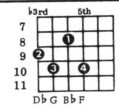
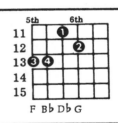

B♭ 9th

C
A♭
F
D
B♭

9th
7th
5th
3rd
Root

Symbol (B♭9)

Melody Chords

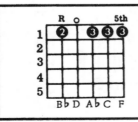
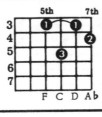
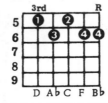
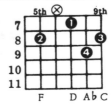
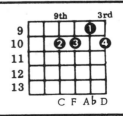

Inside & Rhythm Chords

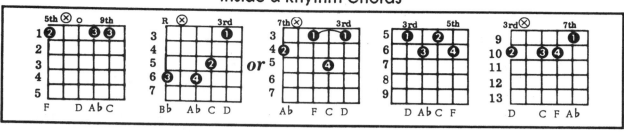

B♭ Minor 9th

C — 9th
Ab — 7th
F — 5th
Db — b3rd
Bb — Root

Symbol (B♭ m9)

Melody Chords

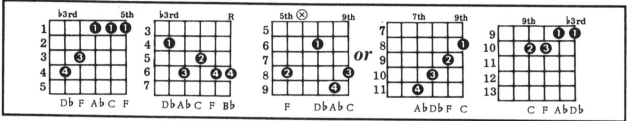

Inside & Rhythm Chords

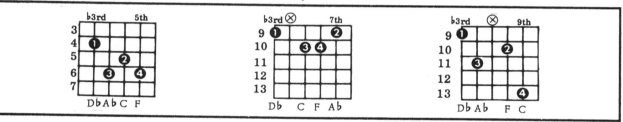

B♭ Major 9th

C — 9th
A — ma7th
F — 5th
D — 3rd
Bb — Root

Symbol (B♭ ma 9th)

Melody Chords

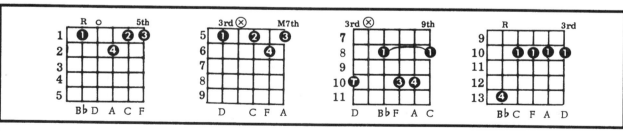

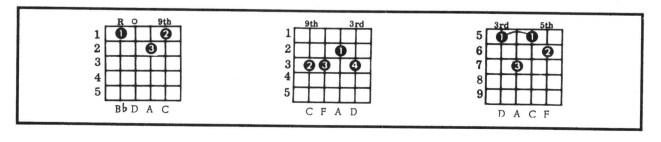

CHORDS

275

Bb Major 9th Cont.

Rhythm Chords

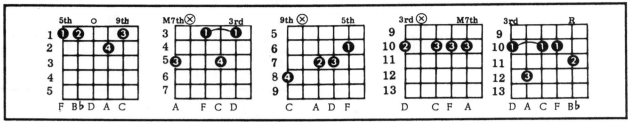

Bb9 Sharp 5th

Symbols
(Bb9+5, Bb9#5)

Melody Chords

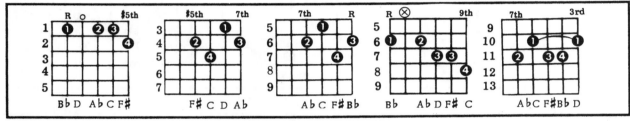

Inside & Rhythm Chords

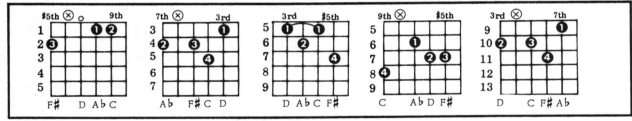

Bb9 Flat 5th

Symbol (Bb9-5)

Melody Chords

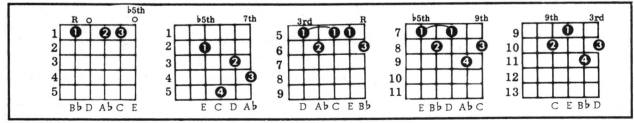

Inside & Rhythm Chords

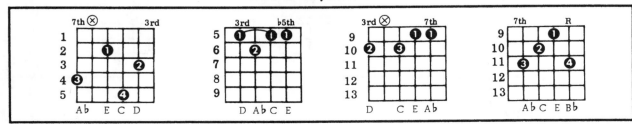

CHORDS